Advance Praise for Jonathan Campbell's
Red Rock

"A rollicking account of how a global genre was transformed as it sank down roots in a very special setting."

— JEFFREY WASSERSTROM, author of
China in the 21st Century: What Everyone Needs to Know

"The ancient rhythms of East meets West have rarely been played out so intensely or at such a raucous volume."

— JONATHAN WATTS, author of *When a Billion Chinese Jump*

"With consumerism the pervasive religion, freedoms taken for granted, and apathy rampant, the West largely has forgotten the power of rock 'n' roll—if not to change the world, than at least to change ourselves (and that is much the same thing). In China, the music never has seemed more vital or necessary, and as an astute listener, sharp journalist, and excellent writer, Campbell does an outstanding job explaining why."

— JIM DEROGATIS, rock critic, co-host of "Sound Opinions"

"No dusty research required, no distant Q&A's necessary, as performer, promoter, writer and pure fan, Campbell was part of the Beijing rock scene when the needle hit the mainline . . . [An] insider's guide to the otherwise impenetrable world of what will become known as the golden period of Chinese rock music . . . pulsing with the energy of the country itself . . . "

— STEVE BARKER, BBC Radio DJ

"A brilliant exploration of the Chinese opening to rock & roll, from a keen observer on the front lines of cultural transformation."

— KEN STRINGFELLOW, The Posies, R.E.M., Big Star

"Campbell is the ultimate Beijing insider . . . *Red Rock* is an entertaining and illuminating romp through the weird world of Chinese rock and roll."

—JAN WONG, author of
A Comrade Lost and Found: A Beijing Memoir

"Campbell's *Red Rock* has the narrative power of a fine novel, and is at the same time a cogent work of historical analysis . . . the benchmark against which all future accounts of the phenomenon will be measured."

—TENG JIMENG, author of
Music-Made America: Popular Music Since 1960s

"Musician, journalist, tour manager, van driver, *guanxi* master, barstool philosopher, old-school Beijinger – Campbell is the insider's insider, and the perfect person to chronicle the rollicking rise of rock in China."

—ADAM PILLSBURY, *Insider's Guide to Beijing*

"Campbell is the most objective observer of Chinese music I've come into contact with over the years . . . It is rare to see this kind of impartiality in promoting Chinese music."

—ZHONG SHENG, Pilot Records (China)

"An enthusiastically written history of Chinese rock music, based on active participation, numerous interviews, and research. [Campbell] succeeds in grasping the particular feeling – and meaning – of 'yaogun'."

—ANDREAS STEEN, author of *Der Lange Marsch des Rock 'n' Roll*

"In this dazzling account of contemporary Chinese music, Campbell convinces us that there is always more than what we think we understand as popular music, there is always more than what we think we understand as China."

—JEROEN DE KLOET, author of *China with a Cut*

"Campbell offers a lively, clear-eyed assessment of both the promise and failings of this potentially transformative cultural phenomenon."

— DENNIS REA, author of *Live At the Forbidden City: Musical Encounters in China & Taiwan*

"Campbell is the most qualified and capable writer to have undertaken this project. In the rock community here, we hold the same respect for the author as China does for [Dr. Norman] Bethune: Campbell has made China's business his own; he shares our hopes and concerns."

— LÜ BO, Scream Records (China)

"Not only is this book a necessary read for anyone interested in the development of contemporary Chinese music and art, but it discusses with real authority an aspect of China's tremendous social transformation that few outsiders have considered."

— MICHAEL PETTIS, professor at Peking University

RED ROCK

THE LONG, STRANGE MARCH OF CHINESE ROCK & ROLL

JONATHAN CAMPBELL

EARNSHAW
BOOKS

RED ROCK

CONTENTS

Acknowledgments

To my parents, who inspired this book and its author in ways they couldn't have imagined.

To my wife, who inspires me every day.

And, to those who yaogun: Those who inspired the march of Chinese rock; those who marched then, and march today; and those about to march.

With a constant stream of Chinese food during my mother's pregnancy, the seeds of a China Hand were sown. My father ensured there was always music around, filling our world with mixtapes. This book results from that combination at least as much as it does from the support my family provided to me despite the distance between us. My only wish is that my mother could have seen it.

I was told to write with an ideal reader in mind; it just so happened that my ideal reader was also my ideal writer. Ian Sherman didn't just write about yaogun the way I wanted to, he wrote about it – and everything else – like nobody wrote about anything, ever. His gig listings were poetry; his live reviews, epic. The writing he did during his struggle with cancer embodied not just an inability to turn off the tap, but the determination of a writer not ready to stop. The tragedy of his passing is about much more than the void where his words ought to be, but that void is enormous.

There are eighty-something people who granted me larger chunks of their lives than I'd imagined anyone ought to be granted, and the resulting hours of conversations meant that researching this book was a pleasure – and editing it down was excruciating. I hope I've managed to convey the excitement that each of you relayed to (and inspired in) me: it was an excitement that was essential fuel for this project.

The comments, patience and general greatness of those who read over early drafts are more appreciated than one could or should attempt to convey in writing. There is also an international network of punk peoples that granted me much-appreciated access to their world. *Rockinchina.com* deserves particular mention for their encyclopaedic and just plain amazing resource.

Team Earnshaw provided invaluable support of my work throughout the long, strange process, carving, despite my best intentions, Something, out of far too many things.

Countless others probably didn't realize their role in these pages, just as I hadn't realized I was doing research. I'm grateful to everyone with whom I've watched, played, argued, discussed and hung around, in front of, behind and among yaogun.

I was extremely lucky to have played and worked with some amazing musicians over the years, both on and off the stage. It started within weeks of my arrival in Beijing, and at t-minus seven days to my departure, I was still playing, still not believing how lucky I was to be doing it with you all. I didn't arrive in Beijing expecting to find rock, and I definitely didn't expect to play it, but I did, and I did, and there is, was and will be nothing like it, ever.

And, Weiwei: You Rock.

This book is not, by far, all-inclusive. There are far too many amazing musicians and people that I believe the world should know about to have possibly included in these pages (which didn't stop me from trying). Thus will my efforts continue online, at *www.jonathanWcampbell.com* where a range of materials spanning many media forms will live. A sampling of the efforts of others can be found in the further reading/surfing section.

Jonathan Campbell,
August 2011

"[Music's] root lies in the human mind's being stirred by external things. Thus, when a mind that is miserable is stirred, its sound is vexed and anxious. When a mind that is happy is stirred, its sound is relaxed and leisurely. When a mind that is delighted is stirred, its sound pours out and scatters. When a wrathful mind is stirred, its sound is crude and harsh. When a respectful mind is stirred, its sound is upright and pure. When a doting mind is stirred, its sound is agreeable and yielding . . . Thus the former kings exercised caution in what might cause stirring."

The Record of Music, *Yue Ji* (circa 425-200 BCE)

"Buddy, what the heck are you playing rock for?"

Second Hand Rose, "Trick" (2003)

1

THE ROCKER'S PARADISE

Do not say that we have nothing.
We'll be the masters of the world.

"The Internationale"

A Scene from the Scene: May 2010

"Arise, slaves afflicted by hunger and cold," they sang in the dark, rain-soaked, mud-covered park in Beijing's university district. *"Arise, suffering people all over the world."*

They were the last Chinese rock fans remaining in the park. They had come from around the country for the eleventh installment of the Midi Music Festival; punks, longhairs, hippies and office workers, singing to a deserted stage and emptying park. The rain that had come and gone over the course of the day came down so hard the festival's plug had to be pulled. Almost twenty thousand people had left the park in the storm's wake. These few thousand stayed, and had taken to singing. Perhaps it was an effort to conquer the storm; perhaps, it was because there was nothing else to do.

"The blood which fills my chest has boiled over," they sang with an intensity that brought to mind their Revolutionary predecessors who, ninety-one years prior – to the day – stood up in the face of international embarrassment and in aid of strengthening their nation. *"We must struggle for truth!"*

"The Internationale," the song they were covering is the soundtrack of the Chinese Communist Party, which was formed in the wake of the youth-led May Fourth Movement of 1919. In 1919, on the day that became known as Youth Day, the kids were up in arms over China's place in the world. On Youth Day 2010, the kids were living in a world overshadowed by their nation, and had different concerns.

"The old world shall be destroyed," sang the rockers, reveling equally in the song and the muck around them. *"Arise, slaves,*

arise!" They would be dubbed "Titos" (*tietou*) – the Chinese word for the former Yugoslavian leader that means, literally, "iron henchmen". It was the word used to describe the festival's first fans, a small and fiercely loyal community.

The word "Woodstock" has for many years been bandied about with reckless abandon to describe Chinese rock and the Midi Festival. But in that moment, even though the gathered masses weren't quite singing about peace, love and understanding, the comparison might just have been reasonable, so long as we recognize that "Woodstock" barely refers to the actual Summer of Love event, but rather some idealized version of a Perfect Festival that embodies the Rock and Roll Life.

"*Do not say that we have nothing,*" they continued, invoking intentionally or not, the words that started China's rock and roll journey two dozen years prior. For a while, a few days before, they did have nothing: Mao Livehouse, Beijing's premier rock venue, was shut down by authorities on grounds of what was called a breach of fire code. "*We'll be the masters of the world!*" Instead of dwelling in the dark, the club took their entire operation to the festival site, setting up a small stage and bar in the middle of the action, and it was one of the best-run stages in the country's musical history.

As its stage lay bare in the downpour and Titos tried to sing it back to life, the festival was rebounding from its toughest years yet. In Beijing's Olympic year, contrary to popular belief outside of the country, events such as Midi were discouraged; 2008's festival was miniscule. Midi's tenth anniversary was in 2009, the year the People's Republic of China turned sixty. Outside of the scope of official celebrations, the festival had no choice but to pack up for its tenth installment and head south to Zhenjiang, a small unremarkable city on the country's east coast with no connection whatsoever to rock music other than a local government eager to attract tourism and no idea what bringing a rock festival might do for them. The next year, during 2010's May Day holiday period – traditionally the time when the festival was held or cancelled – Midi returned to Beijing. It was a triumphant return to the festival's hometown, and a symbol of how far the festival, which began as a showcase for the bands of the eponymous rock and roll school, had come.

As the rain poured down, a muddy mosh-pit ensued and the Titos kept going. "The Internationale" no longer felt so out of place. "*This is the final struggle,*" they sang through the downpour, no longer, perhaps, envisioning the Worker's Paradise of their forefathers. "*Unite together towards tomorrow. The Internationale, shall certainly be realized.*"

Rocker's Paradise is more like it.

As the evening advanced and the storm let up, a cast of some of festival's biggest names took the stage, singing through bullhorns and illuminated by flashlights. The PA system was brought back to life, but the lights remained off. Rap-metal band Miserable Faith, the Titos' Titos, proceeded through an unplugged set and the stage soon became packed with musicians, staff and media. "*Always heading toward Midi,*" they sang, a slight tweak of the lyrics to "Highway Song."

"It was a moment to remember in Chinese rock history," said filmmaker Victor Huey, who has seen and captured more than his share of Chinese rock. "The resilience of the Chinese rock scene to make it happen when the gods made it impossible to perform . . . This may be the moment I have been trying to shoot for twenty-four years."

Suddenly, you forgot how boring rap-metal can be, how bad the sound was, what a mess it all was. Just as suddenly, you started to believe that maybe rock music can change the world; that the underground might actually be a Movement; that its members don't simply run around flipping the bird at anyone who will (or won't) look. That they believe in Something, and are Doing Something. On that night, Chinese rock's future was sealed, and it was a future that couldn't have looked better.

But before we rush to check out what lies ahead for Chinese rock we have to look at where it all came from. China is developing at such a furious pace in so many directions that there is little time for the past. But each step forward is linked to the steps previous, particularly in the case of Chinese rock, where you can go back only so far before you're staring at an empty patch of land.

Another Scene: September 2000

I have hazy memories of my first taste of *yaogun* (pronounced "yow-goon"), the literal Chinese translation of rock and roll. It was just over a decade before Midi's magic moment, and I was a new arrival to Beijing, the centre of China's rock and roll universe (though I didn't know it at the time). The show was at the Oak Club – a dark, narrow space the size of a living room – and atop the tiny stage, cordoned off by shin-high battlements, sat the Wild Children. I remember finding it in a neighborhood of dark alleyways and low buildings, dank and grimy but full of local rock history and flavor. This was before it was razed to make way for a new subway line, condos and a massive shopping mall.

The band's music was, quite simply, beautiful. It sounded to me, in a way difficult to put into words, like China, and I was excited in a way that only a new arrival could be. It wasn't the loud music for which the Oak Club (formerly the Scream Club) was obviously built. It was folk music: unplugged, simple, and stripped-down, with haunting vocal melodies and harmonies that evoked the duo's northwestern hometown and the region around it. I didn't know this about them then, but their music transcended all that. "We've arrived at such a good age," the Wild Children sang; I felt it even if I couldn't decipher their lyrics that night.

Certainly being fresh off the boat and out of a master's program in which I only read about stuff like this affected my perceptions, but the melodies they sang stayed with me in the weeks, and years, that followed in a way that any music rarely had. My excitement may have been somewhat naïve, colored by the fact that I felt like I'd discovered something new, but my love of yaogun is rooted in that first experience.

It's easy to look back on "early days" and lament how far things have fallen, but that's not what this story is about. That night was only one stop on a journey still unfolding: The Wild Children opened their own bar, River, a few months later and it was a living, breathing testament to their commitment to the scene. I'm not waving my cane around as I say that they don't make joints like River any more, but the truth is that they *don't*. Just like how back then, they didn't make clubs like they do now. River, like any good spot, was built upon the foundations of that which preceded it, and inspired people and places around the country, of a size and scope scarcely imaginable in the early years.

Which relates to the question of "Good" vs. "Good For China." Whether the music is good because it's the product of a country still new to rock, or whether it is simply good in any context. That I truly believe what I saw at the Oak Club was just plain Good might well be the result of the shade of glasses I wore at the gig, but I've had time with it, and though hindsight might not be nostalgia-free, I am comfortable with my perception. But that it is a perception is important to recognize.

It's related to my music-filing problem, where I want to protect and provide special treatment for yaogun. I have sections in my musical library – both physical and electronic – for rock, jazz, folk, funk, world, blues and yaogun. What does it mean that the Chinese folk, rock, punk, electro and metal music isn't simply distributed among the other piles? Why separate it? Isn't that enough proof that Chinese music hasn't "made it" just yet? Or is it proof that it is so special it demands its own section?

Thing is, I'm not convinced that the Chinese music I have –
or will have – should be filed in and amongst the other piles. It
would get eaten up in there, never to see the light of day again.
But I'm also convinced that only if yaogun artists were distributed amongst the proverbial piles in the rock world's library,
would recognition be possible that many – not all, but some –
yaogunners are playing international quality rock and roll music. Because there is nothing more patronizing to yaogun, which
is still today finding its bearings, than being completely uncriti-
cal. That attitude, coupled with hype, is downright disingenuous
and produces nothing but mediocrity and inflated egos.

And that's one thing this book is for: To show the world that
yaogun is special enough and can command the respect to earn
its own section, while also being good enough and worthy of
sharing space with the rest.

I've come to learn that yaogun is as much about the highs as
it is about lows that descend to depths unimaginable. Just un-
derneath the façade of the Midi Festival – which has weathered
storms metaphoric and meteorological – are layers of break-
downs threatening an implosion from within. One doesn't say
this merely to burst a bubble, because the bubble reinflates; yaogun soldiers on and always has. One says this to point out the
simple fact that yaogun is hardly ever just what it seems.

Much of this book delves into the steps with which yaogun's
thousand-mile journey began, and how it was that the first generation was coaxed into making them. Its roots lie in the late seventies, when the existence of people, culture, phenomena outside
China was barely recognized by the Chinese, except inasmuch as
it exemplified China's superiority. In order to fully explain how
yaogun became yaogun in its current form, we need to uncover
the foundations upon which the first generation of musicians,
venues, audience and scene were built – whether or not current
rockers choose to acknowledge it, or overcome the short-term
memory that tends to define a large swath of the population both
inside and outside of the scene. Those foundations were carved

out of a political and social situation that seemed to preclude the possibility of anything different, let alone something imported.

Rock and Roll to Yaogun in the New China

In the Beginning, goes the general story, a twenty-four year old named Cui Jian sang a song. It was 1986 when he got up onstage dressed something like a normal person – not like the pop stars with whom he shared the stage – and sang that he, like so many of those watching, had nothing to his name. I was about to say that his now-legendary song, "Nothing to My Name" wasn't created in a vacuum, but the truth is it pretty much was. "Real rock 'n' roll should come from the underground, but China didn't have one," Cui told a reporter twenty years after he first performed the song. " 'Nothing to My Name' just appeared out of nowhere."

There was, at the time, a large cultural void preventing rock from taking off, as the pop singer turned producer Wang Di observed: "From the first time I heard rock, I knew that it had nothing to do with our culture." Thus, to many people it did, in fact, come out of nowhere, and for many people it still doesn't resonate. Which is why, to get the real story, we need to take a couple of steps even further back – back before "Nothing," when there was, well, *Nothing*.

The Cultural Revolution began in 1966 and ended ten years later upon the death of Mao Zedong. It was a decade marked by destruction and chaos when the nation, under Mao's direction and the auspices of "class struggle," became hell-bent on destroying any vestiges of the past to make way for a Revolutionary future. In its wake, there were two kinds of "Nothing." There was the plain-old literal Nothing, in terms of musical options to hear and play, but, even more significantly, there was the Nothing about which Cui sang: the disillusionment and disorientation that so many Chinese felt as their society emerged from Maoism.

The years following the death of Chairman Mao – who was once known as the "Sun in the Hearts" of the Chinese people and who I have heard called, with convincing argument, China's first punk – were defined by a particular and intense confusion. Everything that the Chinese had been raised to believe about their country and their society was being re-examined in the frenzy that was the new policy of 'Reform and Opening'. Society, according to the Party Line, was supposed to be the combination of the efforts of the collective, but some people now saw an out-of-control rush to a me-first mentality. It was these citizens who would be the first to hear and process all that rock music had to offer and, eventually, create a Thing – a kind of music, yes, but also more – called yaogun.

If Western rock blew the minds of young Chinese in the early eighties, Cui's song twisted heads clear off bodies and drop-kicked them across time and space. Western music was one thing, but with "Nothing to My Name" the lyrics were decipherable, not to mention completely sympathetic to so much of the nation's state of mind. Cui's voice was different, too: Instead of either shouting out the slogans of the day like a good comrade or whispering sweet nothings like the pop singers at the time, Cui's groan carried the aches, tensions and restlessness of a lost generation.

The casual follower of yaogun will have heard of the Legend of Cui, and how one night in 1986 he changed everything. But in the internet age it is all too easy to underestimate the significance of such an event. After all, Now is happening; Then is done.

But then you discover Then, and find that Now isn't all it's cracked up to be. The emergence of rock and roll defined the way in which yaogun developed, and continues to develop. Because there was no way that rock in China could be like rock in America or England or Russia or Japan – not, that is, until the new millennium, when societal and technological developments truly freed Chinese citizens from constraints that may not have been physically preventing contact with and absorption of foreign culture, but might as well have been.

While yaogun's later period is about how the music, the fans, the musicians and the scene in general developed alongside that of the West, its early period was marked by music finding its way through the country against unimaginable odds. Forget the struggle, say, over which Beatles album to start with; rockers had to figure out who, or *what*, the Beatles were. When he was sixteen, Zhang Fan fell in love with "Norwegian Wood." "It sounded like a fairy tale," said the baby-faced head of the Midi Music School and Festival – so much so that it inspired him to find out more about the artist. "So I looked up the word [Beatles] in the dictionary, but it wasn't in there." Zhang, and others across the country like him, eventually got together to educate each other; thus did a home-grown understanding of rock emerge almost completely isolated from its source.

Yaogun in the twenty-first century is similar to many other stories of contemporary China in that it is defined as much by its links to and commonality with the rest of the world as it is by an isolation that alternates between unintentional and self-imposed. It's exciting in a way that even the best music can't be, because of the odds.

Iggy Pop and the Stooges, wrote rock critic Lester Bangs in 1970, were "probably the first name group to actually form before they even knew how to play." This is the essence of rock and roll, he continues, and, one is quick to add, of yaogun. "Rock is mainly about beginnings," he said, and:

> [A]sserting yourself way before you know what the fuck you're doing . . . Rock is basically an adolescent music, reflecting the rhythms, concerns and aspirations of a very specialised age group . . . [E]verybody else seems either too sophisticated at the outset or hopelessly

poisoned by the effects of big ideas on little minds. A little knowledge is a dangerous thing.

The Stooges were certainly not the last name band to form
before they knew how to play. It has happened and continues
to occur in the Middle Kingdom with the kind of regularity and
results that are both extremely impressive and monumentally
depressing.

Yaogun is especially about beginnings: The beginnings that
laid the path for the rest of the story. The best yaogun acts have
been blessed with Bangs' "little knowledge." With little more
than shards of information and a lot of "concerns and aspirations" musical and social, these are some of the bands that, over
the years, have kept the yaogun flame from not, to borrow a
phrase, fading away. Not necessarily the most (in)famous of rock
bands to emerge over the past twenty-odd years, they are bands
whose stories tell us about what it is, and was, like to rock China
and, just as important, about how China was, and is still, rocking.

All the clichés about this country are true: old/new, commu-
nist/capitalist, order/chaos, rural/urban, rich/poor and all the
rest. Take your pick of the pastiche imagery that abounds across
the country. Gleaming skyscrapers full of the new middle and
upper class white-collar big spenders flanked by filthy shanty-
towns home to the disheveled and destitute working millions
that build the New China but can't quite seem to join it. Donkey-
drawn carts hauling the bricks that are all that remains of the
neighborhoods paved over to make way for the latest urban
improvement battling shiny new SUVs through crowded inter-
sections. Folding tables set up roadside, where hearty men gather
to guzzle the local firewater at pennies per liter while Chivas
is chugged by the several-hundred-dollar bottle just down the
road in dance clubs as neon-, laser- and iniquity-filled as their
Western counterparts. The thousands of years of history slowly
disappearing in the nation-wide march to an uber-modernity of

no particular kind. An economy kept straight by the State but yet wilder than any West ever imagined. There is more. Much more.

How phenomena of the contemporary world have entered, worked their way through and emerged from the culture of the Middle Kingdom is the story of the nation's last three decades. These were decades which were defined by an emergence from the isolation of the meta-if-not-completely-physical Great Wall, which, save for a few not-so-minor hiccups, tended, over the centuries, to keep out the barbarians and their ideas, and their stuff. But since the end of the Cultural Revolution and the dawn of the *new* New China, China's cities have become places that, in many ways, would not be completely unfamiliar to your average barbarian. What with the concept of borders becoming irrelevant and all, China's contemporary society increasingly reveals phenomena familiar to residents of Beijing and Boise alike.

Like, say, rock and roll music.

Because of this familiarity, international media reports on China's contemporary urban cultures – skateboarding, punk music, experimental theatre – abound, but rarely delve beneath the "hey-check-this-out-they're-doing-stuff-we-did!" quickie. Yes, there was a journey from Mao to mohawks, but as much as the alliteration may work, there's far more to the story than what's at the surface.

Rock music is a culture that represents a sliver of the nation, but it is a sliver that has emerged despite enormous odds and one of many sites of the current ancient-meets-modern, recent-past-meets-present, and communist-meets-capitalist battles being waged in every aspect of Chinese society. It is still up against a mainstream so overwhelming that to most of the population an alternative is literally impossible to envision.

We are constantly told that China is the world's factory; that the era of China is slowly dawning across the globe. Created, like anything else the country has produced, with raw materials and plans brought in from outside, yaogun has blossomed into a very particular form, linked to, but also separate from, its progenitor. Which is why yaogun has so much to teach us about rock and roll.

Yaogun is a many-splendored thing. A mix of people, styles and trends are united under the yaogun banner: a million schools of punks, metalheads, folkies, hippies, hipsters, skinheads, laptop-pers and rastamen. And many more. Their voices and noises rise up in opposition to the all-pervasive pop music of the West and of Mainland China, as well as of Hong Kong and Taiwan, the territo-ries that lie somewhere – geographically, conceptually, generally – between the two. Every permutation and combination of chords, notes, bleeps, beats, feedback, mouse clicks, reverb, melodies and screams combine into a rock scene more varied than it perhaps ought to be. Somehow, barely three decades into its history, yao-gun has already passed through every trend, scene and genre that slowly grew around rock in the West over five decades – while an unprecedented social, political and economic growth period liter-ally swept the ground beneath the nation's feet and continues to do so. Here, in the second decade of the new millennium, there isn't a kind of music you can't find in shops, on stages or coming out of speakers across the country.

But in the early eighties, while the practitioners of rock music in the West were well into their third decade of rocking and roll-ing, the creators of yaogun were only just beginning to hear the whispers of something completely new. Their mixtapes collected the voices of Teresa Teng; of Karen Carpenter and John Denver; of Michael Jackson, Lionel Richie and George Michael; of John, Paul, George and Ringo; of Madonna, Jon Bon Jovi, Axl Rose, Ozzie Osbourne, and more. They put together their own canon because in the early days, 'picky' wasn't something you could be.

Cassette tapes came at first only to the lucky. In the wake of the country's "Reform and Opening" in the late seventies and early eighties, a few Chinese people suddenly found themselves able to do business outside of the Mainland, and they often re-turned home with the first tastes of the pop music with which much of the world was already familiar. Tapes also came across

China's borders in the hands of the few Westerners now able to come in to the country. In the nineties, *dakou* – 'saw-gashed' or 'cut-out' – tapes and, later, CDs made their way in. These were the surplus that record manufacturers marked, with a gash or a hole, as garbage, and sent on via a network of various distributors, ostensibly to the dumps of southern China. Those tapes like, indeed, the yaogun it would inspire, somehow found their way to eager ears. One person's trash, indeed.

Slowly in those early years, a population emerged, eager to find out as much as possible about the music they'd stumbled upon. Slowly, they cobbled together something of an education, and they were eager to share and learn from one another about what they'd found. But it was impossible to control the flow of the new music. It came both too fast and too slow, with no sense of temporal, evolutionary or stylistic context to keep it in check. Without an educational infrastructure, the earliest listeners of rock and roll music in China were simultaneously prisoners of a sort of mixtape nightmare and the recipients of a rock and roll dream come true. On the one hand, it was a ton of new and exciting music; on the other, it was a soundtrack with no liner notes. It was hard – often impossible – to figure out what it was, how it came to be, where it fit, and what it might possibly mean. Even when the source material was available, its context was stripped clean, like so many elements of the New China. What you had was the vacuum about which Cui Jian spoke: It sounded cool, but what *it* was wasn't clear.

The educated class was a strange bunch. Early pirates put together collections of randomly compiled songs, like *The Best Rock 1955-1988*, which advertised "a half century of musical revolution," "systemic appreciation" and "value and enjoyment." There's a mixture of pleasure and confusion over the names checked on compilations such as this one, and the glimpse into the canon-building-in-progress: Bill Haley, Chuck Berry, Elvis, Dylan, Hendrix, the Stones, the Beatles, Pink Floyd ("Another Brick in the Wall"!), The Police, Van Halen, The Boss, U2, Tina

Turner, UB40, Michael Bolton, New Kids on the Block, Jon Secada. This tradition continues today in shops like Rockland, down a windy road just off the banks of central Beijing's lake district, where proprietor Xiao Zhan celebrated his shop's fifth anniversary with hand-picked compilations – like his predecessors, he is passionate about what others ought to hear.

To hear the stories of the early yaogunners' searching, one sees just how much of their lives were devoted to the music, digging in a way impossible to imagine from the perspective of our digital world. They had no choice; it was dig or miss out.

"We really wanted to understand everything," said one rocker, of his mid-nineties rock listening. "The first time I heard Velvet Underground I thought it was kind of noisy and not so great. We never thought 'this is bad, the critics are wrong'. We went to look into why these bands were chosen."

With a giddiness that took over his entire being, the founder of rock venue Mao Livehouse recalled the "good" old days of the early nineties, a "different kind" of good. "We were all discovering a new trail . . . things we didn't understand at all."

Lü Zhiqiang, the man behind Beijing live venue Yu Gong Yi Shan (named for the proverb of the Old Man Who Wanted to Move the Mountain, one shovel-full at a time), remembers "listening with our hearts. We had so few choices, but we cared."

The scale and effort of the first generation's journey is inspirational in a way that contemporary yaogun, and the coverage thereof, would do well to acknowledge and study. There's nothing less rock and roll than to demand respect for elders, and the New China isn't generally a place that looks back ungrudgingly, but true rock and roll, like any culture, is informed, defined and led by its past. And here's the thing: In the current scheme of things, when access is unfettered, it's just too easy to rock. It's still tough to break through, but it's too easy to collect music, obtain instruments, find band members, get gigs, grow a following. Because of that, the older generations are far more yaogun than the kids today will ever be, having come up in and through a world in which most things were impossible. Of course we shouldn't blame young 'gunners for living in a world of easy access. But we can blame them for ignoring the lessons of their predecessors.

Hearing about the discovery of rock in the eighties and nineties, the odds stacked against it and what it meant to those that found it can be shocking. It's easy to forget about how revolutionary rock could be; by the time Chinese kids discovered it, it had already been a long time since rock was supposed to Change the World. But it was literally a revolution when rock hit China. This is not, let us be clear, the "holy crap, rock makes me want to overthrow the government" kind of revolution. The only reason they heard rock in the first place was because China in the eighties was so open. That's the word used by those turned onto rock in the eighties: *open*. At the time, new inputs made their way through segments of the population, and early rockers, like contest-winners on a time-sensitive shopping spree, grabbed everything they could. Eventually, they came up with something resembling liner notes, and paved the way for a future of unlimited mixtapes of a new kind.

Dai Qin, who fronts the band Thin Man, was one of those early rockers. At eighteen, he was singing pop tunes in a nightclub in the Inner Mongolian capital of Hohhot, thinking about what a badass he'd been for walking away from the stable salary of a violin gig in the Inner Mongolian Autonomous Region's Song and Dance Troupe. He was killing it as a singer, making an unheard-of RMB50 (about US$9 at the time) a night, which wasn't only five times more than any other of the club's performers, but was a very good salary for *anyone* in 1992, considering that more than ten years later, your average office clerk was lucky to pull in three thousand a month. But when an Australian introduced him to the world of rock and roll, life, as he knew it, was over. It's impossible to imagine a man who has been since the late nineties the very model of a rock and roll frontman saying "What's rock and roll?" but that's just what he did in 1992. To say that the

Beatles changed his life only barely scratches the surface. When "Come Together" came on, he recalled, "I cried. The hair on my arms stood up. It was crazy! I didn't know what to do with myself. This is what I'd always wanted to do . . . but I had no idea how to do it." What he did was spend every waking hour pouring over the Fab Four, at the expense of not only his club gig. "It got to the point where the Beatles were the only thing getting me out of bed in the morning." He tattooed himself with the band's name, "so that every time I washed my face I'd see it . . . Their music was like a religion to me."

Influential Chinese critic and experimental musician Yan Jun invoked a Chinese saying that speaks to Dai's experience: A drowning man will grab for a blade of grass like it'll save his life. "Sure, it'd be better if it was a piece of wood," Yan said, recalling the desperation of the early- and mid-nineties for his generation, "but they'll grab onto the grass and hold on tight."

The point is that they were drowning. "If it wasn't music, it'd be something else, but at the time, it was music. Life was rough then, we needed something." For Dai Qin, rock was religion. For others, said Yan, it was more than that. "Some people really need these things, like drugs: 'Give me something, I'm begging you, whatever you have.' "

2

THE GREAT LEAP FROM NOTHING TO "NOTHING"

1949–1986

This world is changing,
It only longs to never change.

The Hundred Stars,
"Let the World Be Full of Love" (1986)

Rocking Tiger Versus Dragon

If there was a more unlikely time and place for rock and roll to put down roots than the People's Republic of China in the late seventies, it would be hard to imagine. The Chinese people, Mao Zedong announced from Tiananmen Square to the world on an October day in 1949, had stood up. But the newly upright nation proceeded to spend the next three decades, in terms of engaging with the outside world, pretty much standing still. It would be a long time thereafter before its people started moving to any rhythm, let alone one with a backbeat.

Emerging from a quarter-century of complete isolation that created a maelstrom of confusion, chaos and curiosity, the utter foreign-ness of rock, pop or any music beyond a few Chinese folk songs, revolutionary songs or the occasional classical piece can't be overstated. Music outside of those few options was simply not to be found by all but a fraction of the population until the early eighties. The nation was unprepared for, unable to receive and just plain uninterested in rock music – and most things Western.

There was, however, an exception. Ever since he first introduced the country to yaogun with his instant classic "Nothing to My Name," Cui Jian has been considered Yaogunner Number One, but there ought to be room astride his name for another – even if that name is one of the most infamous in contemporary China. Cui, yaogun's alpha and omega, has been slapped with the label of rock and roll bad boy, but Cui's bad-assingest pales in comparison to rock and roll listener and booster number one, "Tiger" Lin Liguo.

How nice would it have been if Cui confirmed rumors that he learned of rock music at Tiger's feet. "I've heard about Lin Liguo's interest in rock," Cui told me. "I don't know about having heard him play, but I've heard he had a guitar, and he liked music." But let's imagine, for a moment, a not-completely-unrealistic scene anyway: It's 1970, and a nine-year-old Cui, a decade and a half away from his appointment with rock and roll stardom, is wandering through the courtyard of the Air Force residential compound in which he and his family live. His dad, after all, is a horn player in the flyboys' orchestra. Tiger, meanwhile, worked high up in the Force, thanks to being the son of the Minister of Defense, and is no stranger to those barracks. A curious sound wafts toward Cui one day, the sound of an instrument he learns is a guitar. As he peers around a corner, he catches sight of a military man strumming and singing the Beatles, something Lin was said to have enjoyed doing.

"There will be a day," Tiger told his wife, with whom he enjoyed listening to rock music, "when I will let the Chinese know there is such wonderful music in the world." His people found out, eventually, but he would not live to see it.

Tiger's legacy has precluded the possibility of being remembered for being anything but the second-most-reviled (and son of the first-most-reviled) man in a country known for not even treating its friends kindly. It was a long way for Tiger's father, Lin Biao, to have fallen. A highly respected and admired general, Lin Biao became Defense Minister in 1959. Within ten years he was hand-picked to succeed Chairman Mao, but power, particularly late in Mao's tenure, tended to bring at least as much suspicion as it did perks. Whether Mao became paranoid of Lin's rising power or Lin and Tiger became worried about Mao, it is believed that coups and assassinations were planned. Whether it was Lin Jr. or Sr. (or neither) who hatched the various plots worthy of Hollywood (suicide helicopter mission on National Day in Tiananmen square; a fake war with Russia to get Mao in a bunker that could be filled with poison gas; an air strike on the

Chairman's train) matters little to their legacies. They were both branded traitors.

One could envision Tiger plotting a coup to a soundtrack of rock music. He was, at the time, one of the only people in the country to have heard of it, and certainly the only one on record digging it, thanks to the access granted to the ruling elite – access that is also said to have brought him a substantial stash of pornography. There are reports of Tiger, a handsome young man who looks, in a grainy photo, more like college kid than an army official, cruising the streets of Beijing in his convertible jeep with the Beatles blasting from within, passersby responding no different than they would to an alien craft. He's also said to have cruised the country scouting for women to join the team known as "Tiger's Angels," personally overseeing, through two-way mirrors, the requisite physical examinations deemed an essential part of the "recruitment" process.

History tells us that a plane carrying Lins Jr. and Sr., along with Mrs. Lin Biao, crashed under mysterious circumstances into the Mongolian countryside in the wee hours of a September morning in 1971, in the wake of the family's attempted takeover of the country. History is unclear about what happened: Did the plane run out of gas? Was it attacked by the very air force planes Tiger used to command or, perhaps, by missiles? Did the pilot sabotage the plane? All of the above? None of the above? Also unclear is whether or not Lin Biao and his wife had been killed the night before, when rockets were fired on the car returning them home from a dinner with Mao.

With his reputation sealed, Lin Liguo may not have been – may still not be – the ideal candidate to take rock to the masses. Even four decades after his death, his name evokes dread and the personification of the lengths to which power can corrupt. And then there's the rock – and the porn, and the womanizing and the general malfeasance. It's conceivable that all of the stories that color the Lin family legacy were created in the service of ruining them, but the stories do say important things about the perplexing paranoia that defined China in the last decade of Mao's life.

Though they may never have met, Lin Liguo and Cui Jian are joined in more than a metaphoric sense, and not simply as examples of how rock turns good boys bad. A look into the changing state of affairs in the seventies and early eighties reveals that at the time, the decision to rock and the decision to assassinate the Great Helmsman were, to most people, equally ridiculous. Thus it would be some time before anyone seriously took up the rock Mission where Lin Liguo left it.

Something, Elsewhere

When we talk about rock in foreign lands, we talk, intentionally and not, about the paradigm of Rock as Agent of Change. The paradigm is useful, but not to predict a rock-and-roll-led revolution in store for the PRC. What's useful about it is how it paints the picture of the West's understanding of the power of music, and of the West's understanding of China. Rock's history and promise is based on the story of the music rocking, first, American society and, eventually, the Soviet bloc, bringing down the Wall and Communism. This history weighs heavily in the Chinese context, where politics is something more, something different and something all-encompassing; where Revolution with a capital 'R' is not only tangible and strived for, but something that happened and supposedly continues to occur. It's equally important to recognize the limits of the paradigm. The story of Western rock's entering China and becoming yaogun fits, and it doesn't.

The images of rock rebels throughout the years abound, from Chuck Berry adding rhythm to blues and duck-walking his way into the hearts of millions of young girls, and the deepest recesses of their parents' fears, to generations of shock-rockers who eschew subtleties in the effort to remind parents why they might well want keep their daughters under lock and key. In addition to challenging the status quo, rock (and folk) music speared change across Western society at large, in the fights against segregation and the Vietnam War or in raising awareness of everything from famine to feminism.

After the Wall came down, those of us in the Free World learned that a serious swath of the Soviet Bloc was almost contemporaneously in the rock and roll loop, from the moment "Rock Around the Clock" hit the charts, and that there might well have been a line connecting the music and the Movements. In the throes of the Cold War, though, the view from both sides was that rock was not only evil, but that the other guys planted it in our midst to control brains via the booty. The East Germans saw Chubby Checker's "Twist" as an "instrument of the imperialists," while some Americans, who felt that rock hadn't been properly vilified by its link to Satan, insisted that Soviet scientific research rubles were being spent on hypnotizing the youth via the backbeat.

While rock and roll's homeland saw something of the music's protest power, it went to a new level when we learned that it provided the soundtrack for the Prague Spring in 1968 – where, three years before that, Allen Ginsberg had declared that rock "had shaken loose the oppressive shackles of Stalinism" – and for Poland's early-eighties reforms. How better to explain *glastnost* than pointing to Gorby's love of the Beatles?

If rock and roll hadn't brought down the Wall, it was at least a gateway drug that shook the ground to loose the structure. Pink Floyd's performance of *The Wall* in the former no-man's land between East and West Berlin – just eight months after Germans had taken up the album's advice to "tear down the Wall" – connected dots that may or may not have been intentionally linked. (Roger Waters' performance in Shanghai seventeen years later may have referenced the link but didn't have quite the impact).

Legendary producer and musician Brian Eno summed up the greatest irony in the distinction between Eastern and Western conceptions of rock when he said that those living behind the Iron Curtain "believed in the power of art . . . They believed, that it could make a difference."

Something (Wicked) This Way Comes

China's view of art was rooted in the same ground as that of the Soviets. The Party Line, which extends into the twenty-first century, was created in 1942, when Mao and his Communists were guerrillas in the wilderness, nearly a decade before founding the People's Republic. They convened the Yan'an Conference on Literature and Art, setting the stage for the world in which future 'gunners came of age.

"Literature and art are subordinate to politics," quoth Chairman Mao, "but in their turn exert a great influence on politics." The goal of art – a poster, a play or, much later, a three-minute-and-thirty-three-second pop song – was to "awaken and arouse the popular masses, urging them on to unity and struggle and to take part in transforming their own environment." Artists are responsible for the education of the masses and creation of their culture, a responsibility that is double-edged, to say the least. Art wasn't just something you did: It was essential, and in the wrong hands, existentially threatening. Artists were Cultural Workers, as essential to the Mission as the farmers in the rice field and the folks on the cement factory floor, and were seen with a respect befitting this role. As official concerns over rock music increased in this light, so too were musicians' and listeners' aspirations amplified.

As critic and author Hao Fang put it, "To us, China in the eighties resembled the US of the sixties." Both, he said, were defined by "a few people in the cultural realm [who] thought they could change the world." In China's case, these few people understood that changing the world was their job. With our contemporary rock-is-just-music eyes, it's hard to see music as anything more than something to listen to, and possibly, to play. But 'play' is hardly the verb most up to the task of describing what the first generations of yaogunners were doing, and what the music did to them upon their discovery of it. This is intimately wrapped up not only in the idea of the task of a Cultural Worker, but also of the world in which they found themselves.

In 1986, as Cui sang the song that made his fellow citizens long to sing, his country was still reeling from and dealing with the legacy – political, psychological and physical – of Mao's rule. China's sixties were chaotic in a very particular way; this was no free-love-end-the-war type of flower-power sixties chaos. Yaogunners born in the sixties (or earlier) were wrapped up in the almost complete and utter societal chaos that defined the Cultural Revolution. In the late sixties, as American popular music was embarking on something of a revolutionary path, Chinese youths became empowered by a revolution of a different kind, one inspired by an increasingly paranoid Mao. Millions of kids dubbed Red Guards embarked on a campaign of destruction – first, in aid of ridding the country of the "Four Olds" (old culture, old ideas, old customs and old habits), and later, in ridding the nation of "bourgeois elements" or anyone else they decided to mark as Enemies of the People.

Which is, in short, to say that there was an enormous amount of trauma that created, shaped and defined the new nation, as it began to learn to rock.

By the late seventies, the music came to some; somehow they took to it, and then, even more outrageously, took it and used it. Those first listeners found an outlet that enabled them to recognize, work through and express all of the confusion, rage and emotion that defined their generation, at a point in time when even recognizing these previously unmentionables was inconceivable.

Timing was everything: This was a generation old enough to remember living through the tumultuous times of the previous decades, and fully cognizant of the tumult that shaped and predated those times. They came out at the eighties end confused, to say the least, and eager for something, but with no idea what that something could possibly be.

As rock's first converts began to look into and behind the music and the world that created it, an excitement built up. This echoed the general feelings of the nation. There was, beginning in the late seventies, a feeling not only that change had come, but that further change was possible. Change had traditionally come from the nation's youth – from the founding of the Communist Party to the Red Guards mobilized during the Cultural Revolution, to the protest and movements of the mid- and late seventies. In the wake of Mao's death, a generation returned to the education system after it had been shut down in the Cultural Revolution, perfectly poised to Change Things.

Meanwhile, there were the fears of officialdom, summed up – in 1990, no less – by a member of the Shanghai Philharmonic during a seminar on cultural thought:

> The bourgeoisie of the West use pop songs to propagate their view of life and value system. We should never underestimate [the danger] of this. Our foreign enemies have not for an instant forgotten that music can change the way people think.

Influential DJ Zhang Youdai recalled being summoned by a cultural official around the same time to explain the music he'd been finally granted permission to play on China Central Radio. Youdai began with a brief history lesson, but was stopped by the time he hit Elvis. The official didn't want to hear the history of rock, Youdai said. What he wanted to hear was about how rock music had come to be considered a "scourge of biblical proportions." The official had understood that the end of the USSR came "when kids started listening to rock."

Something Emerges, but It Doesn't Quite Rock

After Mao's death, the excesses of the Cultural Revolution were pinned upon the Gang of Four. The Gang, high-ranking officials – including Mao's wife – that had attempted a coup in the wake of the death of the Chairman, made a handy punching bag for the anger and resentment that piled up over the years. Deng Xiaoping was brought back from near political death to lead the new New China into the eighties under a banner of Reform and Opening; "socialism with Chinese characteristics" implied that the nation would slowly rejoin the rest of the world. But music, for most, still comprised a small number of songs that the entire nation heard endlessly on the handful of radio stations broadcasting for a few hours of the day. Only if you were one of the small minority of people who had family members with a job that gave them the brand new ability to travel to Hong Kong or overseas, or if you happened to be their friends, would you have possibly gotten a taste of something remotely different. You might have been a university student (after the universities were re-opened in 1977) who befriended an overseas student with a cassette collection – but you were probably also worried about the potential consequences of such a friendship; ditto for any relationship with a foreign journalist, as the journalist was likely branded a spy from his first moment in-country.

The first taste, in the late seventies and early eighties, of music different from the standard folk or revolutionary song seems, upon reflection, not just harmless, but so harmless that the association might be harmful to yaogun's reputation. If yaogun were another kind of rock – crack-cocaine, let's say – and if the first step on the path to dope-fiend-dom was smoking a cigarette, then one might assume that a balladeer like the Taiwanese pop songstress Teresa Teng is like a can of soda: sugary and sweet and safer than tobacco. Probably not the item that sets one off on the journey that ends face-down in a ditch with track marks up and down your arms and a needle sticking out from between your big and second toes.

But only to the untrained eye.

There was, in those years, an element of danger involved in listening to Teng, who is known in Mandarin as Deng Lijun. That she is a singer in the Karen Carpenter-circa-"Rainy Days and Mondays" vein with the wholesome image of a small-town Homecoming Queen only makes her rebelliousness more insidious. Her syrupy melodies, which were not officially allowed on the Mainland until the late eighties but found their way into stereos and karaoke halls regardless, were for many people the first taste of anything musical that wasn't a product of the Cultural Revolution. Particularly in the late seventies and early eighties, Teng provided an escape from the dreariness of the days before Reform and Opening led to a true opening.

When Li Chi, who would go on to open Beijing's premier live rock venue, Mao Livehouse, was coming of age in the late seventies and early eighties, "there were only Cultural Revolution songs. I could sing them all . . . You can not like them, but there wasn't anything else. I thought *White Haired Girl* [one of the Eight Model Plays deemed politically correct enough to be performed in the sixties] had a few nice melodies, but there was nothing interesting really."

Until Li Chi discovered, as the saying goes, that "Old Deng [Xiaoping] rules by day and Little Deng [Teresa Teng] rules by night." Li recalled the first night, in 1977, that he heard Little Deng: "It blew me away! It was so good! We had a four-speaker stereo system," a rarity for the time. "I went right up to the stereo and sat a couple inches from the speaker all night."

Many an old-school yaogunner had similar experiences: "It was gorgeous," recalled one early rocker. "The voice was just pure velvet. I mean, at the time, I just worshipped it . . . I didn't tell anybody, but I came back home and listened to [Teresa Teng] when nobody else was around."

Zhang Youdai, the DJ credited by many who came of age in the nineties with introducing Western music to a generation, was also smitten with Little Deng. While Li Chi got intimate with his speakers, Youdai was given a hint that this might be something of a forbidden fruit: "There was a guy in the neighborhood that used to play her tapes in his yard. He was a young cool guy; kind of a *liumang* (hoodlum). He had long hair." Zhang's use of *liumang* and "long hair" were descriptives charged with equal amounts of respect for people who dared to exist outside of the mainstream and disdain for the mainstream. Long hair, as Youdai would soon personally discover, was a massive statement of its own. Nearly insane at the time, and only slightly less insane for a decade and a half thereafter, it was a sure sign of mischief and criminality. "He used to play the music really loud on Sunday mornings. I listened once and I remembered the songs."

"Big Sister" Tang Lei is known across the country for her commitment to keeping the south-western city of Chengdu rocking. Her entry into rock was also precipitated by Teresa Teng, who gave the then-postal worker much-needed escape from the dreariness of her job. "Our tapes were copies, and we listened to them over and over until they were such bad quality that we could barely make out the words."

Though Teresa Teng's music comprised candy-coated cheese-laden love songs wrapped in a poofy-dress-wearing, jewelry-ensconced, soft-focused-photo package, her music was nothing less than revolutionary. Her popularity, at first, freaked out the Mainland authorities. They called it "pornographic," "decadent," and worse, and banned it. This illicitness only added another mind-blowing layer to the experience of listeners who had just discovered that there were, in fact, musical alternatives. The authorities eventually came around, offering the ultimate in approval: an invitation, in 1988, to perform at the Spring Festival Gala, which, broadcast on the eve of the Chinese New Year, is the most important television event on the Chinese calendar – an estimated three-quarters of the population tunes in to the show as an essential part of their families' celebrations. Broadcast since 1983, it is a variety show of epic proportions featuring four hours of song, dance, acrobatics, comedy and more in a never-ending attempt to out-do the pomp of the previous year. Teng couldn't make the engagement and it would be nearly twenty years before anyone found out she'd been invited.

To this day, you can still hear Teng's voice in contemporary pop, and her music is a staple of public address systems and karaoke halls nationwide (in a nation as karaoke-obsessed as China, that's certainly saying something). But her impact upon the country was not limited to officialdom and pop. Upon her death in 1995, the album *Goodbye Rock* featured yaogun's contemporary stars performing a collection of Teng covers. Ten years later, a song on Cui Jian's long-awaited fifth album invoked her tune "Little Town Story."

As China's leader, Old Deng, cracked open the gates to the Kingdom, it was only a matter of time before China came up with its own mainstream pop music and an industry that might compete with the Western, Taiwanese and Hong Kong (sung in Cantonese and known as Cantopop) versions that flooded the market. That form, a distinctly Mainland version, was called *tongsu*. While rockers had no choice but to be aware of – and, in many cases, perform – *tongsu*, its relation to yaogun is as the mainstream against which one might attempt to swim. Of course, *tongsu* covered so much territory that it is more useful to think of it not in terms of water, but rather air. Like other industries in the era of the creeping capitalism, a balance needed to be struck between permitted and profitable. Mainland studios cranked out pop tunes in line with officialdom's requirements; singers were brought in after a lengthy "creative" process that combined Approval from Above with as much pop sensibility as could be fit into the Party mold. Here was socialism with Chinese characteristics played out in verses and choruses, a Brill-Building-Meets-Great-Hall-of-the-People; songs written for the People, if not necessarily by the People.

One *tongsu* song emblematic not only of that balance, but also of the early eighties back-and-forth surrounding culture in general, was "Night at the Naval Base." In 1980, Su Xiaoming, a singer in the Naval Song and Dance Troupe, sang the song at a "Rising Star" concert. In the visual mold of Teresa Teng, the clean-cut Su had an intensity behind her ever-present smile that hinted at her military background. In the same way that Teng's songs serenaded a mass audience, Su's song quickly became popular, and one early yaogunner remembers that it was "the first time people heard something that beautiful." The song was about a group of sailors as their ship is gently rocked in the hometown current. As quickly as it became popular, though, the song began to receive criticism from above. The combination of the rousing string section, the recorder solo and the female chorus of "oohs" put it firmly in cheese-pop territory and far from the military-march style that, critics said, befitted a song about the military. Nor did the song stack up lyrically. Soldiers couldn't possibly sleep, it was argued, when they had a nation to defend. It was quickly banned, and slapped with the *ducao* (poisonous weed) label that had been used to describe Teresa Teng, whose style was surely the song's musical inspiration. Like Teng, Su's ban didn't last long; "Night at the Naval Base" was eventually freed from its decadent shackles. Su would later perform it – along with a video featuring soldiers standing on guard, sending messages via flashing lights and, yes, sleeping soundly – on the annual Spring Festival Gala in 1986.

As the Mainland pop machine sought balance between pop and politics, it couldn't crank out hits that compared with its Hong Kong and Taiwanese counterparts. The top ten songs in Shanghai's 1989 charts were all from Hong Kong. The following year, it was seven out of ten. This "cultural competition" between the Mainland and Taiwan/HK, as has been suggested by China scholar Geremie Barmé, helped yaogun: In an effort to see more home-grown talent, yaogun was tolerated. Eventually, *tongsu* found a balance. While still behind in audiences and production quality compared to what has come out of Hong Kong and Taiwan, the Mainland pop industry is now a healthy one.

The pop industry that took off enshrined the singer as superstar. That an artist might require instruments was not just a technical challenge, but also a challenge to the predictability of the carefully constructed song. That the artists might choose to look more like their audiences than the idealized version of a star was illogical, because why would people buy records of someone who wasn't beautiful? The idea that the artists would write their own material made no sense. After all, it was only a select group of Illuminati skilled enough in politics and pop who knew what the People ought to be hearing and how it ought to be sung at them. Singing competitions, an effective way for Officialdom to enshrine and encourage their own popstar model, predated *Pop Idol* in China. In 1987, writes *tongsu* and yaogun historian Andrew Jones, there were already audiences of 700 million – 68 percent of the population – tuned in to shows such as *National Tongsu Contest* and *National Youth Singers Television Contest*. On the one hand, this number and percentage is huge; on the other, you wonder what the other 32 percent were watching, since there wasn't much else on. The combination of televised singing competitions and karaoke's popularity fed off of each other, and hits spread far and wide and quickly while music became synonymous with singing one's heart out. Thus did rock face a huge hurdle that remained as yaogun took off: the "singer" versus the "band"; the "song" versus the "music." It wasn't until they had glimpses of Japanese pop, said early rocker Liang Heping, that folks realized "that the singer and the musicians could be the same people." To this day, an often-added compliment to a pop star is that they "write their own stuff" or that they "actually play an instrument."

Debatably the earliest challenger to the *tongsu* regime was Zhang Xing. Whether or not one might count the eighties star as one of yaogun's earliest practitioners, his reputation and flamboyant lifestyle created the impression, at the very least, of a rock star. American guitarist and former China resident Dennis Rea, who played several concerts with Zhang, remembers the performer as a "dandy" with an "impeccably tailored suit, slicked-back hair and stylish sunglasses." Not exactly the embodiment of rock and roll, but in the early days, this is what one got.

Kids around the country were drawn to Zhang's music, like future Shanghai rocker "Pang Pang" Li Jianfang, who was drawn by the rhythm. There were hints of rocking and rolling in his music, but also sap and saccharine. It's only in hindsight, of course, that we can smile with the naïveté that would have seen Zhang as a threat, though that feeling is tempered by the knowledge that he spent three years in the clink – for violating, according to China Radio International, "the marital laws of the time," which attested to his rock and roll lady-killing lifestyle. But other than Zhang's bad-ass image, there was nothing familiar about yaogun, as it emerged, to enable the masses to accept – or process – it. When not just everyone you know, but *literally everyone* is being weaned on the same cultural teat, the choice to look elsewhere for sustenance is a massive statement. And that's just what the first yaogunners did. And when they left the communal breast, they were hungry.

China Learns (to) Rock: the Party to the Party Scene

"People my age," said Zhang Fan, head of the Midi Music School and Festival, referring to his fellow children of the sixties, "we started life in a very un-free place . . . We experienced it all."

It's a massive understatement. Those of his generation were intimately wrapped up in the shift from the chaos of the end of the Mao era to the complete societal transformation of the late seventies and eighties. Thus were those of Zhang's generation in a particular position to not only be ready for, but to absorb and begin to process something like yaogun. Especially since music played a role in their lives from an early age.

After the Gang of Four's downfall in the wake of Mao's autumnal passing, Zhang Fan recalled, songs emerged expressing an optimism for the future.

"Through songs I got moved into thinking about how things were getting better. That young people were going to be the future. That things are good, the country is opening up . . . That we should contribute to the nation. It made me really happy, and want to contribute."

Only later did songs start to point out problems. The alienation of the post-Mao period and creeping Western culture resulted in the Root-Seeking movement that saw artists across the cultural spectrum engaged in a search for a Chinese identity in and amongst the contemporary chaos. While roots-seeking captivated academics and artists, the masses were more moved by the musical corollaries. Alternatives to the prevalent *tongsu* music, in the form of "northwest wind" folk – a label with which Cui Jian's "Nothing to My Name" would be slapped – and "prison songs" were starting to emerge. The latter proved more controversial, written, as they were, by or from the perspective of ex-convicts and former so-called "rusticated youth" – those "sent down" to the countryside during the Cultural Revolution to be educated by the peasants. These songs spoke directly of those experiences as well as celebrating the vulgar alternative lifestyles of the down-and-out. In April 1985, hundreds of these people descended upon Beijing. Nearly twenty years after being sent down, they demanded permission to return home. Months later, Cui Jian released *Vagabond's Return*, a product of the time before he broke out of the pop world. Though you would have to file *Vagabond's Return*, genre-wise, under EZ listening, its eponymous song was anything but, both in the wake of that event, and to anyone who had been 'sent down' or knew someone who had.

While stylistically different, one common trait held by both northwestern wind and prison songs was the expression of dissatisfaction on some level (sometimes expressed through drink- and smoke-ables), a trait not lost on the authorities. Both the idea of singing from an alternative viewpoint and the content that was sung were certainly rock and roll. And prison songs attracted a similar demographic as yaogun: It was the same underclasses singing and being sung about that were most attracted to prison songs, and the alternative nature of the music also appealed to urban youth. China scholar Andrew Jones reports that somewhere in the neighborhood of three hundred thousand prison-song tapes were sold between the winter of 1988 and the spring of 1989; knock-off compilations were soon also hitting the streets, and the product was selling at a rate that increased as fast as official disapproval of it. The beauty parlors and restaurants that were among the first officially-sanctioned private businesses proved great venues from which to spread the gospel: They blasted the music into their establishments and onto the streets nearby.

If you were just to read about prison songs you might get excited by their revolutionary tint, their anti-authoritarian fervor and general bird-flipping to society at large. But then you take even a quick listen to a clip of a song or two by the man most often associated with the prison song genre, Chi Zhiqiang, and you find music far removed from anything remotely rock, despite all the academic high-fiving. A random sample of the genre's music – from the introspective "Anxious, ah, Anxious" wherein the narrator finds himself in a prison, metaphoric or actual, after separating from loved ones, or the celebratory "Beer and Cigars Are First Rate" – brought karaoke-hall flourishes of electonic baroque bedlam combining pop drumming with synthesized string sections and Chinese instrumentation.

There was more than politics muddying up the path to and through yaogun in the eighties. There was the music itself, which came into the country both too fast to keep track of and too slow to feed the insatiable hunger a generation had just realized they were feeling. Though the amount of music available increased over the eighties, all too often in yaogun's earliest days the sources to which the new recruits turned were of information rather than of music, and it is no wonder that processing it all was far more complex and involved than one might imagine.

In 1980, seventeen-year-old Wang Di was still a few years away from joining the pop world. He attended the high school affiliated with the Central Academy of Art, the school that got fed the top artists from around the country. It was a place whose students you could safely say were different. In addition to being blessed with artistic talent, many were blessed with family members connected enough that they were among the first to be able to travel and work abroad – and to get their children into the school. "We came to rock in a strange way," Wang recalled. "[It was] from a conceptual perspective. I came to think that art was kind of boring, and wanted to get involved in culture. At the time, we were really intense about wanting to find out what it was like overseas." Reading through books and articles on philosophy and culture, which became more widespread as the years went by, the same names would keep popping up: the Beatles, the Rolling Stones, Bob Dylan. Even English learning aided their search, as textbooks were peppered with cultural content in the guise of language learning. "The information came from so many different places," Wang said. That included netting a few foreign friends who aided in the actual acquisition of the music they'd only read about. With stories about the sixties and all the surrounding cultural, social and political context, they weren't just excited about the soundtrack. They were excited about the possibilities that the soundtrack brought.

But because they were contextualizing on-the-fly, the early rockers-to-be were in a strange place. The excitement about the era didn't, for Wang Di, match the music. The first Beatles record he heard, *Abbey Road*, may have been a product of a time in which he was extremely interested, but it didn't quite do it for him musically. "My initial reaction was that it wasn't that special . . . We listened to more ornamental, big rock." It was because, he continued, by the time he first heard the Beatles, he'd already heard his first rock album, an album that "had a huge effect" on him: *Bad for Good* by Jim Steinman, which he heard soon after it was released in 1981. If *Abbey Road* was criticized for overproduction, then there are no words for *Bad For Good*'s production technique. It was, after all, supposed to be the sequel to the legendary, if less-than-subtle *Bat Out of Hell*, which Steinman co-wrote with Meatloaf. The Beatles, it seemed, took some getting used to before they took their rightful place in the rock and roll canon of early rock fans in China.

Critic Yan Jun, too, was less than impressed. "I'd heard the word 'yaogun' before," he said, recalling his first listen to the Beatles in 1988, when he was 15. "I was kind of disappointed at how soft it was. I'd heard that rock was really intense, that it'd make me sweat and move."

Hao Fang, early critic and influential author and translator of many books in the yaogun canon, had a similar this-can't-be-rock experience. Initially, Hao was a big fan of classical music, and of Wagner in particular. "I was a philosophy student," he explained, "so I listened to a lot of classical." As a professor he stumbled into one of the many video rooms of Wuhan to watch *Apocalypse Now*. These pseudo-theatres, which dotted the country into the nineties, were basically living rooms with ticketed entrance where the public could get a glimpse of often poorly-copied movies. When Wagner's "Flight of the Valkyries" provided the soundtrack to the film's helicopter attack, Hao Fang was blown away. But, more significant was the film's final sequence, scored by the Doors' "The End." "[The Wagner scene] was really great. But then to have so few musicians make such a huge impression it was amazing. I realized, wow, rock can be really big." Soon thereafter, he discovered the philosophical powers of rock. It could affect more than just what one heard; it could change your life:

> The biggest impression rock made on me was to show me that there was another choice besides the life of an average person . . . If you listen to rock, the things you initially thought were beautiful aren't as beautiful anymore . . . The things that others think are amazing, you start to think are unimportant.

It was because of the chaotic nature of the learning process that early rockers were both saved and confounded by the music they'd discovered. With a fervor of almost cultish proportions – not so much a drooling, brainless, automaton kind of a fervor you'd see in some wacky religious sect, but more like an exciting, cool and dedicated fervor of an objectively good cause – new converts to yaogun dug, saved, copied, searched, listened and did whatever else they could do to compile collections, spread the word and attempt to understand and process the material.

In 1992, China scholar Andrew Jones followed a posse of rockers who would gather to listen and trade tapes they'd gotten from foreign students living in Beijing. "They listened," Jones writes, "to whatever they could get their hands on . . . It was as if they'd been living in a house without a toilet. The air was fetid, the windows wouldn't open, and the room was so filthy you didn't even know who you were anymore." The music was indoor plumbing, he said. "Rock music was release, in its purest and most urgent form."

These guys weren't *playing* rock, they were *living* it, even before they got on a stage – or whether they got on a stage at all. Not only does this produce a very different product, it is also a shocking thing to behold for a child of rock's motherland. It's what happens when one is faced with one's own culture as processed, reconsidered and transformed by an Other. The choice to rock signaled much more than a simple preference for a particular kind of music that sounded like a good time, but also something slightly less than a conscious decision to overthrow the shackles of oppression. The impression that rock music made upon so many Chinese listeners, from the late seventies to the new millennium, was one that caused something of a life-altering change in their lives, separating them from society at large. Casual listening was just not possible. It's not that the discovery process wasn't fun, it's just that it was also extremely important.

Tapes were passed around, copied and played until they literally gave out. The journey of rock's discovery became part of the larger project of China's opening up. Faced with a new world that existed outside the Great Wall, early yaogunners were on a quest to learn about as much of what was going on Out There as possible. There was a general hunger for information about American culture at the time, and it simultaneously fed and inspired the interest in pop and rock music. It was a time when, surprisingly perhaps, there was a wealth of sources – besides cassettes – to which a Chinese interested in American culture could turn. As learning English became more widespread, culture became teaching aids; chapters in English-language learning books spoke of music, film and more. There were a number of books in translation and magazines with Euro-American content that fed and created the hunger for even more cultural content. Just as *Purple Rain* found its way through the tape players of the yaogun community of academics and scenesters, so too, did William Manchester's mammoth *The Glory and the Dream: A Narrative History of America, 1932-1972* make the rounds.

Because the news of the failure of the dreams of America's sixties either hadn't reached China's shores or else wasn't granted the attention that the era's successes were, there was an intensified passion for the music that proved an aural window into the world of which they longed to be a part. "We didn't really care what kind of music we got," remembers Cui Jian, who was part of the earliest community eager to hear the sounds of the rest of the world. "Listening to these . . . compilations, we thought we were getting the world's best music and all the information as it was coming out in the rest of the world. It was such a happy feeling to know that we weren't backward. We were with the times."

Until the early nineties, there were few places that had music for sale, but there was a small supply of officially available music. Beginning in 1985, there were regular audio-visual exhibitions at which international labels set up booths, but tapes were sold at international prices far beyond the range of most Chinese at the time. "We don't expect to sell very many tapes this time," a Virgin Records representative at the 1985 exhibition told Reuters. "But there's a lot of interest when we show music videos."

The Central publishing house – China National Publishing Import Export Corporation – ran shops that stocked officially imported music, but, as DJ Zhang Youdai recalled, the experience was less than positive. "The tapes were behind these glass displays, so you couldn't really see what they were; it was like a medicine shop." There's also the shopping experience. "Cold," was Youdai's quick description of the record shop staff. Even though "cold" could describe a hipper-than-thou indie record store dude from any major American city, there is at least a theoretical chance for a record-buyer to prove that he's a part of the club. No such luck for young Chinese rockers.

Into the shop they go, where they are met with indifference at best; at worst, the glare of the shopkeepers I imagine fit the mold of the predominantly female middle-aged State-owned store clerk – a State, one is quick to add, whose motto is "Serve the People." With permanent scowl on their faces and a disdain not only for the products they are tasked with selling but for anyone stupid enough to come looking for them, interrupting their tea-sipping, newspaper-reading, shooting-the-shit-with-the-other-dozen-superfluous-staffers-ing, their eyes follow the young rockers and send the message that they'd really rather not have to open the glass cases to let some young no-goodnik eyeball a tape for which they can't imagine anyone being naïve enough to pay actual money. Thing is, in those official collections were some gems to be found, like Bon Jovi and Guns n'

Roses, both of which were stocked by official record shops way back when.

Young rockers assembled collections by grabbing what they could from as many friends, family members and friends' family members as possible. The act of listening to the new incoming music, by virtue of the sheer amount of processing that was required, was a full-time pursuit, only somewhat familiar to music geeks of all stripes. There was certainly a sense of pride, adventure and excitement in the collective journey of yaogunners-to-be discovering the new music. The journey took many forms, from lunchtime listening with a select few classmates around a rare tape player to underground parties where new tapes would be unveiled to an ever-growing in-the-loop community. There are few interviewed for this book that don't remember getting "this tape" from someone – a rare encounter with a foreigner in the early eighties, a classmate, or even, in a few cases, a parent – and finding a third eye Windexed clean and wide open. "Looking back," said Li Chi of Beijing's Mao Livehouse, "those really were the good old days."

There was certainly a sense among the early yaogunners that the journey was a collective enterprise – even if it was lonesome. For many new converts, it was nearly impossible to conceive of the idea of a collective rock and roll experience. While there was a collective vibe to the tape culture that saw the eagerness feed a desire to share, yaogunners through the ages recall their early days with rock music as mind-expanding if solitary periods. These folks had found something that, finally, spoke to them, but also discovered that it spoke to a rare few who were not easy to find. In his 1993 book *Seeking the Rock and Roll Dream*, Xue Ji observed that early rock fans "betrayed their families, because there was no common language left anymore. They spent their time mostly listening to foreign tapes . . . using all their energy . . . They were artificially isolated from the world."

Critic and writer He Xiaoyu remembers the few students in his school that listened to rock music "were not considered normal . . . We'd be hanging out in a room and we'd put rock music on and everyone else would leave." Like generations of teenagers around the world before and since, their answer was to burrow further.

In the face of the isolation that yaogunners chose along with their music and lifestyle, it took a special breed to stay committed. Theirs was the commitment that saw the bulk of a 200 yuan (about US$25 at the time) monthly salary parlayed into tapes and concert tickets, like in the case of Wang Zhuohui who, in 2002, opened Free Sound Records, a CD shop that is one of Beijing's best. "Most of the money I made as a chef I spent on music," he said, remembering 60-yuan ($7.25) tickets for shows at French restaurant-cum-live-venue Maxim's, 10-yuan tapes ($1.25) and CDs at fifteen times that.

Mao Livehouse's Li Chi said that the high price of the albums he bought turned them into something more than simply discs. "I treated my CDs like girlfriends. They were that important, precious and valuable to me."

The prospect of a new tape led one enthusiast to bike his way clear across town, and do the unthinkable: cut class. He biked the fifteen-odd kilometers (about nine miles) to his friend's place, copied the Culture Club tape and rode back to school. The fact that they only got to hear half the record – half the tape had been dubbed over with country music – didn't dull the excitement one bit.

A sense of mission united yaogunners. "There was a real scene," Kaiser Kuo recalled of Beijing in the late eighties, when he co-founded heavy metal band Tang Dynasty. The community that Kuo observed and joined was, early on, possible to penetrate because fellow travelers recognized their own.

"In Beijing, it was so rare to meet people that knew about rock music, so everyone became friends," said Huang Feng, who, thanks to a father working overseas and classmates with parents abroad, was privy to pop early on. As a high-schooler on a field trip to a park in 1989, he saw a bunch of long-hairs and knew he had to talk to them. "They looked so different and unique. One had an AC/DC shirt that was obviously hand-painted." In an age when growing one's hair long was much more than just a fashion statement, for the seventeen-year-old Huang to walk up to the rockers and initiate a conversation was risking perhaps not bodily harm, but certainly life-destroying mockery. But his gamble paid off. The AC/DC fan was none other than Dou Wei, who had just started playing in Black Panther, the Bon Jovi-inspired band that would propel to fame within a couple of years.

Black Panther itself demonstrates this idea of community: It was, at first, less of a band than a collective of musicians. When Kuo was asked to join, he demurred, pointing out that they already had two guitarists. "And they said 'We have a *lot* of guitarists. We have lots of drummers and singers too!' " White Angel was another band that featured a rotating cast of singers taking mainly Chinese stabs at Western pop songs, from Bon Jovi to Billy Joel and Bryan Adams – their 1989 release, *Past Rock and Roll* is not only the second yaogun recording to use the word in its title, but is a window into the soon-to-be stars of yaogun.

Zhang Youdai likens the first years of exposure to rock to an explosion. "That first *hit*," he said, emphasizing the last word by switching to English, "was really a *hit*. When we first heard the Clash: *Wah*! It was so fresh; it inspired us to create something . . . It was really an explosion."

The intensity of the first generation's interest in the music affected the speed with which some music tended to circulate, to the point that it resembled less the real-time tape-dubbing of the early days than the drag-and-drop internet age. Parties were the main forum in which rock fans gathered to listen to live and recorded music. Bars and clubs certainly existed in the eighties across the country, but these were rarely venues for performances of original music until into the nineties. Because anyone who stepped on a stage in any venue needed to have performance permits – a requirement still technically on the books. Venues for rockers who were unable to get permits had to be off the grid.

One source puts the first party at 1984 in the International Club, organized by foreigners, primarily for foreigners. Maxim's de Paris opened a Beijing branch in 1983, and had by 1985 become not only one of the only spots for Western food, but was the top live music venue in town, having hosted a number of parties featuring the rockers of the day. Before Maxim's, there was a small community gathering for the occasional live show at embassies, universities and hotels.

These parties brought a much-needed sense of community: Yaogunners discovered a community, where finally it was ok to have long hair and listen to music that wasn't being played on the radio or TV. Spreading the word was actually less of a challenge, despite what one might suppose, thanks to the tight nature of the community. Long-time Beijing resident Udo Hoffmann, who went from party organizer to festival and concert producer over the course of his first decade in Beijing said, "With ten calls you accessed so many people . . . You had ten people, and they had ten people; at the time, we only had these circles of people."

Zhang Fan remembers what could be considered the rock-party-training ground of his high school days, when he and his classmates would gather for extra-curricular pop music study sessions in the early eighties. The head of the Midi Music School and Festival remembers fondly the experience that was, at once, scandalous and innocent: "Lights-Out" parties, where discovering new pop music was done in the dark. "We called them 'secret sounds'. There would maybe be some wine, a bit of rock music, some Teresa Teng. I remember going to a classmate's house and turning off the lights . . . We'd put on music, smoke cigarettes and just kind of revel in the feeling of freedom." It's certainly an experience to which anyone who's gone to make-out parties can relate, but in this case, the point wasn't to get some couch time with the girl two desks over – at least, not initially. The lights went out not because you were drinking and smoking. The lights went out, in addition to helping you focus on the music, because you weren't supposed to let people know about it. You weren't sneaking off with the hottie from homeroom: You were sneaking off with rock and roll.

The devotion of young 'gunners wasn't merely evident in how hard they listened. It came through in how much they longed to play, and how they decided to learn. There were few examples leading the way. It was rare, even into the nineties, for fans to catch a glimpse of a performance of anything resembling rock music. And so, the education process also involved the newly acquired skill of *badai*, transcribing music through repeated listening. *Ba*: "strip off or skin"; *dai*: "tape." From "transcription," *badai* also came to refer to pirated tapes in general. *Badai* swept through the pop music industry in the mid-eighties, when producers – really, expert listeners and transcribers – would figure out the songs that would go over best, and set about to finding the right singer to fill the task.

Badai was an essential part of the learning process, both in the professional pop music realm, as well as in the general learning-to-rock world. Zhang Fan recalled his time of *ba*-ing as a way to figure out how to play the guitar from the songs he was hearing.

In the mid-eighties Wang Di was on both sides of the *badai* phenomenon, both *ba*-ing and singing.

> Our process of studying music was to copy . . . It was [a] really important part of learning this music. There was nobody to teach us. How could we study? Why were the drums or guitar like this, we had no idea. There was no way to learn these songs at the time . . . With nobody to teach you what other option is there?

Yes, yaogun's roots are in copying, but that doesn't mean that all of its fruit were knock-offs. Certainly, cover bands were the first to emerge, and even bands and artists performing their own compositions produced fruit not far from the tree of their influences. The Rolling Stones are far from the only cover band to have gone on to define their own sound, and yaogun bands were no exception – the difference, though, was that the concept of writing one's own material took some time before it became widespread. First, the early yaogunners had to study. "Rock is from the outside," said Lü Zhiqiang, of live venue Yu Gong Yi Shan. "We had to study a lot. There's a process. In order to create you need to have a good understanding."

Before Filipino surf-rock band Nitaige'er, the first recorded rock-and-roll visitors to China, blew the minds of local rockers-to-be, and before *badai* went big, there were a few opportunities for local Beijingers to come to understand what rock might look like, and how to make it happen. Graham Earnshaw (who also published this book) put together the Peking All-Stars in 1979. Comprised of what would be, over the eighties, a rotating cast of diplomats, journalists and assorted others, they began in the small foreign community, and have been credited with China's first rock show, which took place in 1981 at a Chinese university whose name has been lost to rock and roll history. "The Peking All-Stars were crucial in terms of giving people a sense of what live rock music is; the power of it," said Earnshaw, who adds that when the band asked for requests at that first show they were shocked when someone asked them to play "50 Ways to Leave Your Lover." Point being, the kids knew music; they just didn't know live music. "It wasn't that we were any good, or that the songs were original . . . The Chinese that found their way into hearing us experienced the special power of the music – of, say the opening chords of 'Honkey Tonk Woman'." Simultaneous-ly, they enabled Chinese audiences to interact with foreigners, though through until the nineties, there was still a risk in spend-ing too much time among the round-eyes.

The first Chinese rock band, Wan Li Ma Wang, got together in 1980, out of Beijing's Second Foreign Language Institute. Their repertoire consisted of covers of the Beatles, Bee Gees and Paul Simon. Other bands started popping up in the early eighties, such as the Cao brothers, who played Beatles songs. Cao Jun was one of the country's first guitar heroes. Cao Ping, who worked as a tour guide and eagerly accepted tips in the form of cassettes from his foreign charges, became known as *Lao Yaogun*, "Old Rock," for the intensity of his collection. Many of the biggest names in yaogun through the nineties had begun in bands that formed in the early- to mid-eighties.

As more and more bands formed by the mid-eighties in Beijing, there was something of a scene that started to develop, and both the supply and demand necessary for regular performances. The parties of the early days held a sense of danger that only added to yaogun's rocky reputation as they would occasionally get shut down, or at least draw the attention of the local police – a trend that continued throughout the nineties, and still occasionally to this day. Partly, this was a result of the locations of the parties, which took place in venues ranging from restaurants to international apartment complexes, hotel function rooms, discotheques and even a work unit cafeteria.

By the late eighties, parties would be held pretty much monthly in Beijing, recalled Guo Chuanlin, who formed Black Panther in 1987 – and who himself threw his share of rock parties. At the same time, Shanghai's community would be united by *AV World*, a magazine essential in spreading the yaogun gospel. "Durn" Zhang Haisheng, who runs Shanghai rock venue Yuyintang, recalled monthly gatherings that brought hundreds of like-minded readers together to listen to music and watch videos. Similar gatherings began to occur across the country, eventually paving the way for communities, bands and venues to emerge.

By 1989, Beijing hosted enough bands that six or seven of them could play at a party, which would draw "everyone" in town. Guo recalled one of his biggest parties, in one of the buildings in the Temple of the Moon Park. He had registered with the local authorities – he had to, he insists – telling them there would be, at most, three hundred people in the space that he figured could easily hold three times that. The place was packed to the rafters. At another of Guo's parties, the cops showed up to shut it down. "They told me to refund everyone's tickets and they watched from far away as I set up a table," recalled Guo. In anticipation of getting shut down, he had gotten two big buses to park just far enough away so as to not attract attention, and told each person that came up to the table that he could refund their money or, with a nod to Ken Kesey, suggested they Get On the Bus. "Pretty much everyone chose the bus." The party moved to a theatre, where the bands were able to play.

The promotional campaigns were equally as risky as the actual events, remembers Sheng Zhimin, who made the acclaimed yaogun documentary *Night of an Era* and spent his early yaogun years in the party scene promoting and organizing shows. "We had to look for foreigners in diplomatic apartments to show us where we could post our ads," Sheng told a reporter. "We had to plan out escape routes in case the guards saw us posting them."

He Yong, who would go on to lead his own group and become one of the Three Prominents of the Magic Stone record label, recalled playing at parties in his earlier band, Mayday. His fondest memory was getting paid in what was, until the mid-nineties, the foreigner's only legal Chinese tender: Foreign Exchange Certificates (FEC). Only FECs could purchase imported luxury brands, and the currency was accepted at a limited number of locales. FECs in hand, He recalled, "We'd go to the Friendship Store to buy foreign booze and cigarettes."

From "Nothing" to Huge Thing

Early yaogunners, one starts to notice, came from backgrounds that, in light of the Western rock experience, seem strange to say the least. Many in the first generation were of high-cultural pedigree. They were classically-trained musicians or artists, children of classically-trained musicians or artists. In many cases, these musicians were employed by song and dance troupes, central organizations that not only employed musicians, but like every employer (or, as they were known, "work unit") of the time, they supplied an "iron rice bowl": they housed, fed and provided the musicians with all that was required. In return, musicians gave their lives over to the tight, if erratic, schedule of rehearsals and performances.

And as we learned, those engaged in culture were held in high respect, tasked with the essential mission of education and revolution. Western rock's reputation for inspiring social change, about which young 'gunners had learned, only added to that significance. Critic Hao Fang summed up how far things have fallen:

> Today, the idea is if you have money, you're amazing. The way we treat the wealthy today is how people in the cultural realm were treated then. The first big rock names weren't looking simply at becoming pop stars, and getting famous and rich. They saw their work as cultural. So when rock started it was already placed on a pedestal.

It is important to recognize that though Cui Jian's hit song emerged, basically, from a vacuum, the deep mark upon the nation that "Nothing to My Name" left was the result of Cui first being let into the *tongsu* house he proceeded to set alight. For reasons obvious to those familiar with Cui's yaogun output, he is not eager to delve deeply into his early days in the pop world. "Back then," he said, referring to the days when he sang other people's pop, "was my introduction to music in general. Late 1985 was my introduction to rock." But he was enjoying himself. "From when I was small, I only thought about doing music. At the time, I liked it." He wasn't too particular, back in the early days, about what type of music he was playing or hearing, just as long as he was making music. In addition to songs penned by the official pop world, he sang a number of Western hits, all the while blowing a trumpet in the Beijing Song and Dance Ensemble (now called the Beijing Symphony Orchestra). "Whatever kind of music was okay by me. But what we could hear was limited."

His earliest recordings are rarely mentioned and seem to have been erased from his canon; 1989's *Rock and Roll on the New Long March* is considered his real debut. Other recordings – with his band, Seven-Ply Board; with the pop-singer collective the Hundred Stars; as a solo artist doing Chinese versions of Western pop; or albums like *Vagabond's Return* – are not what people have in mind when they invoke the Great One's name, but they are an essential part of not only Cui's story, but of yaogun in general, showing the state of affairs for rockers and rockers-to-be in the mid-eighties. Cui's pre-*Long March* output featured songs written by Cui with lyrics provided by others and combined, in an extremely fractious manner, with a kitchen sink's worth of musical tools, from straight-up acoustic guitar picking through to the then-brand-new musical technologies. The soft-pop strains bring to mind less rock legend than *tongsu* singer and of the influence of Teresa Teng, the Carpenters and Kenny Rogers. Certainly Cui's signature singing style was present early on, with strained vocals that might be hinting as much at philosophical trouble as they point to trouble in his mid-section, and is noteworthy in the lack of the sugary-sweetness of his *tongsu* counterparts. The material may be far from what one expects of a rock legend, but it contributed to Cui garnering, if you'll forgive the pun, a Name. "By 1986 I could tell that I was famous," he said. In May of 1986, he became infamous too.

The show on which Cui's breakthrough would occur was going to be Big with or without Cui's Big Moment. It was China's entry into the worldwide effort to make huge pop songs for a cause and, particularly when examined in the scope of the past three decades of China's various toe-dips into the wider world, it was a major stop en route to membership in the international community. Already, Band-Aid brought 45 Brits together to sing "Do They Know It's Christmas"; USA For Africa's "We Are the World" gathered 43 superstars; Canada's Northern Lights brought 49 of its finest for "Tears are Not Enough." Producers decided that China's entry had to be bigger, better, stronger and just plain *more* than the others, and so they unveiled "Let the World Be Full of Love" by the Hundred Stars, broadcast from Beijing's Workers' Stadium to the nations' television sets. Like the bidding for and hosting of the World Expo, the Olympics and the Asian Games, or gaining entry into the World Trade Organization, all of which was to come, "Let the World" was China's chance to show the world that it was operating on an international scale – and that their scale was bigger than everyone else's. Various sources that list the globe's post-Band-Aid efforts tend not to mention China's tune, so obviously the world wasn't paying much attention. The important thing, though, is that China assumed that the world was watching.

Simply seeing footage of Cui and his band's first performance of "Nothing to My Name" – online there is a two minute clip, half of which is overdubbed with an introduction to the importance of Cui Jian to Chinese rock – it doesn't seem like such a big deal. Because with all the talk of how important that one performance was to the development of rock music in China, you expect something much more controversial. But that's only if you see the performance of "Nothing" without comparing it to the footage of that which preceded it, and forgetting the context of the nation around it. Cui was part of the Hundred Stars (the official count was actually 107), wearing the yellow and pink windbreakers that were the show's uniform, dancing in the chorus line, lip synching a couple of lines in the everyone-gets-a-couple-lines-but-everyone-doesn't-always-make-it-to-the-mic-on-time title song. "Let the World" is the kind of piece that has a variety of movements: The "Do They Know It's Christmas" knock-off is in the opening movement, featuring sparse (synthesized) strings and a solo piano, building with the requisite bom-ba-pa-pa-bom drum fill while the Stars bring a church-choir feel. In the third and final movement of the song, Cui finally takes centre stage, singing his lines to a tune part disco and doo-wop, the former invoked with the very out-in-front bass guitar and latter the rhythm that you can imagine folks snapping along to at the finale of a Broadway musical – all of which was introduced by a bizarro mariachi motif that disappeared as quickly as it came. Then Cui is at the microphone "singing" words that were never truer: "*This world is changing / It only longs to never change.*" What a wonderful alignment of the stars to see Cui, in this time and place, utter a mere handful of words, "change" being two of them. As he "sings," there is no hint of what change is to come from what seems to be just another member of the windbreakered group. The pop star orgy winds down with a not unexpected return to the song's earlier movements as the stars finally seem to acknowledge the audience with almost frantic waving fits.

And then, we see a different person completely. Gone is the uniform of the hundred stars, replaced by a simple cotton outfit, somewhere between kung-fu-flick protagonist and traditional Chinese scholar, the left pant leg rolled up just above the sock, an homage to the peasant wardrobe – a detail that the camera picks up and focuses upon for longer than might seem necessary, echoing the confusion of so many viewers. The song's opening few seconds are mellow, just some synthesized padding less musical than thematic, but as Cui starts to sing, and visibly strains to reach the high end of the verse's lines, there is a tension. A struggle to reach the notes, but also, were one to read deeply into things, a sign of what is to come. Cui, strumming minimally on his electric guitar, a black Kramer, belts out the first words of the song – "*I have asked you endlessly*" – the audio trailing the video by a large enough factor to make one wonder if words could even keep up with the image of what is happening. The crowd, trained in the art of pop song appreciation, applauds loudly upon the completion of the first line, the "*Hao!*"s ("Good!") ring out above the applause and whistles, and threaten to drown out the second line – "*when will you go with me?*" – which, like the storm that comes in the wake of the calm (the audience, we know now, are blindly and comfortably sailing into their own musical squall, as yet unaware that they are not dealing with just another singer) can't be stopped, even if slightly covered up. The crowd noise requires half the length of the next line – "*But you always laugh at me*" – to die down before silence precedes the words that a generation will come to understand they've been waiting their lives for – "*Yi wu suoyou*" ("I have nothing to my name"). The four-character idiom from which the song gets its name isn't just saying that the narrator's pockets – or, by extension, the listeners' – are empty. The audience would already know the idiom not only from its usage in everyday language, but also, as it has been pointed out, from its appearance in the oft-sung "Internationale" – "*Don't say that we have nothing,*" Communists of the world sing, "*We'll be the masters of the world.*"

Already four lines into one of the first songs Cui Jian had ever written, and the first one of his own that he had performed for a mass audience, we are already almost a full four lines too late to note the most significant element of the song's effect, something that Liang Heping, who played the keyboards that night, has been telling whoever he can find. Liang, who today, with wavy, slightly thinning hair tied into a ponytail, still looks the part of a circa-1986 keyboardist as much as he gives one the impression of an intense orchestral conductor, was almost immediately drawn into the Cui Jian storm. Liang's role at that debut was, at least technically, more than just passing, as he has the honor of being the first person to introduce, musically, the new Cui Jian to the nation: He struck and held the song's first notes. "As he sang that first line," Liang remembers, almost reliving the experience of hearing the song for the first time in the retelling, "my hair stood straight on end. Every other member of the band said they had the same feeling." Something – with a big S – was happening. "It was as if a person had been waiting and longing for something and finally someone sang it out." Songs before "Nothing," he continued, were about "us" – the People. "Before Cui Jian," Liang said, "we had no concept of 'me', 'self' or 'individuality'." Liang likens Cui to Dante: Both men, he said, were responsible for bringing the concept of the individual to their respective eras. "We're six hundred years late," he sighed, though a sense of relief was still detectable. They had made it, after all.

Certainly Liang, after an initial shock, was completely prepared for the fame and notoriety that followed Cui's performance. In his role as house band keyboardist for the "Let the World" concert, Liang wasn't expecting anything more than yet another pop singer he would have to accompany when Cui passed around sheet music and stepped up to the mic in the rehearsal studio a few days prior to the show. "When he sang," Liang started, trailing off slowly as both he and his interviewer realized that words couldn't do justice to the shivers he was re-experiencing nearly two and a half decades after first hearing Cui open his mouth. "After that first rehearsal, I told everyone I knew that we had to pay attention to this guy." Liang remembers breezing through the other staid singers' run-throughs in order to spend extra time on "Nothing," because unlike the other songs they had to play for the big show "we liked it a lot." So much so that Liang spent the better part of the next decade helping to manage, document and promote the man he believes changed everything

The camera pan-out and light fade-in reveal that Cui is not alone on stage. He is surrounded, in fact, by a large number of musicians and unlike the random windbreaker-sporting poppers with instruments completely unrelated to the song along with which they "played," these guys – there are seven of them at least, though it is hard to tell – seem to belong, though perhaps having five guitars on this number is a bit of overkill, like a hip-hop performance where the posse onstage consists of dudes that travel, party, work and hang with the artist regardless of whether they have a part to play in the live show. But here everyone does, at least, have an instrument and handles them with an obvious appreciation and understanding for how they are played. It's the small details, like how Cui's guitar has a cable plugged in, and all on stage are actually playing along, unlike the concert's opening number, in which pop stars fondled the instruments that were obviously brought along for fashion rather than function. Reedman Liu Yuan, dancing on stage right, is swaying and jumping as much as any human possibly can, if not always in direct relation to the music. Cui doesn't move very much, occasionally tapping his leg along with the beat, and sings with the kind of conviction familiar to the pop stars of the day (and down through the ages), but suddenly there seems to be something new afoot, a tension different from the song's beginning, in advance of what it becomes clear will be Liu Yuan's solo – on the *suona*, a reeded instrument that looks a bit like a clarinet with a trumpet's bell on the end. The cameraman's shoddy shooting is part of it, but there is certainly more. In the footage I've been watching online, the camera figures out that the several seconds of headless second guitarist he has been shooting is perhaps enough, and as the second verse comes to an end and the song reaches its second minute, the lens swoops toward Cui, who is obviously building up to something big. Cui's relatively staid stance – save a few knee bends and a little bit of guitar-swinging – explodes, as does the mellow verse, making way for a goose-pimple-inducing, hair-raising, most dramatic of rock and roll moments. Cui doesn't stomp on the distortion pedal here, but the idea and, most importantly, the effect is the same. Of course he needs to run in place: Something Huge has happened. Suddenly, a swooping motion brings Cui's ax up and down as if he was in a hurry to chop whatever lay around waist-height. Over-analyzers could insert a metaphorical enemy of their choice here, which bore the brunt of that first slice of Cui's mighty guitar: the Party, the System, The Man in general. Whatever he swiped at, it died there on the stage.

And suddenly, Cui is Chuck Berry, Elvis Presley and Pete Townshend. And, more important, he is not, anymore, a wind-breaker-wearing member of the pop-singer chorus. His ax-swipe ends with the tip of his guitar aimed at Liu – Clarence, to Cui's Bruce, if we are to take the oft-made comparison to the next level – and here is where China's musical and visceral experience of rock begins. Yes, Cui's lyrics were the first whispers of yaogun, but when the *suona* solo arrives, the song becomes something else completely. It is with Cui's literal leap into Liu's *suona* solo where yaogun truly begins.

Let us pause here a moment to consider just how rock and roll that is. That yaogun began when Cui passed control of his song to the *suona*. Not, let me make abundantly clear, for its East-West fusion, because it is not fusion: It could have been a sax, or a guitar or a kazoo, it just happened to be a *suona*. This is a rock song we're talking about, after all – the Rock Song. The *suona* doesn't make the song "Chinese" rock; geography does that, but only confuses things by doing so. If it is possible to listen to the song with the ears of a new listener – and not simply a new listener to Cui Jian, but a new listener to anything remotely rock – the effect would be almost magical. Proof positive of that comes in the speed with which widespread mimicking of Cui's moves spread through the streets, and in the amount of college kids in the days and weeks that followed trying to sing "like the constipated guy."

One imagines an audience stunned into silence by the shocking sounds coming from the stage. But then one who has experience attending large-scale concerts in China might also doubt that the lyrics, sung as they were through a 1986 PA system into a several-thousand-capacity stadium came through with the clarity befitting the status of clarion call which they have since been anointed. But we know that Cui was heard.

In writing the first yaogun song, it is awe-inspiring that Cui built into it that instant, where the waves parted – or, more accurately, came crashing down – resulting in an instantly-gut-wrenching explosion, indicative of rock music's power. And to be able to whip it out on national television in front of an unsuspecting audience in 1986 in and amongst pop-singer performances only makes it more legendary. It is in this moment, one imagines, where a generation of young dudes across the country all of a sudden realize what they'd really like to do: Move like Cui. And right here begins the third trail, in Liang Heping's roadmap of music in the eighties. No longer is the singer the only participant in the song, no longer are singers and musicians both separate entities. Now, the musicians and singer were one and the same – and they were rocking.

In the final fourteen seconds we are granted in this tiny window on history, Cui bounces, doing a pseudo-running man, alternately machine-gunning his saxophonist and grinding his ax with his midsection, duck-walking and, as much as is possible for this rocker only a few years from first picking up a guitar, waving and flailing his instrument like a man digging for his life. Which, in a way, is exactly what he is doing, and then some. He is digging for his own life, but also for so much more; he is digging to get beyond the Nothing about which he sings, and for the sake of so many others. And though there is a moment where the music seems to have been a bit off – Cui looks around like a mistake has been made – there is a visible point at which one can sense the release that he's finally achieved. And in the wake of the guitar-machine-gunning and fancy-footing, one can just imagine the stern talking-to the suits want to give this kid. And a few sources report on these not-so-positive reviews of the song and show, but they are almost too cliché to be believed, as if this is the part in the movie where the Establishment hears what the new crazy kids are playing and tells them, with no concept of being potentially proven wrong, that they are making an ungodly racket in which nobody is interested.

At least one official in the audience of that landmark performance is reported to have "left angrily," accusing the singer of letting loose "monsters and demons." Another high official is quoted saying: "What having nothing? Isn't it a slander directed at our socialist homeland? Is it possible that he is saying that we have nothing now?"

"You could say that singing that song [at *Let the World*] was dangerous," Cui said, almost twenty-five years later. But, he adds, he had essential support from those in charge of the concert's production, who knew exactly what Cui would unveil. Wu Luqi, one of the show's producers, recalled in the documentary *Night of an Era*, that "Cui Jian . . . was basically crying" when he came to them in advance of the show. "He said 'You don't have to pay me anything. Just let me perform.' " They did, and with foreknowledge of what they were unleashing, said Wu, "We were determined to make popular music play a role on the political stage."

Cui's fate wasn't sealed by angry official reactions – at this particular show. *Let the World Be Full of Love*, the album, was released two months after the concert and featured, in addition to the title track, a Cui Jian single by the name of "Nothing to My Name." In 1987, though, he did fall victim to the campaign against bourgeois liberalization, the first of many times he'd bump up against the authorities.

In early 1989, he released *Rock and Roll on the New Long March* on the state-run China Travel Audio-Visual Company record label. He was back on big stages, performing in March at Beijing Exhibition Hall. And the *People's Daily*, the officialest of official newspapers, wrote in 1988, about the significance of "Nothing to My Name":

> Why has Cui Jian received such a warm reaction? When you hear that melancholy, heavy-hearted tune, when you sing along with those disconsolate lyrics, it always feels like you're spinning out the sadness in your guts . . . What the song exposes is the feelings of a whole generation: their sadness, their perplexity, the feelings that pour out from the bottom of their hearts. The song's use of the deep desolate tone of the folk music of the northwestern plateau, and its coarse rhythms are well suited to its purpose . . . "Nothing to My Name" can also be called the seminal work of Chinese rock. It fuses European and American rock with traditional Chinese music, creating a rock music with a strong Chinese flavor.

Cui believed there was more than just the song itself that caused the reaction. It was his pop roots that added to the effect:

At the time, people just thought I was a mainstream singer, because nobody sold better than I did. That meant that [the songs I performed] were commercial songs, they couldn't think of it as rock. It was only when I called the album *Rock and Roll on Long March* did people start to say [what I was doing] was rock. Before, everyone thought it was pop.

It's debatable whether the words "rock and roll" were the most scandalous in the album's title. Certainly they signaled Cui's separation from the pack with whom he used to run, and yaogun is, to this day, not a word used lightly. But its combination with the last two words was definitely a poke with a sharp stick. The Long March, the near-mythological and epic retreat-cum-rally of the Communist Party during the Chinese Civil War, was not only the embodiment of the Party's persistence, but remained, and remains to this day, one of the essential elements of the story of the liberation of modern China. With his New Long March, Cui was signaling that yaogun was to be the new banner under which the nation would be liberated.

And an increasing number of troops soon joined his march.

3

SO WE'VE GOT "NOTHING."
NOW WHAT?

1986–1989

*Comrade Cui Jian has worked very hard,
and he is a good comrade.*

Beijing Song and Dance Ensemble spokesman, 1987

Step One: Learn from the Visitors

While Cui Jian's legend-making performance in 1986 was certainly one of yaogun's Great Leaps, it wasn't until the tail end of the eighties that yaogun really took off. After Cui's televised unveiling, he continued to perform, but as far as the mass audience that now, if they hadn't before, knew his name was concerned, it wasn't with any regularity, and it wasn't in the context of a rock show. Cui performed "underground" along with the growing number of bands sprouting up as yaogun remained, for all intents and purposes, at the fringes of Chinese society. Cui Jian's March 1989 concerts at the Beijing Exhibition Theater to celebrate the release of *Rock and Roll on the New Long March* represented yaogun's real widespread launch, and the beginning of something resembling a mass live music culture. Prior to Cui's album release concert, there were only brief glimpses into what a rock show might look like, which is why the handful of overseas performers able to visit China in the eighties – who, like the cassette collections of the first generation, may not have, exactly, *rocked* – proved so essential to those about to rock.

It's hard for those of us reared in a society in which live music experiences are a normal occurrence – whether it's Barry Manilow, Barry White or the White Stripes – to appreciate what an early 'gunner experienced attending his first live show. One's body said one thing and the security forces – always, in large-scale events, a constant presence – another. To the physically confusing situation we can add the intellectual confusion of a concert-goer not knowing what to do with the thoughts and feelings that were bubbling to the proverbial surface. "Rock was new," recalled Xiao Nan, whose band Cobra played around the country and world from 1989 through the nineties, "so the audiences were naturally attracted to it. It was as if they had no control over their reactions . . . Their reaction was physical."

Midi Music School and Festival head Zhang Fan's education in the power of live music – a lesson he'd apply in his career – came in high school. His band – with four guitarists backing Zhang on vocals – didn't just win the school's Battle of the Bands in 1985, they dominated. "The other groups were basically doing karaoke," he said. "The show was in the cafeteria, and everyone went *wild*. They were dancing on the tables. It got so the principal had to pull the plug because things got too crazy." And that was with a set list that included "Sailing" and "On the Bayou."

Critic and experimental musician Yan Jun's 1991 serenade of the object of his affections showed an even fiercer side to what music might make you do: Setting up below her building, he and a couple of friends sang Cui Jian and Taiwanese folk-popper Luo Dayou songs. The group quickly attracted onlookers – and a lot of them. "All of the sudden . . . they started lighting fires. They lit the drapes, anything they could . . . People went crazy!" (Except, one hesitates to add, the girl.)

Actual gigs were happening by the late eighties, when Kaiser Kuo said he'd already performed in cities around the country. "Bands would go out and do these weirdo tours," he said. "There'd be *xiangsheng* [a traditional comedy performance resembling an Abbot and Costello routine], a juggler, a magician, a ballet troupe, a song-and-dance ensemble and a heavy metal band." Gigs not unlike those he described continue to occur with a regularity that seems hilarious – until, that is, you're in the rock band following the guy who slaps classical tunes on his cheeks.

If the late eighties saw the beginnings of a circuit beyond the party scene that defined the decade's live rock, the fact that foreign acts coming to the Middle Kingdom were a rarity goes without saying. It wasn't until some years into the millennium that catching a show by a visiting artist would be much less than a once-in-a-lifetime opportunity. The mere fact of these acts being foreign was essential to giving the masses – and, in particular, the musical minority therein – a window into the international live experience. In the eighties, it wasn't easy to get into the country (officially) unnoticed, and it would be some time before a club level emerged; thus did the few visitors perform on large platforms. Those that made it in the eighties were a strange collection: French electronic music pioneer Jean Michel Jarre (1981), Filipino surf-pop band Nitaige'er (1982), Irish folk outfit the Chieftains (1984), English pop duo Wham! (1984), sixties surf-rock legends Jan and Dean (1986) and German pop-rock band BAP (1987). What they all had in common was their deep effect on yaogun. Those that didn't make it but attempted the trip over the course of the eighties are also noteworthy, and included Queen (outbid/foxed by Wham!), the Rolling Stones (done in, reportedly, by Mick's bad behavior at the Chinese Embassy in Washington, DC) and Men at Work (who were told that Wham! had "overstimulated the youth").

In 1982, when cover band Nitaige'er (their Chinese name seems to be the only way they are remembered) came through Beijing, Guo Chuanlin and his friends were already interested enough in rock music to have gotten a band together. Sort of.

Q: When Nitaige'er played in Beijing, did you already have a band?
Guo Chuanlin: (pause, thinking) "We had already started,"(pause, more thinking) "to have a few people," (another pause) "that started to get together."

The reaction of Guo, soon to become Black Panther's manager, to the show included the statement "We had no idea a guitar could make those sounds!" Makes you wonder what, exactly, his band sounded like. Apparently, the band sounded like Nitaige'er; Guo's cover band, he said, covered the Filipino cover band.

Wham!'s 1985 visit changed everything, wrote Cui Jian in *Time* magazine in 1999. Guo also recalled that Wham! show: "We

Red Rock

all went to see that concert . . . We lined up the whole night to buy tickets . . . A friend had told me how good they were, but they were *way* better than he said." In his book *I'm Coming to Take You to Lunch*, manager Simon Napier-Bell recalled that Wham!'s Beijing audience at first copied the motions of the expats in attendance, who were standing up and dancing. Eventually, a wave of confidence took over until, "With no in-built sense of self-control, some of the Chinese kids [got] dangerously overexcited. People danced around the terraces, not with style and rhythm, but with manic swinging arms, pouring out energy like punk rockers on speed."

Wham!'s influence on the local scene is more than a little ironic, given the fact that, despite appearances to the contrary (tapes were manufactured and distributed around China as well as provided with the price of admission), they only came to China in order to garner press that could be exploited in aid of breaking big into the American market – a technique that is arguably still employed to this day. Not only was there no talk of a return to the Middle Kingdom after the initial trip, but, according to the man initially responsible for the documentary film of the China tour, there was little interest in the Middle Kingdom while they were there. "I was struck by [George Michael's] total disinterest in China," wrote Lindsay Anderson, yanked from the project by Wham!'s management, Sony, who decided he hadn't put enough of the band in the film. "His vision only extends to the top ten."

The Wham! concert certainly tested the boundaries of what was possible in the country in terms of large-scale events. Napier-Bell's memoir of the process of acquiring the requisite permissions, permits, contacts and technical requirements necessary (no small feat) notwithstanding, as well as the authorities' reticence and simple ignorance of what happens at concerts was manifest in limits on audience actions. While Team Wham! knew that they were dealing with a nation that had no context or understanding for what a pop show might look like, and that they were testing the limits, they still sent a breakdancer to run through the shocked crowd, nearly ending the concert before it began.

Logistical problems, unsurprisingly, had also threatened Jean Michel Jarre's 1981 performances in Beijing and Shanghai – performances that have arguably as much to do with yaogun as Wham!'s. At the risk of the appearing to swallow whole Jarre's version of events, the China concerts were certainly monumental in the grand scheme of things Western gaining entry into China. "I knew from the beginning," Jarre told *Billboard*, "that . . . a lot of people would see my visit simply as an attempt by a French artist to become celebrated as the first Western contemporary musician to play concerts in China." Like George Michael, Jarre had already achieved a large amount of international fame and success by the time of his China trip, but his first trip to the country wasn't to perform.

In contrast to Wham!'s admittedly means-to-an-end relationship with China, Jarre's concerts resulted from several visits. In 1980, he first visited Beijing, where he lectured at the Central Conservatory and left behind a synthesizer, and in his wake the school set up an "electronic music study group." On that trip, Jarre met with an official from the Cultural Ministry. "I had a feeling she was enthusiastic about the idea of my playing in China," he said. He made two more trips – one for extended talks about a potential tour and collaboration with Conservatory musicians, and another to scope out venues. A year and a half after his first trip, Jarre was waving his hands through the beams of his laser harp for bemused crowds in Beijing (two shows) and Shanghai (three shows). Jarre would later release an album of the concert, which featured not only Chinese songs – a move that to this day remains the quickest way to a local audience's heart – but also a Chinese orchestra, who played with him live. Traditional Irish group the Chieftains also added local musicians to their 1987 concerts and the release that followed.

Jean Michel Jarre and Wham! seem to have been free of any constraints upon their performances, other than the technical and logistical efforts it took to get them onto the stage in the first place (to power the Jarre's shows, it is reported that power had to be cut in surrounding areas of Beijing). Not so for Jan and Dean. According to one report on the duo's tour, officials in Shanghai, worried about the effect of featuring a disabled performer – Jan Berry was partially paralyzed in a near fatal car accident – told the group that Jan's portion of the show would have to be cut. "I was told that seeing a handicapped person reminded most of the older people about the Cultural Revolution, when many people were maimed and killed," Dean Torrence later told a reporter. "I figured that was their call." Whether or not, as the band's web-site puts it, audiences in Shanghai "witnessed, firsthand, a rising student unrest resulting from Communist oppression," (the line that some sources draw between their show and the events of Tiananmen Square three years later is less than direct), the events were certainly testing grounds for the live experience from both sides of the aisle. The security detail seemed to have been as unprepared for the dancing in the aisles as was the audience to have been thusly inspired.

Step Two: Learn From Cui Jian (Again)

As challenging as it was to get visiting performers onstage in China, the journey of local rockers to a stage above ground was more so. Sure, you could play at Maxim's or at a ballroom in a foreigner-friendly hotel or diplomatic residential complex, or at the other temporary party venues that encompassed the live music scene at the time, but even though there might well be a few hundred people that showed up, you were still under-ground – often literally. As Cui Jian was finishing up the record that would become not only his "real" debut, but also yaogun's, the situation first stymied, and then inspired, those around him. Musically, they were on a Long March of their own through the *tongsu* jungle blindfolded. But when it came to everything else – record release, distribution, promotion and more – their proverbial ears were plugged and mouths taped shut as well.

There was no model upon which to base the promotional campaign that would follow the release of a record like *Long March*; the only vision of the future Liang Heping, who had by now joined Team Cui, and others could envision was one of constant uphill struggle. Against the odds, they decided to aim high. "I don't remember whose idea it was," said Liang, "but someone decided that he should play a solo concert." Because if you're going to go down fighting, it might as well be in a blaze of epic proportions. Concert dates were set for March 12 and 13, 1989, in advance of a trip to perform in England and France. And while the concerts themselves were mythic and awe-inspiring in a way that only could happen when a hero takes the stage, the story of *getting* Cui to that particular stage is perhaps more significant.

The idea of a solo concert was virtually unprecedented. At that point, concerts featured a cast of singers, none of whom tended to have enough material or star power to go for long enough on their own. But in Cui's case, there were obstacles that most others didn't face. In a previous live appearance, alongside a slew of pop singers, he drew ire from authorities for performing "Nanniwan" and "Rock and Roll on the New Long March." It was hard to know which song had pissed off the government officials in attendance more – the former was a revolutionary song about a mud-filled gorge that Cui had covered in a yaogun style; the latter played with the most untouchable, mythic and seminal event in the Chinese Communist Party's history. Both songs were now tarnished irreparably at the hands of a young whippersnapper too big for the britches he had rolled up in further mockery of his elders, superiors and his entire nation. Cui was barred from the stage the very night of the performance. Being unable to perform on major stages was something that Cui was very soon going to get used to, spending much of the nineties in a purgatorial state that didn't outright ban him from the stage but made it nearly impossible to find his way onto one in Beijing.

So Liang went to work. "In the West, it's simple," he said, about what happens in advance of a new recording. "Take the Beatles. They had a manager. They had a market. They promote the record, and that's it." But in late 1988, China had no Brian Epstein, or any rock and roll managers at all – or rock and roll, for that matter – and Beijing was no Liverpool. Thanks to the particular market and societal conditions of the time, it's doubtful that even a genius in the Epsteinian mold would have been able to pull off a beast as removed from the norm as was conceived of for Cui. Cui and Liang may have been experienced at navigating politics and music in the *tongsu* sphere, but Cui's record didn't fit into the extant paradigm and nobody with any political sense was going to get involved with rock and roll on a new Long March. Indeed, it's a triumph that there was a record label willing to put out the album in the first place. But since there was a record coming out, its release had to be Different, and thus did yaogun kick off with a two-concert run.

"There was nobody suitable to put on a show like this," Liang recalled, immediately realizing that there was so much bush to whack in the yaogun jungle that they'd need a team. At t-minus one month to go-time, Liang started to get a group together to split up the tasks that were required to make it all happen. First, the requisite car-repair-shop owner and music fan – a man who would, much later and more famously, lead the Twelve Girls Band, a group of instrumentalists gathered under the auspices of combining traditional Chinese instruments with synthesized contemporary music and, of course, general hotness – was brought in. He knew a guy who knew a guy and pretty soon Team Cui had enough hands, skills, *guanxi* ("connections" only scratches the surface of a concept that encompasses a combination of skills, from flattery to flat-out bribery, proximity to power, and general character by which it becomes possible to gather juice and Get Things Done) and know-how to put together one of the most important events in yaogun's history.

Twenty years later, the aforementioned car-repair-shop owner, Wang Xiaojing, sat wearing mirrored sunglasses in front of a camera crew to talk about his role in putting the show together, and how geography played as much of a role as *guanxi*. The concert was less sanctioned, he explained, than it was not prevented from happening. "I asked Cui what I could do to help. He said that the things they couldn't get done involved public relations and the public security bureau [the local police]." When Wang discovered that Cui's last controversial gig – the one that "got out of control" is as much detail as he went into – went down in Beijing's Eastern District, he took out a map and went to "some friends" in the Western District. With the accompanying hand gestures that revealed briefly his gold-watched wrist and cigar-cradling fingers – the accoutrements, one guesses, of his work with the dozen women rather than the solo rocker – he explained that those "friends" helped acquire the necessary permits.

They sold every ticket for the two shows. "We didn't give away a single ticket," said Liang. "Reporters had to . . . buy tickets too." In addition to the fact that people knew Cui's name, the press went to town covering the concerts. The added bonus, Liang added, what really put things over the top, was the irony that has haunted rock and roll oppressors from day one: The ban on Cui only further whetted the audience's appetite. With those two concerts, Cui kicked off a new era yet again. Yaogun stood up on the television sets of the nation in 1986. Three years later, it hit the big time, joining the nation's sanctioned culture on major stages.

And then there was the record celebrated in the concerts. Liang Heping's efforts to spread the word about Cui, which began the moment he first heard the man sing in a "Let the World Be Full of Love" rehearsal room, were to pay off in a very different manner than he had expected.

As Taiwanese-Mainland relations improved in the late eighties, there was more potential for cross-Straits collaboration.

Though Rock Records enjoys fame for its investments in yaogun via imprint Magic Stone through the nineties, there was an earlier Taiwanese player in Kedeng Records, a company partnered with major label EMI. Chen Fumin, a singer/songwriter who worked at the label, came to Beijing to meet musicians and, through a cousin, came across Liang, who happened to have a Cui Jian demo handy. "He had never heard anything like it," recalled Liang. "He was shocked." Chen took the demo back across the water to play for his colleagues and convince them that this was, in fact from the Mainland – "Nobody believed that this could have come from Beijing," said Liang. Chen was put right back on a plane with a directive to sign Cui, and *fast*. Thus did *Long March*, via Kedeng and EMI, receive overseas distribution before it hit Chinese shelves.

Cui's record sold very well across Asia, at a rate that brought two extremely important, if completely unintended, consequences. The first: taxes. Cui was the first Chinese artist to sell well overseas. To call the tax laws at the time unfair to locals doing business outside of the country would be a major understatement, and Cui decided to take the issue to court, becoming the first person to sue the tax department. The decision – against Cui – wasn't a surprise, but, said Liang, "it was something we needed to do." Indeed, the law began to change soon thereafter. Unintended consequence number two: Cui blazed yet another path, the rock tour. But not quite yet.

Suddenly: Nothing, Again

We've arrived at the point in yaogun's story – and China's – that has colored perceptions of the Middle Kingdom arguably more than anything Mao Zedong did in his lifetime. We have come to

1989, a year that, in the context of China talk, is preceded by such an enormous shadow that it blocks out everything around it. In the yaogun context – like so many others – it is the lens through which everything is captured. Over the course of its first full decade in China, rock did an inarguable amount of unshackling, opening up possibilities for a generation in desperate need. But in the context of rock's promise – that it is the soundtrack, in short, to freedom – June 4, 1989 is surely the only test of rock's promise that matters. In fact, what matters even more is not rock's role in the events leading up to June 4 as much as what happened to it in the aftermath.

There is no shortage of references to "Nothing to My Name" as anthem to the demonstrators in the square in 1989. Hearing, twenty years later, the invocations of the word "anthem" in discussions of the current rock scene, your author is reluctant to join in the chorus of assigning that kind of status to any song, but will allow that the song was certainly on the minds of many protesters, and Cui's wide-spread popularity was already established, via both pop and rock music he debuted earlier that spring. But there were other, less rocky tunes being sung. According to China scholar Geremie Barme's account, hunger strikers sang Luo Dayou's "Orphans of Asia" and Qi Qin's "Probably in Winter," and public address systems broadcasted them as well. The people in the Square weren't all young'uns who knew the latest pop tunes from Taiwan, so the set list of songs sung in the Square included "The Internationale," "We Workers are Powerful," "The Guerrilla Squad," "I Love Tiananmen in Beijing," and even "Frere Jacques." But it was as more than just a part of the soundtrack that yaogun was wrapped up in the events of the spring of 1989.

Wu'er Kaixi, one of the more (in)famous student leaders, said at a conference in the fall of 1989, "Chinese rock and roll influenced students' ideas more than any of the theories of aging intellectuals on democracy." Given the choice between heavy reading and heavy metal, well, *duh*. But on the other hand, most yaogunners across generations share the belief that through the music they gained entry into another world that enabled them to see alternatives. As rock critic Xiao Yu put it, "Rock is a door; after you open it, you look at things differently." Russian rock critic Artemy Troitsky said the same of rock music in his homeland: "[Rock] meant fight your parents. It meant: You are free to do what you want, no matter what the seniors say. It was a form of fighting back, a reaction to oppression, a catalyst for change." Reading political theory was one thing, but singing along with Axl Rose did far more – and joining Cui Jian in a chorus took that all even further.

One yaogunner recalled that "all the big names" were in the Square, though the attendance of rockers didn't necessarily mean that they participated in or identified with the movement, as the early days of that Beijing Spring were a spectacle that drew people regardless of affiliation. The Taiwanese singer-songwriter Hou Dejian, who had moved to China in defiance of the Taiwanese ban on travel to the Mainland, was a regular fixture at the Square. "Heirs of the Dragon," his controversial and popular song about the link between all Chinese, was another of the songs sung by the gathered masses. Proto-punk He Yong brought portable generators, amps and his band Mayday to the Square for what would be their final performance, singing, as writer Andrew Jones recalled, the song for which he is still best known, "Garbage Dump": "*Is there hope? / No! / Tear it down!*" Cui Jian, too, made a few visits, one of which was in late May, before martial law was declared and after the hunger strike had begun.

"I came with about a twenty percent hope of performing, and eighty percent of just coming to see you all," Cui said on the recording of the four-song set that made the rounds on the internet in the summer of 2009. Some of the hunger strikers found the music a bit much, but they were far outnumbered by the masses thrilled to catch this rare performance. What the recording captures is far beyond what any other bootleg could ever do. While "Nothing To My Name" wasn't on the set list that day, Cui did perform the scathing "Piece of Red Cloth." Before starting the song, he recited its first five lines, while asking anyone with a cloth to put it over their eyes:

> *That day you took a piece of red cloth*
> *Covered up my eyes and covered up the sky*
> *You asked me what I saw I said,*
> *"I see the happiness" This feeling made me so tranquil.*

The imagery of the red cloth was lost on none of his audience members. On an August day in 1966, one million red-armbanded Red Guards gathered at the same Square in which Cui was now performing, and watched their generation's superstar put on his own piece of red cloth. With Mao's donning of the Red Guard armband, the Guards' status and involvement in the Cultural Revolution was established – with the blessing of their Chairman, they proceeded to wreak an unprecedented amount of destruction upon the nation. By the late eighties, red armbands were still in use, but were re-appropriated by other, less intimidating and violent members of society: so-called "public security volunteers," from security guards to retirees, who gather on street corners under the auspices of neighborhood committees. Even now, red armbands are still used by volunteers of all types, ostensibly identifying themselves as some form of security or keepers of the peace. In the run-up to the 2008 Olympics, the weight of the red armband was heavy enough to spur a swap to a chest badge.

In his performance in the square, Cui ends the song by repeating the first four lines, leaving the crowd with the words "I see the happiness" as he exits the stage. "Goodbye friends," he said, and there is pandemonium for the last minute of the recording. There is shouting; most of it is unintelligible, and some of it consists of people screaming Cui's name. Even more chilling is the combination of the intense screaming that cuts through the crowd noise shouting nothing in particular and the distant sirens that remind the listener of what would happen to the gathered crowd, and so many others, not two weeks later.

In the wake of June 4, the nation was disillusioned. Confusion reigned among citizens before Tiananmen over which of the New Chinas was theirs: the China that "stood up" in 1949, that which was reinvigorated with the rehabilitation and rise to national leader of former disgraced official Deng Xiaoping, or the one which featured Reform and Opening Up. Realizing the lengths to which their government could go in acting against its own people also had serious effects. There was severe psychological and existential dismay, but the situation also had a major effect on Party-People relations. As a result, the Party decided to pull back in its vision of governing every element of every citizen's life. It was better to grant limited freedom, they believed, than to risk another movement.

The Party's message: Don't challenge us politically and you can pretty much do whatever you'd like. Go abroad, listen to rock music, become a prostitute. As long as your grey-area/illegal activities aren't up in our face and, more importantly, as long as the line in the sand remains uncrossed, we're all good. The central authorities' endorsement of leader Deng Xiaoping's economic vision – a vision that put him on Mao's bad side in the first place, and one that culminated in his 1992 tour of China's south during which the phrase "to get rich is glorious" came to the fore – was their bet that the citizenry would prefer economic prosperity over political freedom. It quickly became clear that all it took to ease the central government's fears of another uprising was allowing their people to make money.

Novelist Wang Shuo, one of the most influential contemporary pop cultural icons in the country, said, "What didn't happen through June 4 will happen through rock." That may have sounded reasonable in the early days. Even though a minority were further inspired by the events and of the increased amount of debate leading up to the massacre – critic Hao Fang, for example, said that 1989 is the reason he started writing seriously about rock music – things did not change for the better. With the new ground rules in place, many were led away from yaogun and, indeed, away from intellectual debate of any kind – debate which had flourished in the decade prior to the Incident.

Wang Weihua (also known as Wei Hua or Wayhwa), who fronted the early-nineties band the Breathing, embodies, to an extent, that tension between being spurred into action and backing off in the wake of potential trouble. The daughter of an army official, Wang began as a radio journalist, and moved eagerly to China Central Television's brand new English newscast in 1986, just in time to report on the student demonstrations that year. Two years later, she co-hosted the network's Spring Festival Gala, the biggest show on Chinese television. In the weeks prior to June 4, she produced a story, which was never run, about the hunger strikers. After her story was spiked and she heard Prime Minister Li Peng refer to the students' behavior as chaos, she told *People* Magazine in May of 1989, "I felt cheated, I just wanted to cry for the whole country." In her first interview with an overseas outlet, she barely minced words, saying that the nation's leader, Deng Xiaoping ought to consider retirement. After that, the interview requests came flooding; ABC's *Nightline* introduced her as "a brave journalist who says Deng should resign." In the wake of June 4, it was unclear whether she'd been fired or left before it came to that. "I'm not even really interested in politics," she said in the days after the crackdown. "I'm not sure whether speaking up is worth risking everything." "Everything," in her case, was Something, what with her family background and stable job. She joined the Breathing, whose rock was influenced by the hair and power-ballad bands of the late eighties – a band that began with Chinese ballads and Madonna covers – before embarking on a solo career in the nineties.

But it wasn't all bad news for yaogun. In the ensuing months, there was a freer atmosphere in which potential yaogunners could operate. Meanwhile, the angst and confusion of the fallout from June 4 fed into a new affection for the music and the culture that surrounded it. And with the national rush to riches now fly-ing openly in the face of the socialist upbringing of its citizenry, there was arguably more fuel for the rock and roll fire. Gao Qi, an important rock force throughout the nineties, in bands the Breathing and Overload, explained the change. "Pre 1989 we were idealistic. Post 1989 we are realistic. Since 1989, a lot has changed. Some people are still writing songs about the govern-ment, but I don't see the point. Now I write about how we can live, what our purpose is."

Yaogun did keep rolling and, indeed, thriving, in the new post-1989 landscape, contrary to expectations. Nicholas Jose, an Australian diplomat and novelist reported catching a gig within months of June 4 featuring a band called 1989, I Love You playing covers for a "capacity crowd of dancing youth." The show culminated, Jose said, with a "strange and deeply ironic" cover of "Without the Communist Party There Would Be No New China" that was compared to Jimi Hendrix's "Star-Spangled Banner." It was, said Jose, a "weird, cacophonous, twenty-minute improvisation that could be interpreted as a musical re-enactment of events still imprinted on everyone's mind. It was electrifying. Nothing was said, and nothing need-ed to be said."

The fallout from June 4 created the context in which yaogun bands were able to do large-scale shows in the first years of the nineties. "Without June 4 things wouldn't have gone as smoothly for rock music . . . There is a delicate connection," said Liang Heping, a member not just of Cui Jian's TV debut band, but also of the team that managed him. There was Cui's tour in support of Beijing's Asian Games, Beijing's Modern Music Concert, multi-band bills in Shenzhen and Shanghai, and more – all of which might not have happened without that event.

There existed a bit of wiggle room for rock music to exist, and a stage upon which it could be seen by a large number of people. The Modern Music Concert was a two-day event held in Beijing's Capital Stadium in 1990 featuring six yaogun bands and a reported 18,000 spectators each day. That the word yaogun was avoided was subordinate to the reality that it was featured in a way previously unimaginable. Yaogun's role in the recovery process was invaluable, perhaps more than it had been to the initial explorers that found and took to it in the first days of rock's entrée into China.

Cui Jian's Asian Games tour was a beast of another kind. Liang was convinced that it was a good idea for Cui to perform concerts in support of the upcoming Asian Games that Beijing was hosting in the fall of 1990. Slowly, Cui was convinced to consider it. "The Asian Games are international," Liang reasoned. "China is in the midst of a reform and opening; we'd been closed off for so long. We should take any opportunity we have to open to the world." It was, he emphasized, not in aid of the government, but helping aid of the country. "So that we can open up even more." Rock music needed support, he added. "Through shows like this, the government can see that we're not doing anything bad . . . Otherwise, they'll keep [rock] down forever. Whatever you say, they'll never listen."

Cui had agreed to the idea before June of 1989, but plans were delayed after the events in Tiananmen Square. By September, though, things had cooled down enough to continue the planning. At the time, nations around the world spoke out against China and the Games, while support was waning at home. According to a source quoted in the *LA Times*, "The Asian Games Committee is in big trouble . . . Chinese people are not interested in the Games at all. In fact, they're hostile toward them. They recognize them as a propaganda tool."

Wang Xiaojing, the car-repair-shop-owner-turned-impresario behind Cui's 1989 Exhibition Center shows, found an Asian Games official who liked the idea of the Cui Jian fundraising tour, but said that approval had to come from his boss, who was at the time working the post-June 4 spin circuit, visiting fellow Asian Games nations to convince them that all was on schedule and things would go smoothly. His boss, who hadn't heard of

Cui Jian before his trip, was ecstatic about the possibility, thanks to the second unintended consequence of the success of Cui's debut in Asia (itself a product of June-4 fallout): Cui's name kept coming up during the official's Asian travels. As long as lyrics passed muster, Cui was cleared to hit the road. He got permission in November.

Things on the Rock and Roll on the New Long March Tour went both extremely well and extremely badly. Cui and his gang were thrilled by the reactions; their chaperones, not so much. The problem was that despite all appearances, Cui was not on a Cui Jian tour. Though the understanding was that their support of the Asian Games was showing support for their nation, the reality was somewhat different. "It wasn't just Cui Jian there as an individual," Liang said. "He represented the Asian Games, and the government." The front section of each hall's audience was comprised entirely of local government officials, who, at the behest of the central authorities that sanctioned the tour, had to provide local support. But the local officials were also responsible for what happened in their territory, which created a major problem for them in light of both Cui's behavior and that of the crowds, who were getting increasingly excited as the tour went on. By the third stop, Wuhan, complaints were already coming in to headquarters. The tour was cut off after Chengdu, the fourth stop on a tour that was supposed to hit major cities around the country in three segments.

Meanwhile, the crowds were eating it all up. "You wouldn't believe some of the footage I got," Liang Heping said of the video he took on that tour. "The leaders had never seen anything like this."

The recollections of a Chengdu rocker present at the final stop on Cui's Asian Games tour exemplifies how the music mattered:

> We never got any release . . . [I had] cried every day [after June 4] . . .
> Cui Jian rescued me. [His music] comforted my soul, reassured me.
> I am really thankful for this concert. If not for rock, I would've gone

mental. I was in real pain at that point; I'd spend days at home crying. It brought me back.

The Sichuanese capital had also experienced serious violence on June 4, and it was with that in mind that things seemed to come to a head in Chengdu. Tickets for the concerts – initially there were two shows planned, but a third was added – were RMB15 (about US$3.25 at the time) and went for RMB60 (US$13) on the black market, recalled one fan whose monthly salary was RMB70 (US$15). But the concerts, all of which were sold out, were about something more than money could buy; it was the kinds of feelings that moved one fan to push past security and run onto the stage to embrace Cui – not out of rock star crush but the result of the pent-up emotions that the concert allowed to be released. "When Cui Jian played the last song," the fan in question said, "suddenly I felt a real peace; I was really moved. I felt a pain. I cried. In my heart, there was pain, there was trouble, and there was excitement."

Out from Nothing, Again

As the nineties saw national energies poured into economic development, lingering political problems were often swept aside in the rush to modernity and wealth. But China's success story didn't enrich all of its citizens, and for more and more people, rock music remained an essential tool of survival. Beijing-based critic Yan Jun was raised in Lanzhou, an industrial western Chinese city hit hard by the privatization of the nineties. "[It] was hopeless. Tons of people in Lanzhou lost their factory jobs; lots committed suicide," he said. "So many people had no way of surviving. Lots of people turned to prostitution. And young people then had no way of getting a job either. They saw what was happening with the adults." When Yan hosted a radio show in 1996, he saw first-hand how rock was, for many people, not simply something to listen to:

> My listeners were all students, young people, military folks: really depressed people. These were the people that listened to rock music. [They] were looking for something new [and] saw rock as a new way of life, and that life could be even better . . . I got tons of letters . . . I put on Godflesh and it moved people so much they cried . . . It was a great thing I did, moving people to thinking about how to be happy, getting them through a rough time.

Listeners and yaogunners, whether or not they realized it, were making an essential choice when they chose to rock. They were choosing a life outside of the mainstream, yes, but even with a sudden ability for individuals to exist outside of the direct control and care of the state, those choosing rock chose to eschew the goals of the rest of the country: the wife, the job, the car, the house. In recent years, this choice is less controversial, but still seems odd to the bulk of the population. When yaogunners speak of their experiences listening and playing, there is more than just music at stake here.

While 1989 was a point at which the floor fell out from under the roller coaster ride that defined yaogun's early period, it was not, by a long shot, the end of the ride.

4

MANY THINGS, MORE NAMES

1990-1996

*The entire country was busy making money
and we were busy making noise.*

Yang Haisong, P.K. 14

Another New China

Shedding its eighties skin, and diving headlong into the nineties with a modernization and outlook that was unprecedented, China was, yet again, recreating itself. Yaogun was swept along on the journey, for better and for worse. By the time the decade came to a close, China was as different a nation as yaogun was a different beast.

Yaogun's ranks swelled. By 1992, according to China scholar Geremie Barme, there were already calls for Cui Jian's "extermination," and a number of rockers began to come out of the woodwork and into a landscape that was more and more suited to – or, at least, less and less opposed to the idea of – domestic rock. In the early days before the pirates pulled into port, a selection of yaogun records were selling across the country.

The situation was enhanced by the growing availability of the music. Radio stations started to play, and shops started to stock, a growing amount of rock – including yaogun. Stages appeared around the country, particularly in the decade's first weeks: Beijing's Modern Music Festival and multi-band bills in Shenzhen and Shanghai all occurred in 1990. The party scene grew out of its underground hovels; new bands emerged to populate the underground while older names hit a growing number of stadium stages. Soon, there existed various undergrounds, and the scene spread out geographically and stylistically as a growing number of new recruits joined rock's ranks.

Cui began the decade in the good graces of the authorities, but that didn't last long. While he put out three records and performed around the world, the situation at home was downright purgatorial. There were no written edicts preventing his music from being played on the radio, or preventing him from performing major concerts, but over various periods both occurred. The back and forth symbolized the decade's scattershot climate.

With yaogun suddenly more than just one name, other rockers followed and benefitted from the philosophy outlined in the Reform and Opening of the nineties. Writing of Tang Dynasty in 1992, Andrew Jones speaks to yaogun's new mission: "Their goal is to be the best rock band in China. If they're going to overthrow anything, it will be Cui Jian's monopoly on the word 'superstar.'"

Geremie Barme, writing the same year, saw yet another group of groups aiming for the rock stage: "The frustrations of many of China's wannabe rockers are not necessarily aimed at party elders but rather Heavy Metal commissars and rock 'n' roll apparatchiks who are hesitant to share the stage with the up-and-coming."

Turning Up the Radio

The nineties began much as the eighties had ended: With a growing number of new ears attracted to rock, isolated and faced with a nearly impossible task of finding, or imagining, other like-minded souls. Thus, radio became a lifeline to rockers once a select few DJs were able to get the music on the air. In the pre-internet age, radios were bulletin boards, encyclopedias and stereos all rolled into one. Pop music, Chinese and foreign, was not unheard of on the airwaves in the eighties, but was rare. Until the early nineties, the music on FM radio (AM was for news) was primarily classical, and no station had yet gone twenty-four hour. "They'd play 'The East is Red' and sign off for the night," Radio DJ Zhang Youdai recalled. One rock enthusiast recalled the day in 1986 when he and his fellow fourteen-year-old friend heard the first broadcast of the *Billboard* Top Ten. "My friends and I were interested in foreign sounds, so we recorded it and listened to it over and over. It was probably the first time we heard anything Western on the radio."

But the amount of Western music on air was nowhere near to meeting the demand of an increasingly hungry and growing community. That would change when Youdai took the airwaves.

In 1990, an American named Kenny Bloom attended one of Zhang Youdai's college parties. Not quite the keg-in-the-dorm-hall affairs one might associate with a college party, it was a weekly university-sanctioned dance held in the cafeteria. "They'd mostly have waltzes, ballroom dancing, that kind of thing," said Youdai, but the *pièce de résistance* was the "little bit of 'disco' at the end": Richard-Clayderman-with-a-disco-beat would often end the evenings. Youdai was an early adapter not just of Western music, but of cassette tapes, a collection of which would accompany him wherever he went – whether in cabs or restaurants, he'd ask that they be played; he became a regular rock-party savior when he stepped in to prevent the equipment guys from controlling the between-band soundtrack with the one "usually crap" tape they'd brought. It didn't take long before everyone was calling him Youdai – "*You*" ("to have"), "*dai*" ("cassettes"). His university party gigs came slowly. He was granted permission to play a song or two before he was given a weekly gig for the bulk of his student life, attracting, in the process, students from around Beijing.

Youdai remembers being the subject of Kenny Bloom's constant and careful watch, and his knowing nods with every song that went out over the speakers. "He'd look at me and say 'Hmm, Peter Gabriel; hmm, the Clash.' " Still early in his DJ-ing career, the closest anyone at school had come to this kind of interaction with his music was to tell him to turn it off. After Youdai's set, Bloom approached, with the perhaps more-than-a-bit-too-obvious "Hey Mr DJ." Which, it turns out, wasn't obvious to Youdai. "I had no *idea* what that meant! I'd never heard that word before." Bloom's company, KB Communications, had been producing "Foreign Music Hour," which introduced American music on China Central Radio. The show, which ran at the decidedly un-rock-and-roll hour of eight o'clock on Sunday mornings, consisted of a playlist and a script that had to be submitted to the station's foreign affairs office for review a week in advance. Bloom brought Youdai into the project in early 1991, and Youdai proved his worth by submitting a script on John Lennon that was approved by the censor. "It was really annoying work," said Youdai, "because if they found a problem with the script, they'd go and find me."

Youdai had floated the idea of hosting the show himself, but met with a brick wall. The show's voice, which read the script, was literally one of a handful of Voices permitted on the airwaves. But the Chinese transliteration system just about guaranteed that international artists' names would be unrecognizable, even to those familiar with the music. The ensuing cross-cultural misunderstandings would be hilarious if one didn't know how seriously listeners took the music. So Youdai suggested he go on the air alongside the announcer. "I was told to not even think about it. That it was impossible," he recalled. "It's the Party's mouthpiece," he was told. "How could we possibly let *a guy like you* go on the air?" A "guy like Youdai," referred to his haircut.

"They *really* didn't like the idea of Zhang Youdai going on air [with] long hair," said journalist Steven Schwankert. "On the fucking radio!" The previous year, the *LA Times* reported that Evening News guitarist Xiao Yiping had his hair cut forcibly by Dalian police after his band played a gig in the northeastern city.

By 1992, the "Foreign Music Hour" had ended, and Youdai was introduced to a former jazz DJ who had brought his record collection to Beijing from the US. Though Youdai barely knew anything about jazz, he saw it as an opportunity to learn. This time around, he was allowed on air, becoming the station's first actual host. "Of course, it was prerecorded, and I had a 'co-host' – the announcer."

But it was a start. *Jazz Train* lasted two and a half years; with different shows through to today, Youdai continues to program jazz.

In the early nineties, recalled Youdai, radio was hot, particularly because of the new phenomenon of call-in shows. "Everyone went wild. Suddenly, radio was far more popular than TV." When Beijing Radio asked Youdai what he'd like to do for them, they not only agreed to his suggestion that he do a rock and roll show, they told him that it was perfect timing, because they needed a rock guy. In 1993, "Rock Magazine" went on the air every Thursday afternoon, though it was quickly rechristened "New Music Magazine": The station may have wanted a rock guy, and yaogun may have been allowed on the airwaves, but "yaogun" as word was *verboten* – in Chinese; the English name, which Youdai said regularly on the air, didn't upset those upstairs.

Chen Yi, who since worked at yaogun and international labels, has fond memories of the show: "It was the happiest hour of the week," he said, his happiness increased by his ability to hide his headphones so he could listen during after-school classes.

Soon thereafter, Youdai added a weekly blues show to his schedule, exploring the roots of rock and roll. "I'd only recently learned about [rock's] roots," he said. He co-hosted a fourth show devoted to pop music and, in 1994, added "Anyone Can Play Guitar," which was everything its name suggested. The how-to show enjoyed widespread, if short-lived, popularity (it lasted a year), with a format of inviting guests to teach licks to listeners. Its first episode featured a lesson on "Hotel California" by one of the early local guitar greats, Cao Jun, thus, perhaps, pinpointing the source of a scourge of contemporary China: The ubiquity of the Eagles' classic (in its unplugged form) everywhere from dive-bar stages to hair salon speakers to shopping mall sound systems across the far reaches of the nation. But the show also had a positive effect on yaogun: Many a future rocker snuck headphones into class to hear the show.

Another Beijing superstar DJ in the early nineties was Chang Kuan, though he was something of a star before he was a DJ. Once a bad-boy rocker with his band Baby Brothers, he smoothed out his sound and rose to prominence early on. Zhong Sheng, who heads yaogun label Pilot Records, remembers listening to Chang Kuan's show and hearing, for the first time, "Smells Like Teen Spirit" as well as Metallica. In 1993, Gao Qi – who had led rockers the Breathing and later thrash (later pop rock) band Overload – also had a radio show, which covered ground even heavier: "Metal Kingdom" sent some of the world's most extreme metal across the airwaves for just under a year.

Youdai's fame, meanwhile, translated into the ability to be one of the few hosts allowed not only to program his own shows, but also to broadcast live. Youdai recalled that after the station leadership got to know him – after, that is, they got past the long hair – they became genuinely curious about him. "They said things like 'You're a good guy, why are you like this?' that kind of thing," he recalled. After convincing them that there was a logic at work behind his commitment to and interest in the music, he was given something resembling special powers. He did the first radio interview with Cui Jian and was the only person allowed to play Cui Jian songs on the air. But he wasn't completely bulletproof. "There was a lot of music I couldn't play. Like most of Tang Dynasty's stuff," he recalled. "And every year around early June I couldn't do live shows." He was still considered a potentially "dangerous" person playing music that was "sensitive." Indeed, he still is to a certain extent. "They tend to move my timeslot around – it's still sensitive, what I do, so they put me in crappy slots. I'm living on the edge. Sometimes the edge is dangerous."

With shows that covered territory a fair ways across the Western musical spectrum, Youdai's name spread across the country, but he was not alone. Li Chi of Mao Livehouse remembers that Shanghai was further ahead Beijing in terms of radio. "There was lots of foreign music on the radio [in Shanghai]: jazz, country, rock, pop. I recorded radio shows every day." Shanghai's earliest rock DJs were Zhang Lei and Sun Mengjin.

Sun continues to be an active critic and promoter in Shanghai, his reputation cemented by the following his radio show garnered. Unlike Youdai, Sun was on the air at a more reasonable rock hour: ten in the evening.

"He had such a big influence. He spread rock across Shanghai," said "Pang Pang" Li Jianfang of Crystal Butterfly. Lu Chen, who would found one of the nation's quirkiest and most interesting bands, Top Floor Circus, was first turned onto the "strange sounds" of rock via Sun's show.

O Yang broadcast rock to Tianjin beginning in 1992. "William" Wang Hui remembers not just being introduced to music by Tianjin radio, but to the community: "They had a hotline, and I called to find more people into rock," he said. "They broadcast my ad . . . and people would page me and let me know what was going on." These days, it's William who does the "paging": he runs the city's RIFF Livehouse.

Tianjinner Song Ping heard O Yang's broadcasts, and was inspired to make broadcasts of his own, in the early aughts at his university station in Zhenjiang, a town that much later appeared on the yaogun map, with the Midi Festival. "They never told me to stop putting on rock, they just told me to keep it low and don't talk about politics. They just assumed rock was political, violent, all that." Indeed, if it weren't for some quick thinking and sweet-talking on his part – a skill that seems mandatory for yaogunners that wish to last – he may not have gotten a show at all. When confronted by a high-ranking school official (or, to use Song's English, an "old lady") who told him he wasn't allowed to put on rock music, he reached into his collection and pulled out Elton John's "Tiny Dancer" in the hopes of lulling her into a calm place. "I said: 'This is rock, too!' She said: 'Huh, not bad. More like this.' " While Song knew well that the music he was playing was sensitive, he also knew well that the school authorities had no ability to discern the content of the music that went over the air. "There are different ways to fight for rock. I made them happy, and was able to keep doing what I wanted."

These days, it seems to be even more difficult to get yaogun on the air than in the past. Partly it is due to the commercial pop industry's near monopoly of the airwaves, and the pressure from Upstairs to ensure it stays that way. But there are other forces at work. One DJ at a Central radio station in Beijing confessed, in 2005, that she could only "sneak on" Cui Jian songs, that she "can't really play them." How does one "sneak" a song on the radio? One simply doesn't mention, either before or after the song plays, who or what it was. In the past, she added, the station higher-ups "didn't really worry about rock music on the air, because they didn't pay much attention." But things changed. "They're afraid of *trouble*," she said, emphasizing the last word by saying it in English. The beauty of this general aversion to "trouble" is that all it takes is the invocation of the possibility of it by an authority figure – the local police precinct or cultural bureau turning down a festival permit application, or pulling the plug on a concert, or a radio station manager who perhaps might not be secure enough in his position to risk getting a phone call – and all debate ends (the word "safety" is similarly employed). When I asked what "trouble" might mean her response was simple: "Nobody knows."

While radio helped unite yaogunners, its main problem was that it wasn't up to the task of enabling listeners to translate their interest in and love of the music they were hearing into acquisitions. There was the perennial language barrier. How would one propose to look for Elvis's albums? Under the transliterated *Ai'erweisi*? Under his Chinese name, "Cat King?" By his English first name, or family name? And how would you spell that, anyway? Meanwhile, shops seriously stocking the rock being played on the air were years behind the advent of what little rock radio existed.

Zhang Haisheng, who runs Shanghai yaogun institution Yuyintang, remembers the early days in Shanghai. "You couldn't buy real tapes," he said. "On the street there were copies of tapes that people brought from overseas, that was it." Many had to stick to recording the radio. Li Chi, Zhang Fan and many others were eager to show me the boxes and shelves they had devoted to recordings of the radio shows of their youth.

Heavy Metal: the Mistake Heard Round the Country

"Yaogun started out with a mistake," guitarist Kou Zhengyu recently told the website Mogo.tv. "In the beginning, everything was metal." That one of heavy metal's most noteworthy performers would consider his music's early introduction as the wrong foot upon which yaogun got off is not a dismissal of the genre, or of those that brought it to the fore in the early days. Had that first "mistake" not been made, Kou almost certainly would not be wielding an axe in two of yaogun's better known acts, Suffocated and Spring and Autumn. What's interesting about Kou's interpretation of rock's rotten roots – and he is not the only one that believes yaogun comes from a tainted source – is that it comes around about the same time he complained about the lack of metal coverage. "I don't know why, maybe it's the kind of people we are, but so much media lacks any metal coverage," he said. "We're also part of the rock scene, and actually, we're a pretty big part of the rock scene. It's not that I want to steal a place for us, it's that there *is* a place for us, and I want to take it . . . Why is nobody paying attention?"

That question is a reasonable one to ask, because metal deserves its place in the yaogun story, past and present. Rockers from across the country recall that the earliest local bands were at least somewhat metal, and those musicians tended to be the first generation of rock teachers. Today, metal scenes abound in cities large and small. To wit: Heavy-metal mag *Painkiller* has more readers in the northeastern cities of Changchun and Harbin than anywhere else.

What makes Kou's statement especially interesting isn't that metal isn't considered a part of the scene: It's that metal folks might *care*. This is perhaps the result of the community that built up around metal, a community whose roots go back to the days when the project of filing and decoding the incoming music was communal; the eventual isolation was the result of the changes that colored China's nineties, when the available inputs and options seemed endless. Though the nineties began with metal as the epitome of the rock and roll dream, they didn't end that way.

Yaogun's metallic foundations created a very specific type of rock, a rock that was defined by long hair, tight leather and relatively intricate vocal, rhythm and guitar work. The imagery of metal did as much – if not more – to attract a following than did the sounds. "The metal look works for Chinese males. This shit sprouts out of our heads quite naturally," said Kaiser Kuo, grabbing his long locks in *Global Metal*, a film documenting the genre's cross-cultural travels. The metal look, he added, resonates with the look of the ancient Chinese warriors. "Long hair means martial prowess." Kuo's first band, Tang Dynasty, took things further with their Chinese-flavored take on the genre, and not just musically – the band was reported to address each other as "swordsman." Glimpses of guitar gods, drum kings and idolized frontmen on videos and album artwork from overseas, where metal was enjoying a heyday of stadium-sized proportions, were hard to resist. It's little wonder that the first rockers were drawn to it and why they might be reluctant to look far beyond the genre: Everything else sounded lame.

Shanghai rocker Pang Pang, who would in the late nineties play poppy rock in the vein of Brit-rockers Suede, initially found the band "gay" in the face of metal. And don't get him started on the Fab Four. "The Beatles weren't rock, only metal was." When *dakou*, the marked-for-trash music that found its way to China in the early nineties, flooded the landscape you could spot a metal record a mile off so rockers' searches focused on fonts, logos and hairstyles. Few rockers who were buying music in the *dakou* days can say that their early purchases were *not* heavily metal. "Because I was so into metal, I didn't listen to a lot of Chinese bands," said Zhong Sheng, second in command at Pilot Music. "I thought Cui Jian had no energy. That was the music that my neighbors were listening to. The more metal I listened to, the more heavy it needed to be. I was all about the metal."

Grunge-funk-etc rocker Zhou Ren recalled the late eighties and early nineties as a time when "it was hard to dislike metal."

It was a shift from the yaogun of Cui Jian in many ways. Rock Records' first *China Fire* compilation in 1992 fed off of the tastes of the day. That it was mostly metal showed the current and near-future direction of the music. The release of debut albums from Tang Dynasty and Black Panther drove the point home, bringing two very different kinds of metal to the fore. Their successes both inspired a new generation and rode the wave of metal's popularity. They are the only remaining first generation bands that still perform, and whether or not they are still considered true yaogun is not the point. What's important is that they continue performing music – on television, radio and in stadiums – that is more rock than their pop counterparts, and their actual-rock roots are part of the story that the mainstream media tells about the band.

Black Panther represents not only the lengths of yaogun's battle for recognition, but also the strange path it took to get there. Manager Guo Chuanlin's intense devotion, combined with a healthy dose of dumb luck and a few strategically placed supporters in an environment that was just as likely to be wide open as it was to be suffocatingly closed, allowed Black Panther to achieve the popularity that Guo had envisioned. "I promised that as long as everyone was devoted to this band, we'll be famous. They laughed! They didn't believe I could do it."

Black Panther is rooted in the metal-ish sounds of Bon Jovi, but also looked to Wham! for their inspiration, creating a finished product that sounded less metallic – in the heavy sense – than it looked. Not invited to Beijing's Modern Music Festival,

Guo found his own gig for Black Panther and six others, in Shenzhen, which caught the attention of major labels. Guo's initial meeting with BMG, he said, was sabotaged by Wang Weihua of the Breathing, who sat in for Guo's translator and talked up her own band rather than Guo's. Fortunately, Rock Records' Hong Kong company Jinshi stepped in and the band's debut was released in Taiwan and Hong Kong in 1991. While the band waited for the record to come out in Mainland China the following year, Guo convinced a producer at China Central Television to spend two minutes of a fifteen-minute news and culture show profiling the band. It was a risky decision for the producer, who was at the time young enough and, perhaps more importantly, enough of a fan of the band to roll the dice and broadcast the segment. The producer was suspended pending an investigation; the band shot to superstardom. "After that," said Guo, "I could organize a real national tour . . . If something was on CCTV, that was the signal to the rest of the country that it was something to promote." Wherever the band went, local officialdom eagerly rolled out the red carpet. Things snowballed from there, hurling the band onto the pages of the *People's Daily*, the most official of the official newspapers – a report that won over JVC Records, who initially said they couldn't be involved with a music not approved by the government, to sign the band.

Black Panther remains one of the most popular bands in the country. Having just celebrated their twentieth anniversary, they continue to perform in stadiums around the nation, though many yaogunners would argue that they left their rock roots early in their development. After all, their widespread fame emanating from their first album was as much the result of syrupy ballads like "Don't Break My Heart" as it was on hard-rock hitters like "Shameful." The latter is a Poison-esque rocker with the kind of lead guitar licks that directly bring to mind the head of hair banging to it; the synth padding, tom-tom rolls and backup "oh-woahs" are ripped right out of Bon Jovi's playbook. The former, far more popular, features the titular chorus in English, and has all of the rock and roll power of a Richard Marx song. But context is everything, and for a young generation to see a band of its own join the rock pantheon was essential.

"We feel a stronger sense of responsibility when we are making music now," lead singer Qin Yong told reporters in 2004. "It's hard. But hardships drive creativity." Whether one believes that they face hardship in superstardom – or, for that matter, produce anything worthy of the term "creative" – to disqualify them from the rock canon is not just to neglect their initial impact upon the scene as a band that broke through. Their fame enables them to take the form of rock music – overtly and at times embarrassingly in the yaogun context, commercial – to the masses, educating audiences about the existence of that phenomenon that Guo Chuanlin had to explain to most people he came across so many years ago: the *band*. And among the airbrushed waifs with backing musicians who are either absent or in the darkened background, possibly playing, possibly not, that dominate the pop world, it's nice seeing guys with guitars, who earned their stripes in the days before stadiums conceived of their existence.

Tang Dynasty presents a similar situation: Rooted deep in yaogun, they are seen as having crossed that line, now inhabiting the land of pop. When they began, though, they were, for many young rockers in the early- and mid-nineties, not only the entrée into the rock and metal world, but the benchmark for the imports. Their rise to the top of the admittedly small pyramid of first-generation bands did come swiftly, though despite appearances, they were not rock stars from the get-go.

When introduced to Ding Wu in the fall of 1988, American student Kaiser Kuo recognized immediately a man destined to front his own band. Perhaps they hadn't envisioned a debut in a Peking Duck restaurant, but they took what they could get. The band's first incarnation featured Ding, Kuo, Kuo's college bandmate Andrew Szabo, and bassist Zhang Ju.

Tang Dynasty's first real shot came when they were approached to be in a film about a fictional Beijing rock band. Szabo's ethnicity precluded his appearance onscreen, so Zhao Nian, who had played with the band in its first rehearsals, was to appear in the movie. Filming was scheduled for the spring in a Beijing suburb, and the band took up residence in the nearby worker's dorms of the Hotel Mövenpick. The script was lame, recalled Kuo, but the project was hard to resist, offering hours of rehearsal time and hard-to-find gear with which to do so. "We were in paradise." Until, that is, the events of the early spring in Tiananmen Square ended the film before it could begin.

In the wake of June 4, the foreigners were forced to return home. The band continued, with veterans of the mid-eighties scene Zhao Nian and Lao Wu joining the fold on drums and guitar, respectively. Kuo would occasionally play with the band after his return to China in the early nineties, joining again for a brief period ending in 1999.

Their slot at the Modern Music Festival whetted Rock Records' appetite. The label had, through subsidiaries, just released Black Panther's debut in Taiwan and Hong Kong, and they quickly scooped up Tang Dynasty.

A Dream Return to Tang Dynasty came out in 1992 and sold a reported 700,000 official copies in China; almost 1.5 million more copies were sold across Asia. The video for the album's title track was nominated for MTV Asia's International Viewer's Choice Awards in 1993 (they lost to an Indian pop-rock act), but that it made the list was a big deal. The record got *radio play*. The video was getting played on Channel V, the music video station under Rupert Murdoch's Star TV, broadcast out of Hong Kong (and into pirate satellite dishes across China, and later via television stations sharing content with the music video channel).

Dream Return is the genesis of heavy metal in China – even if it isn't quite as metal as one might expect. Kaiser Kuo may have put it best: "The record was important. And amazing for that time. But not anymore." It rocked harder, and differently, than the other contenders for China rock supremacy. It has been widely praised for its combination of ancient Chinese themes and sounds with modern metal (Iron Maiden, Black Sabbath, et al), though prog rock (Rush, King Crimson, etc) is also an important touchstone. Not for nothing, then, did the label hope to de-emphasize the band's American connection in Kuo.

In the early nineties, the band packed stadiums in China, and went to Germany, Japan and Hong Kong. They lived like rock stars. And, like so many before them and since, that's when things started to turn. Drugs were taking their toll, stalling efforts for a follow-up record. In May 1995, bassist Zhang Ju died in a motorcycle accident. The band's future looked dim. Though the entire community mourned Zhang, the band barely made it through the recording of the compilation dedicated to his memory, *Goodbye Zhang Ju*. Lao Wu, a hero to a generation of guitarists-to-be, left the band; Kuo rejoined. A replacement for Zhang was found, and a deal with Jingwen Records, a Mainland giant, was signed in 1996. Sales of their sophomore release, *Epic*, released six years after their debut, were good – a reported 80,000 cassettes in the first five days in Beijing alone – but there were complaints about the quality of the record from within the band and without. More significantly, it had entered a world light-years from the one in which the band first appeared, a world in which yaogun could no longer be defined by a few major players. By then, the big bucks were gone, and a new generation of bands was on the rise. Soon thereafter, Kuo again left the band – there were troubles over a woman, and tensions over the NATO bombing of the Chinese embassy in Belgrade. Lao Wu rejoined, but it still took until 2008 to release their third record, *Romantic Knight*.

These days, Tang Dynasty occupies that curious space between pop and rock star. They are widely known as a rock band, but their reputation in the yaogun world tends to be harmed by their widespread fame. In 2007, the band was featured on China Central Television in the studio preparing for their third album, which is, depending on your perspective, either the epitome of what the band has done perfectly right or absolutely wrong. Anyone who has both seen *Culture Express*, a program on the network's English-language station, and appreciates rock music would find the band's appearance on the show as anathema to yaogun. With a thickly accented introduction by a smarmy-grinned and over-bodily-gesturing host and a narrator parroting language about which he seems to have no understanding, you wonder if this is what the band had in mind in 1993 when they were asked by a German reporter about appearing on Chinese television. The band was dismissive of the idea at the time, not because they couldn't envision themselves on TV, but because they knew it would be a long time before they were allowed to appear. Observation changes that which is observed, here more so than anywhere. When you hear the official voice talking about Tang Dynasty's seminal role in China's heavy metal scene, you start to wonder whether Tang Dynasty could possibly be a metal band. And about who's won: The Man or the Band.

But that mainstream success, said Yu Yang, one of the founders of metal magazine *Painkiller* and *rockinchina.com*, was only the result of a strong underground. "Real metal culture has always been a sub-cultural thing," he said, adding that Tang Dynasty's success was really the result of metal's incubation below ground and its exploitation by Rock Records. The success of Tang Dynasty and Black Panther paved the way for the metalheads that followed.

Getting it on Record

In a 1991 *China Youth News* article it was observed that the music of the Mainland was "obsolete" and "incapable of engaging the psychological changes of our youth and equally unable to satisfy their musical needs." Accepting rock, the article continued, would strengthen pop. Otherwise Mainland music would "fall far behind in its ability to keep up with the increasingly refined popular listening tastes" and Cantopop (the Cantonese-language pop coming from Hong Kong) will dominate. The article ends with a warning that Chinese rock will drown in the coming floods of Western rock if it is not encouraged. "The Beatles once sang 'Give Peace a Chance'," the article concludes. "How about giving rock 'n' roll a chance?" As the nineties went on, it was clear that authorities generally did just that, and yaogun briefly flourished.

As yaogun aimed for the stars and the national mission switched from being solely concerned with politics to a vision familiar to capitalist roaders vilified in the years before, it was inevitable that the two would meet. The big bucks that 'gunners had heard about, through a combination of circulated articles and round-the-campfire-type stories, apocryphal and actual, told amongst the early scenesters. With the emergence of an actual record industry, or something like it, it seemed everyone had the chance at something resembling rock and roll fame.

In the early nineties, Rock Records, a Taiwanese record label that had met with some pop success in the late eighties, set up Magic Stone to handle yaogun. Its arrival on the Mainland was met with initial excitement and optimism, particularly as compilation record *China Fire* hit shelves in 1992 (Volume II and III came out in 1996 and 1998, respectively). The compilation was essential in showing the nation and region that there was Something brewing in China. Magic Stone scooped up rock and rollers, including Black Panther, Tang Dynasty and the trio of artists (Dou Wei, formerly of Black Panther; He Yong and Zhang Chu) known as the Magic Stone Three Prominents.

Yaogunners were enjoying the ride. Tang Dynasty bought motorcycles and instruments. "They really believed that they could live like full-blown rock stars," said one source. And they did, for a while. With new rock bucks came rock accoutrements:

Drugs of all kinds found their way into the scene, influencing music as much as minds. Hashish was rolled up in the rock scene from the get-go, thanks to its tradition in the communities of the various minorities, mostly Muslim from the northwestern provinces, who had settled around the country. These ethnic minorities were logical bedfellows for rockers, as both groups were considered outsiders. Meanwhile, its domestic pedigree and the large number of northwestern transplants in cities meant that hash was always easily available.

"Weed was normal," recalled documentarian and filmmaker Sheng Zhimin. "There was always a bit of that at parties." It seemed that in the early days, nobody was too concerned with the ramifications of getting busted with a bit of brown. A story circulated that one rocker, when asked by the police to reveal the source of his hash, replied "Van Halen," which was duly noted. Foreign names – names, that is, of actual people – proved useful, particularly those who had once resided in-country. One former and future resident recalled that during their time away from China, their name was oft invoked enough to produce a "thick" file.

Over the nineties, raids scooped up a number of 'gunners. Luo Qi, whose intense rock voice led the hard-rock-meets-synth-cheese Compass and her own solo project (and who is famous for her missing eye, taken by a smashed bottle in a bar fight), didn't so much get busted as much as put herself in harm's way. One account of her July 1997 Nanjing bust has her asking a cabbie to take her somewhere to score and winding up in a police station; the other has her comatose in a bar and coming to asking for treatment. Either way, she wound up on a three-month "recovery" that saw her emerge as an official anti-drug spokesperson. "I did promotion free of charge," she told China rock scholar Jeroen de Kloet. In a twist whose irony was not lost on Luo, she added that her clean start enabled her to access publicity impossible in the past. "Now I have become a role model as an ex-heroin user and am on TV . . . I have been interviewed by many government papers and they forget that I'm a rock singer."

Things turned more serious, said filmmaker Sheng, after bands signed with Magic Stone. He recalled a loss of innocence for the scene in general, with an emphasis on – not to mention the possibility of – rock stardom. And then, there was the change in drugs. "There was more heroin. This represented a big change. That's when people died." Zhang Ju, Tang Dynasty's bassist, whose drug habit wasn't a secret, died in a motorcycle accident in May 1995. Wu Ke (aka Xiao Ke), the guitarist from Dou Wei's band Dreaming – and the subject of the soul-searching that colored Sheng's documentary *Night of an Era* – died in September 1996.

Drugs were "pretty much everywhere," recalled one rocker, remembering a scene divided, for a time, between those who used heroin and those who didn't. Musically the drugs had an effect, and not necessarily a good one. Certainly more than a few rockers followed in Kurt Cobain's footsteps, having studied up on the man that was an idol to many, despite knowing full well how that story ended. One rocker spoke of the time wasted on music far more conceptual than listenable, music inspired by a conversation with a camel.

By the late nineties, the heroin period ended. "People either died," said one rocker, "or were done with it." But there were other drugs to keep rockers occupied in China as in the rest of the world. The crossover between the dance music and rock scenes was the result of a lack of proper venues for either, and it was inevitable that punks, rockers and ravers would wind up at the same parties, introduced to the same drugs: ecstasy, speed, cocaine. A member of the punk scene who saw the evolution of the drugs in that community recalled that things changed quickly by the end of the nineties: from hash to acid; from "fuck the disco" to partying at raves. "It's a reflection of the fact that we're talking about teenagers. One day you're a hippie, then the next day, you're something else." Electronic music, and accompanying raves and drugs, spread at the end of the decade, its membership comprised of a familiar mix of the same *liumang* – hooligans – initially attracted to yaogun.

Yaogun stardom, though, was not entirely roses. "When you saw where these guys lived," said journalist and observer Steven Schwankert, " 'making it' was lower standard. They had a Beijing Jeep [the local version of the Jeep Cherokee]. That was the sign of success." But in relation to even the new moneyed classes at the time, it was something; there were only a million privately-owned cars in the country in 1992.

Other labels swooped in. Hong Kong's Red Star released albums from Zheng Jun and Xu Wei, two artists who rose to national prominence, as well as for Cobra. After two hit albums, Black Panther switched to JVC in 1994.

But, let us pause, if only briefly, for perspective: "It wasn't that there were tons of bands that weren't recording," said Tang Dynasty co-founder Kaiser Kuo. "By 1992 or 1993 . . . if you could get fifty people to show up to a gig, you could probably get a record deal." That would change over the course of the nineties, only to return as punk, and later, "indie," emerged. Meanwhile, Black Panther's 1992 debut is reported to have sold 1.5 million (legitimate) copies in China; the record went platinum and they were playing in stadiums, but even in 1995, "one of their biggest problems," wrote Schwankert in *The Wire*, was debt.

By the time the Three Prominents and Tang Dynasty appeared together in Hong Kong in 1994 for a concert the likes of which the island had never seen, yaogun had either peaked or bottomed out. There was the high of record sales, publicity, stadiums and the newly acquired vehicles and instruments. But for some, that's when things got ugly.

Filmmaker Sheng Zhimin recalled becoming disillusioned right around then. It was, he says, at the Peninsula, a five-star hotel that is still among Beijing's higher-falootin' joints, for a 1993 party to present Black Panther and Tang Dynasty with platinum records that he started to become conscious of a fish-like odor. "I was there, wondering how on earth they got such a luxurious venue. Something had changed. It wasn't the scene I was working for, so I quit," said Sheng.

Dennis Rea, the Seattle guitarist who lived and performed in China in 1989 and toured there for seven years thereafter, agrees. "In a cruel twist of irony, the Chinese rock revolution was brought down not by gun-toting Public Security agents but by the virus of corporate rock culture," he writes.

Rockers quickly saw that the labels were less than ideal. In Sheng's *Night of an Era*, Magic Stone Prominent Zhang Chu speaks about how yaogun at Magic Stone was eerily like those early *tongsu* days, where the singer was the star. Zhang, like others, was told, in so many words, that the releases would be under the frontman's name. "On the contract it was pretty clear," he said. "They gave me a choice: be selfish and sign, or consider everyone else and leave it alone. We were the first generation of musicians dealing with a problem of commerce. And we went through a lot of pain."

Zhang's fellow Prominent He Yong recalled that the situation was brand new to yaogunners:

> They didn't have the time or energy to explain . . . the commercial system of the industry. The contract [was] based on their rules and we just took a look and signed. We didn't get it . . . and there wasn't really anyone around who did get it . . . You could say we were not on the same page when negotiating with the company.

Niu Jiawei, who worked for Magic Stone soon after the company set up shop in Beijing, takes this one step further:

> The company made a LOT of money. But nobody else did. I wasn't sure at the time what the real financial picture was because they wouldn't let me see the books. But bands never seemed to get anything beyond their advance – it seemed to me that the company had made back the advances, but there was nobody to ask these questions, so nobody got any answers.

Yet for all the talk of success for early metal and yaogun – including the Magic Stone Prominents and the several bands thereafter – the bottom line was still the bottom line. "Turned out," said Yu Yang, a co-founder of both *Painkiller* Magazine and *rockinchina.com*, the label "wasn't such an overwhelming financial success." Magic Stone left the Mainland in the wake of the Asian Financial Crisis of 1997. Whatever their financial legacy, it paved the way for the next generation of "indies," which rose up just as Magic Stone was on the way out, and to which we will return later.

Rock Records' online presence, Weiku, offered bands an early taste of the online music industry. Bands culled from around the country got paid to post songs that were voted on by users; with enough votes, a record deal might follow. The model only lasted a brief couple of years, and Rock's "rock" years on the Mainland ended – the label's story over the last years of the nineties reveals a company done in by competition both legitimate and not.

Pirated music was as much one of the valleys of the yaogun coaster as it was the foundations upon which it was built. For the labels, sailing their proverbial ships through the infested waters that were the Chinese market, it was simple math. "In terms of piracy, back in the nineties, you could take your legit sales figures and add a zero," said Magic Stone's Niu Jiawei.

"For every album we pressed," adds American David O'Dell, who also worked for the label, "there were ninety-nine (pirated) albums."

But the labels themselves, their bands and their fans would hardly exist were it not for piracy. Yaogun was built, after all, on a foundation of *dakou*, the cut-out recordings chucked from the West toward Chinese dumps and on to a network that ended in record stores of a special breed. At first, piracy was restricted to overseas material, which seemed to be selected on a completely random basis. Eventually, pirates got into the local rock game, but even in the early days of yaogun piracy, young fans had unprecedented access – the kind of access you might associate with the internet era – to local music.

Solo artist Wang Yuqi, who has played for Second Hand Rose, Mu Ma and others, remembers the late nineties as a golden era for record-buying. "There was good distribution, there were lots of stores," he said, recalling an album by thrashers Overlord that he found in a small town. "It was easy for people to find out about things. There was one TV station, one radio station." In the yao-gun world, the scale was even smaller. In 1996, when Wang found that album, there were a total of six yaogun releases, according to the meticulously compiled *www.rockinchina.com* database.

The shelves of arguably every rocker that listened to music on forms that predate the mp3 overflow with *dakou*. If one were looking for metaphoric meaning, a parallel with rock and roll's own journey from West to East, one could certainly find something alluring in the form of the tapes and CDs from which gashes were sawed, holes punched and chunks cut. Unwanted in the land that birthed them, countless rock recordings were sent to the dumping grounds of the Middle Kingdom, where they made their way through the country, doing in new territory what they no longer could at home. Learning from the Soviets, the Chinese authorities worried about American efforts to subvert their youth with the music; despite the vernacular hurled at the music and the evil therein, they never could have imagined that they would have to protect their citizens from literal garbage.

Beginning in the early nineties, *dakou* albums made their way into the hands of a new breed of businessperson. "In the early nineties, everyone was 'doing business'," recalled Mao Live-house's Li Chi. "No matter what their job was, everyone was 'in business'." Li remembers phone shops – that is, shops offering public phones – crammed with "businesspeople" of all types each trying to out-shout the other with their calls for buying and selling – this was, after all, in the days when getting rich was just about glorious, and hordes were lining up to 'jump into the sea' of money-making. Whether or not overseas record labels were complicit at some level in the operation – there are theories that see the situation as analogous to charges that tobacco manufacturers were complicit in international cigarette smuggling – *dakou* was an immeasurable boon to yaogun. More so than even Cui's unveiling of "Nothing," or of DJ Zhang Youdai's broadcasting of it and other songs, it put the music directly into the hands of the masses, bringing the listening experience directly to the rocker-to-be in a way that the internet would build upon in the near future.

Dakou shops sprouted like wildfire, containing, in their often-closet-sized spaces, completely unsorted piles of more music than could be imagined. It made for a challenging experience, rewarding in a way that can only be felt by spending hours wading through music so crappy you didn't realize they still sell it (and that they don't, actually) and coming across the one record you've been looking for since you were a kid.

"For the most part, the early shops' only strategy was to separate tapes and CDs," remembers Wang Zhuohui, who runs Free Sound Records, one of the longest-lasting sources for (legit) local music in Beijing. In the rare shop that split the selection by genres, it had to be the customers that stepped in. While not always places amenable to hanging out, if individual record stores didn't serve as community centers like their counterparts in the rest of the world, they were at least generally confined to an area of town where yaogunners knew they'd likely run into like-minded souls.

Nanjing had a neighborhood like this, where Yang Haisong began his yaogun journey. First, he discovered that there were others like him around. And on one fateful day, he met a Beijinger that parlayed two important pieces of rock news. The bad news was that Kurt Cobain had committed suicide. The good news was that there was a Beijing rock scene. Thereupon Gao Jingxiong, the visitor from Beijing, handed Yang his band's demo. That band, Underbaby, would kick off the punk scene in Beijing. The meeting between Yang and Gao would connect the two in a way that made it possible for Yang to move to Beijing with the band that would become P.K. 14, which in turn rose to the top of the yaogun heap in the early aughts and has remained there through five albums and more than a decade.

Beijing's university district, Wudaokou, was one of the capital's centers of *dakou* shops. One shop in particular proved to be essential to the formation of Hang on the Box, the all-girl alt-punk band fronted by Wang Yue. She and her soon-to-be-bandmate Yi Lina started hanging out in the neighborhood as high schoolers, with Hao Fang's book on Kurt Cobain as a guide through the endless bins of *dakou* tapes. The shop owner's organizational system was simple: the good stuff was behind the counter, the decent stuff was on the counter and the rest, for pennies, was on the floor. Wang hit the jackpot on day one: "We found the Meat Puppets on the floor. We told the boss that it was awesome, that he really should put it behind the counter." After, that is, putting their money down. They'd go three or four times a week, and the boss took a shining to the "bargain bin babes," eventually hiring them on to help sort through the piles. "We got really good at fixing tapes," said Wang, since tapes invariably got gashed too hard. The boss showed his appreciation by passing Wang an electric guitar – she previously had to make do with the acoustic that was the limit of her parents' benevolence – and it was working there that netted Wang the third member of her trio. "She was wearing pretty cool clothes when she came into the store. I asked what she was looking for, and she said she was looking for punk and alternative stuff . . . I put on the Clash, 'Should I Stay or Should I Go' and we exchanged contact information."

Radio DJ Zhang Youdai was not a fan of *dakou*, but he was a fan of the type of shop that could bring a band together, and he was eager to encourage others to amass collections as big as his own. "Opening a record store was the most logical thing for me to do," he said. His eponymous shop lasted from 1994 to 1998. The shop stocked imported CDs and a few demos. For a while, he split space with his number one fan, writer and critic Hao

Fang, who was to books about music what Youdai was to broad-casting music. But it was a tough business. His discs weren't imported through fully above-board channels. He had to pay up front for products he didn't know he could necessarily move. And at RMB120-140, or around US$15 at the time, the products were far out of most peoples' price range. "I wanted to make my shop like my home: A great place to hang out," said Youdai, and according to all reports, he'd accomplished that.

Chen Yi, who went on to work for Beijing rock label Scream and then Warner Music, and hosts the regular online radio show "Tangsuan," cut his teeth in the music business at Youdai's shop. "I had the feeling that I knew the customers even though we just met," said Chen. "It was because of our interest in music. I met a lot of people through that store."

Youdai remembers the balance not quite struck between love and money. Hanging out and listening to music was a long way from putting down upwards of twenty bucks for an album. "You can't live off culture," said Youdai. "Both Hao Fang and I realized that."

Three Kinds of Live: the Parties, the Stages, the Festivals

With permanent and purpose-built live venues absent until the latter years of the nineties, the hipoisie – artists, musicians, writers and others, as well as an increasing number of a variety of expats – gathered in a rotating cast of venues for what were dubbed "parties." Before helping to form influential metal band Tang Dynasty, Kaiser Kuo played his first gig at a Peking duck restaurant. Radio DJ Zhang Youdai recalled, with fondness, a restaurant in the Temple of the Sun Park where the stage was a collection of beer crates. To this day, the man behind Mao

Livehouse, Li Chi, can't walk by a cafeteria without having a flashback of the parties he attended on many a Saturday night at Sushanna, which was an office canteen during the week.

Li Ji, best known in the new millennium for his hip Thai and Vietnamese restaurants, was a major player in the party scene, opening a string of party venues that would thrive for a moment until the inevitable shut-down. "He did wonderful places; absolutely amazing places," said Udo Hoffmann, who himself organized parties in the late eighties and early nineties before branching out to produce festivals. "These were places that were never really recreated." Partly, one adds, because of Hoffmann himself. "I'm personally responsible for closure of two of Li Ji's places," he said, citing parties that got a little too festive, perhaps.

A highlight of the mid-nineties party scene was cover band Five-Point Star. A product of Inner Mongolian Dai Qin's obsession with the Beatles, the band studied the Fab Four with an unimaginable intensity, which was rooted in Dai's life-altering encounter with the music. They realized, for example, that John played guitar and sang, and Paul sang and played bass, so that's what they did. When they found out that Paul played left-handed, they had to call a meeting to talk through whether or not Dai was going to have to relearn his instrument for the other hand. Their first trip to Beijing ended badly. In the six months they'd spent there, they'd blown all their money and, in their one glimpse of the local scene, realized that they couldn't compete. Three months of intense practices later, they returned to Beijing, made a call to a party planner, auditioned, and immediately got a gig. "You have to understand," said Dai Qin, "we *studied* the Beatles: their voices, the visuals, *everything* . . . We were like soldiers with our practicing." The party at which they debuted featured upwards of ten bands, and they stole the show, becoming known as the Mongolian Beatles. "Everyone was shocked, especially the foreigners." On the strength of that gig, friendships were made and the band was inundated with requests for party gigs, of both the underground rock variety or the much-further above-ground embassy gatherings and hotel bars. "For hotel gigs we got 200 *yuan* a person, sometimes three," said Dai. "You could cab around the entire city for twenty, so it was a *lot* of money."

Parties eventually gave way to clubs, and Dai, who would later front the band Thin Man, was there for one of these permanent-ish venues. He ran Angel's, which he says was the country's first live rock venue for the year it existed, roughly 1996-1997. "I didn't know what a livehouse was," he said, using the English-by-way-of-Japanese "word" that has found its way into the yaogun lexicon. "But I knew bands should have a place to play." Angel's wasn't destined to last; with starving musicians congregating there, financial troubles were virtually assured. "I gave away the bar in drinks," he recalled with a smile, the investment not his to give away.

The mid-nineties saw the emergence of several venues like Angel's, which had regular events that were becoming less "parties" and more "gigs." Large discos remained important venues for shows requiring more space than a tiny bar, but there was less need for them as the millennium approached.

But there was, still, as the earliest converts to Teresa Teng and Western pop music had found, a sense of danger in attending parties. Until even around 2000, remembers journalist Steven Schwankert, you never knew if the shows you were going to would last an entire set, since the cops tended to wait until after things started before pulling the plug. "So there was always an edge . . . It was the idea that you were listening to outlaw music." While nowhere near the extent of the nineties, contemporary yaogun, played in clubs and festivals across the country, is still occasionally plagued by "incidents" reminding audiences that they haven't come all that far.

For some, things started to go downhill soon after the rock party scene's heyday of the early nineties. One mark that a scene has sprung is the number of scenesters up in it doing nothing more than aiming to be seen. In Schwankert's 1995 article for *The Wire* magazine, one organizer and band manager bemoaned the direction that things had taken:

> In the late eighties, if you held a rock party, everybody was there to see the band, they were serious about the music. Now, it's a social thing. The people want to talk with their friends, have a few drinks, dance, listen to whoever's performing. Money's too important now. They don't listen to the message.

As parties populated the underground, there was a fertile plain upon which stages were built out in the open from the very first days of the decade. The Modern Music Festival, two days in February 1990, provided a literal platform for bands, and kicked off the decade with a positive jolt. In terms of the ability of the live experience to connect with its audience, it would have been rare for any show to be a less than revelatory experience. Cobra's Xiao Nan recalled audience reactions that went beyond what one might expect of those seeing her all-female band in yaogun's early days:

> Back in the nineties, audiences had the impulse and instinct for rock. At the time, people were more pure. They'd never seen anything like this and they reacted very strongly to the music . . . They only had our shows to go on. They didn't think too much about what kind of music we were, or are we popular, or wear the right clothes, or perform well. They were moved because we were playing.

The excitement over live music moved people in different ways. When, in the first days of June 1989 Tang Dynasty set out on tour alongside STG, a band comprised primarily of Tang Dynasty members, they discovered how easy it was for fans to believe that they were superstars. STG sat out the first of two gigs in Qiqihar because one of their members returned to Beijing, objecting to the tour's route. The crowd turned ugly when STG didn't play, setting fire to the ticket booth in anger. STG, like Tang Dynasty at the time, had foreign members, which made the promoter's claim that they were Michael Jackson's backup band that much more believable.

American guitarist Dennis Rea, who performed around China between 1989 and 1996, noted in his memoir *Live at the Forbidden City* the intensity of the audiences that attended his shows. Rea brought his Taiwan-based band, Identity Crisis, on a small China tour in 1990. Their shows in Chengdu – which marked the first visit by a Western rock band to the city – were sold-out affairs attended by thousands, while hundreds more were turned away. "Students at one of our . . . concerts at Western Medical University shattered a large glass door trying to force their way into the hall, while others climbed in through second-floor windows. At one show, an audience member drummed on a desktop so zealously with his fists that he actually broke his hand – and he later insisted that it had been worth it!"

On an autumn 1991 tour of Chengdu, Chongqing, Kunming and Guangzhou with a group of Americans united under the name of The Vagaries, Rea performed at Kunming's National Defense Arena for four thousand fans. Not exactly a subdued affair, dancing and cart-wheeling spilled out of the seats, and even onto the stage. At the post-show dinner a drunken provincial cultural minister announced, "I have seen the power of rock and roll!" Unbeknownst to the blitzed bureaucrat, this was only a small taste of yaogun's power.

The following year Cui Jian rolled through town and "power" only began to describe the event. When musician Liang Heping tells one about "the most amazing footage" he has, one should drop what one is doing, and immediately join him in sifting through decades' worth of tapes of Cui's concerts, underground jam sessions and festivals. One should also prepare to be amazed. The footage that Liang showed me is difficult to describe, other than to say that the audience seems to be literally going insane. Not quite in the young-girls-crying-after-getting-a-glimpse-of-Elvis kind of a way, but in something resembling the ecstasy and sheer emotional re-lease of the sudden enlightenment – less zen-master mellow than whirling-dervish-snake-kisser-tongues-speaker wacky.

One of the reasons Liang believes things were so intense was because of the short glimpses people got of the Chengdu shows that ended Cui's Asian Games tour, which had been, against the odds, broadcast. With two years to reflect on the clips they'd seen of a Chengdu audience going mental, it still comes as a sur-prise that the original two shows weren't enough for Kunming: Four had to be added. The intensity of the crowd, said Liang, in-creased with each concert. "At the time, there was a lot of tension building up inside of so many of the young people in Yunnan," Liang said. "It was a huge release for the audience; far more in-tense than in the north . . . There's *never* been a show like that. In terms of Cui's interactions with society, Kunming in 1992 was the absolute peak."

Andrew Jones, writing in *Spin* magazine that same year, tells of a Chongqing concert featuring Tang Dynasty, Black Panther, Compass and Cobra. Despite having not yet released any albums, and without much in the way of advanced publicity in those days when Cui was, for most, the embodiment of yaogun in its entirety, "they were greeted by the audience with a frenzied rush toward the stage and a hail of flowers." Tang Dynasty bassist Zhang Ju was given a teddy bear by a girl who climbed onstage. Local officials seemed just as confused as the audience, doubling the security for the next day's show and canceling the third. When China scholar Orville Schell saw Cui Jian perform in the eastern city of Nanjing that same year, he met fans that had come from the northwestern city of Lanzhou – a thousand miles away.

It wasn't, in the first years of the nineties, easy to get these massive shows lined up; there were few people experienced in what was required logistically and technically, and nobody seemed to know exactly what political mojo was needed to pull a concert off. Hair-metal band Black Panther's manager Guo Chuanlin became, by dint of necessity, gifted in the kung-fu of

Getting Shit Done in the early nineties. In 1989, when finding a sponsor for the equipment his just-formed band required, he learned just what he was up against.

"This type of thing," the man said when Guo explained the concept of a rock band, "doesn't exist."

Black Panther would not only exist but thrive, as would Guo, who began as a party organizer and quickly graduated to large-scale traveling concert. Though he found the southern city of Shenzhen "relaxed and open," it was an effort of massive proportions to pave the way for the five-band bill he took there in 1990 – and thanks to the too-hot-for-officialdom lyrics of Baby Brother, he nearly didn't ever get home, his name comprising the entirety of the list of those responsible for the show's content. Arranging the 1993 concert that would be Black Panther's big Beijing break required not just a serious dose of chutzpah and various levels of official permission, but a big financial promise to a senior citizen's charity, and the extraordinary powers of a fiery Long March survivor able to scold her way through all permit-issuing departments. What he got for his troubles was what he called a "pretty successful" outing: Limited in his movements to the sightline of the head of the cultural bureau, who assured the young 'gunner that he'd be hauled away should anything remotely untoward "happen" during the show, Guo oversaw a concert featuring nine police department security details and more national officials in attendance than any other concert previous.

Cui Jian was the first 'gunner to leave the Motherland for performances. Between 1988 and 1992, he hit Korea (performing at Seoul's Olympic Games), England, France and Japan. In 1993, he, along with metal band Tang Dynasty, pop-rockers 1989, dark new-wavey and all-female Cobra, early electronic artist Wang Yong and a jazz band led by Cui's reedman Liu Yuan were bundled up and sent to Germany under the banner of the Chinese Avant-Garde. Organized by Udo Hoffmann, who had lived in Beijing for four years prior to the tour, the goal was to change the impression of China colored by the events in Tiananmen Square. It was, said Hoffmann, "to show that there are young people in China doing things which are similar to those in Germany . . . That there is a society which was able to digest young people going in different directions."

Putting the operation together was not easy. Obtaining passports for yaogunners who had never left the country, finding funding and figuring out the logistics of several simultaneous tours of Germany, all while keeping the information away from the Chinese Ministry of Culture, who might pull the plug on the tour and its organizer. But the most challenging part of the whole thing, Hoffmann said, "was convincing the Chinese bands that it could work. Most people thought I was crazy."

But it paid off. Demand for tickets to the shows outstripped supply by an exponential factor, and footage reveals an audience with minds blown – perhaps more by the sheer existence of the artists rather than the music they performed. But a mind blown is a mind blown, and it was an important a first step in the journey that both audience and musicians require in the process by which the music and its reception improves. The tour was educational for the Chinese as well, bringing them new insights into international-standard performance and travel, and also into the impressions of China held outside the country, particularly via the eager local press.

Cobra, being all women, were especially sought after, and their experience with the German media made them rethink their outlook. "So many reporters asked if we were a feminist band," said keyboardist Yu Jin of their time in Germany. "I'd never considered this. We answered really simply: 'We want to play music, it's fun.' "

"We aren't feminists," guitarist and vocalist Xiao Nan told a Chinese reporter after returning to China. "But we want to use the band to prove the existence of the social value of women."

By 1994, Taiwanese label Magic Stone Records had their fingers in just about every part of the yaogun pie. They'd scooped

up the artists who had come to be known as the Three Prominents – He Yong, Zhang Chu and Dou Wei – and bestowed upon
Tang Dynasty and Black Panther platinum records. To follow up
on the hit releases, they decided to take all of the aforementioned
artists save Black Panther to Hong Kong, to see how the band
might fare on the island. The concert, "Chinese Rock Power,"
was to be held at the Hong Kong Coliseum and would, like
Chinese Avant-Garde before it, test yaogun's reception outside
of its homeland.

Most reports point to an amazing success. *Most* reports.
Hong Kongers were obviously impressed with the music coming over from the Mainland. "It was the first time they'd stood
up to watch a concert," said He Yong. The footage, in addition to
showing He Yong at the prime of his rock and roll life, shows a
crowd loving every minute.

But Dou Wei remembers things differently. Watching footage from the concert it is obvious from the glimpses of Dou we
are given that he is in a different headspace – and his musical
journey over the years adds to this impression. At the end of the
concert, all of the performers gather, reveling in the show they've
just played. When we see Dou, he seems to be in a world of his
own; looking at the antics around him with a combination of dis-
gust nearing anger.

"Our feeling coming off the stage was a lot better than the
feeling while we were playing," Dou told Phoenix TV in a 2008
interview and continued, registering his discontent that the label
released the live video without fixing the mistakes that he said
were in the performance. "My feeling about that concert is that
there were more negatives than positives." All the talk about how
that was a so-called "spring of new music," said Dou, "is a con."

Yaogun was not only tested in its forays out into the world,
but also as the outside world came to yaogun. As yaogun became
worthy of the large stages popping up across the nation, there
was an increase in performers from outside the Middle Kingdom. Though the environment improved, rock, particularly that

of foreigners, remained sensitive and subject to censorship. Paul Simon performed in Guangzhou in 1991, and while he wasn't personally the victim of censorship, his show was. Dennis Rea writes that Cui Jian, like much of the yaogun population, headed down to check out what was to be a half-empty 8,000-seat arena show. Simon and his band had skipped the pre-concert hang-out session arranged by the American consulate to introduce the northern rockers to the visiting musicians, but had agreed that Cui should come onstage for renditions of both "Scarborough Fair" and "Nothing to My Name." Cui didn't make it past back-stage, though, informed by local officials that the show would be canceled if he stepped on the stage.

BB King opened Beijing's Hard Rock Café (a place that has had virtually nothing to do with yaogun for many years) in 1994. Roxette and Air Supply both hit Beijing in 1995. "Although at that time, almost every musician in China was focusing on heavy metal, Roxette's [concert] still shocked them," wrote one Chinese fan on a bulletin board on the Swedish band's website. "It's the first time we [saw] a 'World Class' band . . . live." Pointing out that while Wham! blazed the pop band trail, the fan adds that nobody in China knew the British duo, while Roxette had some-thing of a fan base when they passed through. And knowing all about the varied tastes of young yaogunners, we can assume more than a few had at least a tape somewhere with "The Look" on it. "Their [visit] will never be forgotten," concludes the post.

Beginning in the mid-nineties the number of bands visiting China increased exponentially, and yaogun has felt the effects. It is in the small-scale venues yaogunners have gained, and con-tinue to do so, the types of lessons from their more experienced brethren in arms necessary to move things forward. Most small-scale gigs featuring international artists in the nineties occurred – and still, for many, occur – under the radar. They were thus not generally subject to the kinds of censorship that may have been (and remain) on the books but is not often enforced with serious vigor.

As the punk scene took off, more visits resulted from its international network. Jonathan Leijonhufvud, a Swedish citizen raised in Hong Kong and Beijing, was involved in some of the earliest club-level punk that came into Beijing. He brought Japanese punks Pridebowl and Envy to Beijing in 1997, before Scream Club even existed to house them, and converted a number of young rockers. Soon thereafter, Swedish punks International Noise Conspiracy boosted the nascent punk scene in 1999, creating a fiercely loyal following that remained when they returned six years later (and again in 2009 when, due to last-minute problems at the Modern Sky Festival, what would have been their third tour was canceled).

In addition to kickstarting or detouring a scene, there were more practical lessons to be learned from the visits of overseas yaogun compatriots. There is the Show, for one, which is something that bands all over the world have been studying. Rapcore, a genre that would proliferate through the early aughts, was arguably kickstarted as much by pirated Rage Against the Machine albums as it was by a visit from a band known as Gorgon, about which scant information is available. On the run from a year-long stint at a hotel in the southern city of Changsha, the band squeezed in a show at the CD Café in 1996 and, said one witness, altered yaogun's course. "That gig changed a lot of rock and roll," recalled Liu Wentai, American bassist and producer, who at the time was a member of Zhou Ren's grunge band. "This was the first time a Beijing audience saw what was coming from New York . . . Everyone in music scene went to that show."

Dai Qin, who had by then already formed Thin Man, which took Rage Against the Machine as a major influence, remembers seeing them. "We were shocked," he said, the smile getting bigger as the memory of the gig got clearer. "They used the venue's crappy gear, but they had so much energy!" It was energy of a kind they'd never before seen.

In light of recent huffaws involving visiting artists upsetting their local hosts, or being prevented from visiting in the first

place, we might look at the history not just of visiting performers, but of the varying degrees to which officialdom wielded
influence over them.

Post-Olympics, any mention of international artist visits to
China invariably leads to the invocation of Bjork's name, and
the Incident that, we are told, cursed the live landscape for generations.

It would have come as a complete surprise only to those who
hadn't looked, even briefly, into the artist. When Bjork ended
her March 2008 Shanghai show with the song "Declare Independence," tacking on, at the end, the yelp heard round the world:
– "Tibet, Tibet!" – Bjork's pro-Tibetan, and pro-a-lot-of-minority-
groups, leanings were no secret. She did, after all, perform at
the Tibetan Freedom Concert in 1996 and 1997, and punctuated
performances around the world with the same move, substitut-
ing "Tibet" with "Faroe Islands," "Kosovo," and "Aboriginal
peoples of Australia." But what happened in her wake did come
as a surprise, despite the increasing cool in the pre-Olympic
air experienced by many familiar with the grey area of the live
music sector. The fallout from the incident may well have been,
in the grand scheme, a ripple in the pond, but in the context of
the moment it was more like one of the waves in the stormy sea
that was pre-Olympic China. The nation was busy putting on its
meet-the-world face – which, contrary to many outside expectations, meant tightening more reigns than it loosened – while pro-
Tibetan and Beijing demonstrators made a mess of the Olympic
Torch relay in city after city around the world. One doesn't have
to have watched China for very long to know that it doesn't take
well to slights from the outside.

While Bjork's move caught the world's attention and talk of
the inability for artists of any kind to visit China thereafter flourished, the reality was less black and white – not unlike the shade
of color currently governing the live music industry, where all
is okay until it's not, and where rules governing lyrical content
local and international, as well as permits, licenses and more,

were on the books before Bjork and remain so. As in so many other realms in China, legislation and enforcement are two very different phenomena.

It's not a situation simple enough to blame The Man. Sure, The Man put laws concerning censorship of lyrics on the books in the first place, and yes, in the international musical context, this might well be a law too far. But hey, if you want to play the game, you have to know the rules. If anything, we might blame – it should be added, only partially – The Men, since the central authorities have far more arms than faces, and it is the local guys, fearing the downhill trajectory of the proverbial poop, that tend to throw up the biggest roadblocks.

Bjork's Incident was only the most widely-reported of its kind of late, and we would do well to recall that Bjork not only performed at Beijing's Workers' Gymnasium in 1996 without in- cident, but one rocker remembers that in the months leading up to the gig, her image and voice was everywhere, including on the officially-run China Central Television (CCTV). Officialdom reared its head a year before Bjork's first visit, when Roxette was told that the lyrics to "Sleeping in My Car" – the most scandal- ous of which appear to be: "*Sleeping in my car – I will undress you / Sleeping in my car – I will caress you / Staying in the back seat of my car making love, oh yea!*" – weren't suitable for China. The male half of the duo was quoted as saying that they'd initially agreed to the changes, "but didn't change them in the end." The Swedes emerged unscathed. Roxette: 1; The Man: 0.

In 2002, the Rolling Stones' *Forty Licks* greatest-hits album was shed of four eponymous licks – "Brown Sugar," "Beast of Burden," "Honky Tonk Woman," "Let's Spend the Night Togeth- er" – as was their 2006 setlist. In advance of a planned (alas, not consummated) Britney Spears tour, cultural officials demanded show organizers guarantee that Spears not wear anything too revealing as part of her stage show. One can imagine officials from "relevant departments" lining up to carry out the "strict reviews" promised by the China News Service.

Harry Connick, Jr.'s big band sat out many tunes during his 2008 tour, a situation resulting from the mistaken submission of an old setlist to the authorities. Had Bjork not shouted for independence just days prior to Connick, Jr.'s show, it's likely the band would have been able to play the songs they'd rehearsed – and brought the sheet music for. With such sensitive timing, the band instead saw, first hand, the official censorship process: Officials showed up an hour before show-time in Shanghai and physically crossed songs off of the setlist. "Due to circumstances beyond my control," said Connick in a statement, "I was not able to give my fans in China the show I intended."

If the Pet Shop Boys are granted permission to come to China, it's likely that they won't be playing "Legacy," a song from their tenth album, which was released in China in 2009. The China version of the album featured the song sans vocals after objections were raised (the song hints at the transience of governments in one line). "Does the Chinese government really fear the power of a song to bring about change?" asks Pet Shop Boy Neil Tennant (one might reply: "Doesn't the lyricist believe it?"). The answer isn't clear, though obviously the 1942 conference on art still holds serious sway. That Public Enemy could perform "Fight the Power" at their 2007 Beijing Pop Festival appearance, or Roger Waters could lead an audience to chant that they didn't need any thought control earlier that same year only clouds the issue.

Many artists, meanwhile, are precluded from a trip to the Middle Kingdom based on prior acts – performing, say, at a Tibet Freedom Concert, or appearing with the Dalai Lama. Unless, of course, the artist comes less than officially – which is still, despite the rising large-scale concerts arriving in the Middle Kingdom, the main method for music to be brought from overseas to China. Club- and bar-level shows, while technically subject to the same laws as those that see songs removed and clothing potentially covered up, in reality are often too small-scale to attract attention. And so, for the moment, while Britney is told to cover up or stay away, bands like the International Noise Conspiracy, D.O.A. and countless others tour clubs across the country with nothing protecting unsuspecting audiences from potentially scandalous lyrics. Or outfits.

But back many years before overseas visitors would come with anything resembling regularity, and as parties slowly gave way to venues, it was inevitable that the Festival would become an ideal for which to strive. Certainly, as more and more bands filled stages of all sizes, festivals – like the ones they'd seen on videos, and read about in books and magazines – would have been the natural progression. But, for the most part, it was only late into the nineties that the concept became reality, and it is the exceptions that, particularly in contrast to the millennial festival-ian explosion, make for a different kind of window into the times. It's also important to note that the Chinese festival clock didn't begin ticking with the be-all and end-all Midi Festival, though its dozen-year history is worthy of commendation in light of the experiences of its forbearers. None of its predecessors may have lasted, but they were essential pieces of the whole that tend to get trampled in the quick contextualization that seems to have no time for the world before Midi. But before Midi, in theory if not in practice, there were a few beacons of hope on the festival landscape. Whether things really began in 1990 with the Mod-ern Music Festival isn't really clear, because the event's Chinese name labeled it a "concert," but the idea – two days, many bands – certainly helped things along; likewise did various multi-band bills in cities around the country also add to the fervor.

In 1990, Udo Hoffmann hosted what he calls the first rock festival in China. It was an indoor event at the Friendship Hotel, which was already a regular spot on Beijing's tiny yaogun map. But on this occasion, there was a theme, and a thousand attend-ees. "We built a big Berlin Wall, then an acoustic band played in front of it," he recalled with a huge smile. "A bunch of artists, many of whom are now quite famous, painted on the Wall, and then rock music brought the wall down." That event, he said, was the first he did "with a real open impact." Impact indeed. "Someone told me that a city official heard about the show and said 'hell opened its gates'." Which didn't stop him from thinking bigger: Moving the event outdoors, he envisioned – and nearly got – a massive festival. Two days before the big day, the event was officially cancelled, though Hoffmann allows that "maybe it was never permitted." By then, he said, 5,000 tickets had been sold. On the day of the show, Hoffmann, the hotel's PR manager, and over a thousand policemen awaited the crowds – which, even in the days before IM, SMS or even cell phones, already knew not to show. Which is either inspiring – seeing how tight-knit the scene was back then – or else, depressing – even as they bought their tickets they knew it'd never happen.

Around the same time, filmmaker Sheng Zhimin, then involved in the party-organizing scene, was contacted by the organizers of a Temple Fair-type event in the Beijing suburb of Miyun. The carnivalesque fairs have traditionally been held around the country in conjunction with Chinese New Year, and tend to feature a throng of humanity and stall after stall of various edibles and drinkables. But bringing in Sheng, the organizers were after something a bit more, and Sheng was after even more than that. "It was exactly like the case now," Sheng explained. "There was a company that wanted to make some money, and they told the local government that doing a festival would be a good idea."

Sheng and his "artistic director" immediately had visions of Woodstock and the other videos they'd seen. The event, they were told, would be held in an amusement park, which was only half true: The area set aside for the concert was right smack dab in the middle of a roller coaster. "The thing would zoom by constantly," Sheng recalled. There were other problems to sort out as well: Eye-high grass grew wild and there was no company qualified to build a stage of the scale they were envisioning. So Sheng and his crew came up with a plan. Acquiring a truckload of wood and a posse of local workers and with images from their video collection in mind, they ordered the construction, guiding the workers with the call to make the stage taller than a person. They got a three-meter-high stage and topped it with a simple lighting rig. It was only when they went to adjust the lights that they realized they had no ladders tall enough for the job. Cranes were brought in.

Sheng's initial lineup was decimated by a rash of drug busts that put a chunk of the rock scene behind bars. His attempts to free the jailed rockers with official letters from the Miyun County government and his own protestations were in vain, and then some. Seen yapping with the cops, Sheng was assumed to have been the mole that got the group busted in the first place.

With a drug (-bust) -free lineup in place, it was show time and Sheng was in heaven. "Waaaaah!" he remembers thinking, as the first band started and the lights came on. "It's *just* like on TV!" But there was a tone, and pause, in his retelling that indicated there was a "but" to come. "But," he continued:

> There's like a thousand people. And at first that feels good. But then, I look around and realize that ninety percent of the audience is local peasants, none of whom have paid to get in . . . There were maybe one or two hundred people that came up from Beijing, but most of them haven't paid either; they're our friends, they're artists or whatever.

So Sheng and his friends got their festival after all, free, one might add, looking for the bright side, of any of that messy financial stuff that gets in the way of a good time. And most importantly, it sure *looked* right.

It's easy to dismiss the naïveté of Sheng and his cohorts in their quest to replicate the festival experience they had longed for as the silliness of youth and of yaogun's early history, but until very recently, when qualified staging, lighting, sound and security outfits emerged, there wasn't a whole lot of difference between their strategy and that of so-called "successful" festivals.

Radio DJ Zhang Youdai glimpsed his first live show outside of his native land in 1996, when he covered Cui Jian's performance at Roskilde, continental Europe's biggest festival. "There were a hundred thousand people in the audience, for four days and nights of performances," he told the *Southern Weekly*. "I was shocked and excited. That's when I started to have the fantasy of putting together China's first festival." Alas, his plans for the shores of Yanxi Lake, sixty-odd kilometers (about forty miles) from Beijing, were not exactly to result in yaogun history. Droves of fans from around the country arrived to discover that the festival had been canceled. "No electricity," people were told according to one attendee. It was a situation with which yaogunners and festival boosters would have no choice but to become acquainted.

In 1998, critic Huang Liaoyuan was approached by someone who wanted his help to bring three Beijing bands to a disco in Zhengzhou, the capital of Henan province. "I said, 'let's do it bigger'," Huang recalled, a dozen years later from the comfort of an office atop his thriving art gallery in one of Beijing's Art Districts. "This guy was really up for investing." Three bands in a disco became the biggest show the country had seen: Nine bands in a stadium in the "small" town (population: 5.5 million) of Xinxiang dubbed New Music China Xinxiang Concert. You'll note the absence of both the word "festival" and "rock," but try telling that to the thirty thousand people in attendance, including the few thousand who rode a chartered rock and roll train, singing the whole way. "We spent a million *renminbi*, and got back 1,080,000. We made eighty thousand!"

As the underground started to emerge as a place where a band could exist long term, more smaller-scale events sprouted up around the country. In Guangzhou, Hai Liang, along with other members of the band Zhaoze (formerly known in English as the Swamp), put together the Kaiping Festival in 1996, which they held for five consecutive years. "Smaller cities were a bit more free," Hai said of the decision to do the festival in the town just over an hour outside of Guangzhou, presaging the situation that exists well into the millennium, where the festival map hardly corresponds to population distribution. "If you knew the local government, things were easier," he said, adding that they sold it as a "youth music festival" because it was "easier than saying it was rock and roll."

Writing through the Racket

As musicians in China faced overwhelming odds against achieving any kind of legitimacy – or even acceptance – so, too, have critics been on an uphill climb to show that rock music is not just worth playing or listening to, but important enough to be written about. But what was arguably their earliest and most important work was less that of the critic and more that of teacher. The environment necessitated that critics play multiple yaogun roles; if they only reviewed records, their reviews would be lost on a populace who wasn't, for the most part, prepared to take in critical prose about a music that was little understood. And on top of that, the critics themselves were new to the game. "We were a bunch of amateurs that came and went before the word 'music critic' ever existed," wrote Hao Fang. At first, they concerned themselves primarily with overseas artists, but as more domestic bands emerged, they not only covered them, but also eventually played a role in getting the bands gigs or, at least, promoting the gigs through their channels.

Huang Liaoyuan and Hao Fang were two of the first critics to appear in mainstream press and books introducing Western music. Huang began writing rock columns before publishing his book *World Rock Overview* – which features sections on history, stars and lyrics – in 1992. Through the nineties he continued writing, but also began working in the music business, in production and publishing as well as at a label. He became Tang Dynasty's manager and then jumped into the music festival sea, beginning with 1998's New Music China Xinxiang Concert (he put together a festival in the northwestern desert in 2004 and a ten-band bill in the east coast city Ningbo in 2009), and picked up management of space-pop-rock band Ruins and Second Hand Rose, a band that creates a fun blend of progressive rock and traditional Chinese opera and comedy. In 2004, he shifted across the cultural plane, opening the Beijing Art Now Gallery and representing several emerging visual artists while continuing his yaogun work.

In 1992, Hao Fang's *Connect Your Soul to My Line: Pop Music in Mass Culture* was published. In contrast to Huang's more how-to approach, it took a more academic tack, a factor of his headspace at the time. "When I started, I took music as a form of learning, a high form of art. I didn't want to write like a journalist, and I didn't want it to be simple . . . I had a lot of questions in me as I wrote." His goal was to show that pop music, which was being dismissed as fluff at the time, was in fact capital-c Culture. "There was nobody really paying attention to the seriousness of pop music," he said. 1993's *Wild Blooming of Wounded Flowers: The Bondage and Struggle of Rock*, continued the effort, while translations of books like Henry Rollins' memoir of Black Flag's days on the road *Get in the Van* and *Please Kill Me: The Uncensored Oral History of Punk* brought previously unknown details of the rock and roll life to 'gunners. His Kurt Cobain bio, *Radiant Nirvana*, put serious rock writing on the map in China like nothing before it. Released in 1996, it came at a time when other critics were coming to the fore of the national yaogun consciousness.

One would have to put radio DJ Zhang Youdai in the same category as Hao and Huang. Youdai spent most of the nineties with at least one rock show on the air, and has certainly pulled his weight in the education of those about to rock. Hao Fang was and is one of Youdai's biggest fans; he sent the DJ – whom he hadn't yet met – a copy of *Wild Blooming* with thanks for "keeping me company" while writing (Youdai said he was touched by the gesture). In fact, it's rare to meet a Beijing 'gunner with memories of the nineties who doesn't list Youdai as instrumental in their musical education.

Just as there was limited action outside of Beijing, so, too, were there actors. The Shanghai-based Sun Mengjin and Lanzhou-to-Beijing transplant Yan Jun both serve as good counterparts to the slicker Beijing-based Youdai. All three garnered a radio following, but while Youdai tended to the (relatively) bright and shiny side of things, Sun and Yan dug into the gritty side of rock and yaogun. Sun was a Jim Morrison devotee whose hope for the future of yaogun is the kitchen-sink-crooner Zuoxiao Zuzhou, perhaps most often described as China's Tom Waits. Yan ran with Lanzhou's down-and-out – who were punks before people had the vocabulary to thus describe them – and upon moving to Beijing, stuck with the emerging darker yaogunners of the late-nineties. Both Yan and Sun, poets of some renown by the way, were concert organizers in times and places predating proper venues, pouring their own income into the efforts. As the millennium dawned, they would prove to have more of a role in the national conversation – which they had helped to create.

If that conversation was kickstarted by any one publication, it was Hao Fang's book, *Radiant Nirvana*. Ten thousand copies hit the streets on its first print run, but far more people than that read it the first time around, said Hao, based on all the letters, kudos and reports he's received – and not just from the usual suspects. There were the punks, to be sure, but there were also executives. He spent such a long time and huge effort on the book, and amassed such an enormous collection of research that he found he was better informed than many of the reporters from overseas who later visited him for interviews. "I spent more on photocopying than I got for writing it," Hao recalled with a laugh. And it's not just from the hindsight of a stable career in the television industry that he casually dismisses the project's economic equation. "It wasn't a commercial project," he was quick to state. "It was just to understand what was happening at the time." Hao had always wanted to write about Cobain. "About his moods and his conditions, and what it says about society. I wasn't setting out to write an encyclopedia." What he did write was a bible.

He never expected many people to read *Radiant Nirvana*, and certainly not to embrace it as they did; his mixed feelings about its effects on people are proof of that. Kids unfamiliar with rock music picked up and took to the book in a way that was shocking. And there were other surprises, like the letter from a middle school teacher berating Hao for inspiring, through his writing, one of their students to name their basketball team Rape Me. The name, said the student, "sounded cool." But that paled in comparison to the depth to which many readers were moved. For many, the book became, in Hao's words, "an important weapon" for countless kids who sent him letters he couldn't bring himself to read. "You were writing about me," they told him – going through nasty divorce, tough times at school, and on and on – "not Kurt." The news that a distraught reader committed suicide hit hard; a major regret for Hao was not making it clear that there were, for Cobain and others in similar situations, alternatives. With more than a dozen years since the book's publication, Hao's hindsight seems to embody the difference between the thirty-year-old still-new philosopher-cum-rocker living in exciting yaogun times who wrote the book, and the more realistic and experienced forty-something that now sees the need for a more balanced picture. "When you write a book, you never think about how it might impact people. You might not think much of yourself, but others could take you quite seriously."

A good many people took him seriously, and took up the challenge laid out in the book: They took yaogun in new directions. Punks from Wudaokou to Wuhan soon picked up where Cobain left off, as did musicians from a range of backgrounds along with critics and critics-to-be from around the country. Hao said that his "dissatisfaction with society" informed the book; its subject represented that feeling. He was not alone in looking at Cobain and seeing his own reflection. "We strongly identified with him because we shared the same anger, irony and intro-spection that he had, and that was the general feeling at the time; no one captured that sense of disillusionment like he did," Hao told *Time Out Beijing*.

Nirvana's recordings were available before the publication of his book, but their spread increased in its wake. But Hao is also eager to temper the reception to his book by pointing out that it was a sad situation that led to its success: "If rock was a normal thing, the book wouldn't have had such a big impact."

And in the days to come, rock did become marginally more normal, thanks to efforts of the critics mentioned above and a growing number of others joining up alongside of them. But first, a detour into the somewhat more abnormal times of millennial yaogun, and of China.

5

THEY HAD NOTHING;
WE WANT IT ALL

1997-PRESENT

Kurt Cobain allowed [young people] to realize that punk and alternative is not only a choice of music, but a way of life as well.

Hao Fang, music critic and author

From The Scene to Many Scenes

By the late nineties, the Scene was no longer the single-celled organism headquartered in Beijing that had started the decade. It traveled across the country. The music changed. As yaogun diversified, suddenly there was no yaogun standard. Extreme forms of metal emerged; punk appeared and broke into a thousand schools; meanwhile, much unclassifiable "alt" spread across the landscape. And more was brewing, all leading to an environment more conducive to rock, and to rocking. Compilations were once limited to Rock Records/Magic Stone, whose *China Fire* series was essential to any yaogun library and the genesis of the compilation, which remains an important element of yaogun. But there was quickly far more music than they could compile alone; by the mid-nineties they no longer held a monopoly. As new collections of music spread through the nation, bands and bands-to-be had both a goal and inspiration, while fans discovered the range of what was out there.

Meanwhile, as the nation grew more accustomed to its new, if ever-shifting, identity as a member of the rest of the world, yaogun started to look less like an enemy and more like just one of those things with which a modern inhabitant of the globe might, if they wanted, deal.

The decade began with yaogun centered in the Chinese capital, and while Beijing remains yaogun's headquarters, it has been many years since it was confined there. The Midi Music School, which opened in 1993, was a siren that drew rockers from far and wide – and remains so to this day – increasing yaogun's ranks by siphoning the supply of hometown heroes elsewhere.

A rock education brought 'gunners to Beijing, but until recently, the post-graduation access to infrastructure, like rare rehearsal space enjoyed by many a Midi-ite, kept them. But by the middle of the decade, the community expanded, and so, too, did the infrastructure. Shanghai and Guangzhou, generally grouped with Beijing in the "first-tier city" category, saw small scenes early on; the former gaining from its financial legacy, the latter from its proximity to Hong Kong and its radio and television waves. While Beijing became Music City, PRC, many young'uns stayed or returned home, and scenes outside of Beijing grew to become more than just second-class shtetls. Wuhan emerged, first as a punk-band breeding ground, and then, in the last half-decade, a mandatory stop on any rock and roll tour thanks to the efforts of the community around local club Vox. Chengdu's Little Bar spawned a scene more varied than even its own residents can believe. Changsha, Dalian, Kunming, Nanchang, Nanjing, Shijiazhuang and a hundred more "small" cities (the aforementioned have no less than 5 million inhabitants) emerged as home to bands, venues and audiences eager to take in all that yaogun has to give. When Cui Jian initially envisioned his Rock and Roll on the New Long March Tour in 1992, it was modeled on the pre-PRC idea of going from town to town "liberating" the populace through yaogun. Cui may not have personally brought the nation into the fold, but between his own efforts and those of his progeny, yaogun's map now looks surprisingly liberated and had begun to go that way by the end of the nineties. Bands that used to struggle to put together a five-city tour – or even find a hometown spot transformable into something resembling a venue for music – now hit almost two-dozen cities around the nation.

As more players joined all sides of the industry, yaogun's web became tangled. Likewise for the nation itself; China had begun the decade on its own and wound up joining the world in an unprecedented fashion. Hong Kong returned to the Motherland in 1997, the tenth anniversary of Tiananmen came and went, China won the right to host the Olympics and entered the WTO. Reporters appeared in rock clubs and longhairs appeared on TV. Oh, and the internet changed everything.

On the Record, Off the Beaten Path

As the scene expanded in terms of membership, musical style and performance opportunities, the record industry opened up as well. A space for smaller record labels without the budget or power of a Magic Stone began to open up. There was more music ready for release than the big guys could – or wanted to – handle. Cue the chickens and eggs. Did the rise of labels cause scenes – alternative, metal, punk – to sprout or vice versa? Does it matter? Into the breach stepped a few brave souls, and China had its own indies, competing not with major labels as much as with a growing multitude of nameless rivals: pirates, filesharers, downloaders.

One of the most oft-seen faces of Chinese indie music in the new millennium would be familiar to indie-rockers the world over: moptop haircut, large and thick black glasses just this side of nerdy. In this case, his name was Shen Lihui, and his record label, Modern Sky, epitomized the image of an indie label as much as its boss epitomized the image of an indie rocker. That it is impossible to legally be a truly independent company publishing music, literature or magazines in China – all of which Modern Sky did or still does – is a matter of semantics. The music that Modern Sky releases, with a few pop exceptions, can certainly be filed under "indie." Shen Lihui had first found decent success with *Yaogun 94*, a compilation that was his attempt at showing the nation what else was brewing. It wasn't that one-man operation Modern Sky allowed for a flourishing of an alternative to the rock stars of the day, but that Shen Lihui recognized the large amount of talent toiling in the underground.

While many now describe Modern Sky as more of a PR agency than a record label, one undeniable element of their success is that their image – visual and musical – has stayed consistent. The label's debut album, from Shen's own band Sober, was bright, if slightly tempered by the moan familiar to fans of Oasis, Pulp and Suede through which Shen sang. A compilation followed; it was Shen's second but Modern Sky's first, and it introduced a new group of bands, of which a handful – Sober, New Pants, Supermarket – would go on under the label's banner. Compilations quickly became a Modern Sky staple, and sub-labels, beginning with Badhead in 1998, have enabled the label to diversify its content without seeming stretched too far across the map. While metal and punk had defined the first and second halves of the decade, respectively, Modern Sky turned attention toward a third branch of nineties music, which was, for the most part, more hopeful than the material that had came before and would come after. "The market was ready for music that didn't say 'we're fucked'," explained journalist Steven Schwankert.

Modern Sky tended toward the poppy side of things – and still tends to aim for somewhere between commercial and hipster sound – while simultaneously creating something of a media empire with its many projects. *Modern Sky Sound* magazine began publishing in 1999, Shen's No. 17 Bar was one of the capital's best live venues in the late nineties. In the new millennium, after a brief downturn, the label's brisk advertising and design business brought them from the brink well into the black. In 2007, Modern Sky entered the music festival business with their eponymous festival. Their Strawberry Festival came in 2008. "Modern Sky was really great from 1997-2000," said "Johnson" Ding Taisheng, who is now the label's promotions director. "In 2001, things weren't great. But I only realized that later . . . I decided to leave when it got to the point that they couldn't pay my salary." In 2005, when he returned to the company, he said, "things had really changed.

They had developed a lot. They were working with lots of big companies and had become more of a PR agency."

The label provided space not only for the happier side of the Brit-pop-influenced artists of the late nineties, but also for the harder-to-define artists not quite punk enough – or too early – for Scream, another similar label that emerged in 1999. Eventual critics' favorite Zuoxiao Zuzhou's No, and the intense and abrasive noise rock of The Fly found a home at Modern Sky (and its subsidiaries), alongside the bright early electronica of Supermarket. Another band that exemplified Modern Sky's overall image and sound – until its 2010 break with the label – was New Pants, a band that began with Ramones-ey punk, eventually adding an extra dose of happiness and fun to create a lo-tech disco-punk-ish version thereof. The band's rare ability to mix that peppiness with good humor and a borderline unhealthy obsession with retro alongside Peng Lei's experience in film, meant that they were able to break through in ways most others couldn't. Videos that featured homemade claymation, homage to over-the-top Hong Kong kungfu flicks and more showed that the band could take – and make – a joke where most other rockers couldn't. The video for "Dragon Tiger Panacea," the band's ode to kungfu epics, contains a kernel of truth when one of the band receives, from a guru, a vintage synthesizer, the type which has become an integral element of New Pants' sound. Their video for "Equal Love" (the translation, official though it is, misses out the full effect of the original "Barbarians Have Love Too") could have been culled from outtakes of Black Panther video shoots, playing, as it did, on the hard rock influence of the early bands. New Pants recast itself from their usual retro-tracksuited oversized-indie-glasses-sporting shy geek-types into the embodiment of the early yaogun upon which they were raised, complete with cut-off-jean short-shorts, strategically placed handkerchiefs, tight jeans, biker gear and cock-rock posturing in a rare joke upon themselves. New Pants made yaogun history by performing at California's massive Coachella Festival in 2011.

Scream Records, meanwhile, opted for the heavier, louder and faster end of the yaogun spectrum, quickly cornering the metal and punk market. "Scream's purpose was very simple and clear," said Chen Yi, who spent three years at the label. "It was to keep the development of yaogun going." It was also, as founder Lü Bo has often pointed out, a method for documenting yaogun's evolution. In a 2008 article for *InMusic* magazine, Lü laid out the company's two "operational principles": Low cost and the avoidance of signing long-term contracts with their artists, both of which are essential to the label's mission of documenting what's happening RIGHT NOW. Chen added that a band like CMCB, which calls themselves hip hop – and had the outfits and swagger to match, as well as the DJ that was *de rigueur* for the heady rap-rock days of the early aughts – were representative of the bands that Scream worked with. "These are bands that got well known in the underground. The process was very short. We signed them and put the record out quickly," said Chen, adding that their process produced ten albums a year plus a couple of compilations, so there was little time for much beyond bare-bones efforts. It was only after a stint at Warner Records, Chen said, that he discovered "what releasing an album really needed. Scream was more like a small workshop." But there was no disparagement in this characterization, as Chen is quick to point out. "The idea was to release the most representative stuff. Because of that, it has to be done quickly . . . It was the best way to document what was going on. This was the stuff that was being performed at the time."

In contrast to Scream and Modern Sky, Pulay Music and Entertainment started turning heads with their big ideas, signing, to start things off, Cui Jian. Pulay, which grew to take on several stars and a few underground bands, was set to take advantage of American producer Matthew Clark's live recording skills. The plan was to produce concerts and release live albums and use piracy to their advantage. "We want to flood the market with live recordings," said Clark, the label's international representative and the producer of the compilation *Beijing Band 2001*. The hope was that people will "pirate the hell out of us" so that audiences will be inspired by the recordings and head to live shows, for which Pulay would acquire corporate sponsors and thus be able to afford to keep going. Pulay slowly disappeared from the yao-gun landscape, while the more "underground" labels continue to this day.

Meanwhile, critic and musician Yan Jun began releasing albums in 2001 under the banner of Sub Jam. "I decided to release good music my friends were making," said Yan. Describing his methods as "anarchistic," he demanded no contracts and gave artists complete control over copyrights. Labels inspired by the Sub Jam model have sprouted up around the country, in a situation similar to the rest of the world whereby bands don't necessarily need big (or mid-sized) labels to get their product out there. While there is generally little, if any, money involved in operations like these, the plus side is that there tends to be no money-related strife either.

Miniless Records represents another segment of the recent rise in alternative labels, following the same vein as Sub Jam. Founded by a group of like-minded friends in 2006, it is technically centered in Shanghai, but isn't necessarily *of* Shanghai. Co-founder Han Han, who was then based in Hefei, a nine-hour trip west of Shanghai, said that the label works more as a platform than as a company. "Miniless is like a posse," he said. "We didn't get together to do a label, we got together because we're a bunch of friends. It's like a big family." A laid-back family, at that: There are no contracts with bands, which, in spite of Han Han's grunt work at the grassroots level of show promotion, organization and general helping out wherever he can, has scared off more than a few artists. And because of the nature of the label, bands on board still have to pull their weight in time and money.

"We don't have financial support and every *yuan* flows from the musicians and it'll flow back into the hands of them," Han Han told music blogger and writer Jake Newby. "Which means we are basically a platform rather than a company trying to make more money. That's bad sometimes." But then, with no contracts, bands can come, go, stay, work or chill at their own pace, and if something better comes along, they're free to follow it elsewhere. Bands remain masters of their own domain, for better and for worse, because the label focuses on promotion and a bit of gig-booking, while the rest is up to the band. But what they get in return is a sense of community that would seem unattainable in any profit-driven enterprise.

Scream and Modern Sky certainly lead the indie charge in the late nineties and early aughts, and while they brought a large number of artists to the fore, few are the bands that speak of happy arrangements. Like artists on the more commercial Magic Stone, many are convinced that the space between actual sales figures and those reported to them was larger than they were being lead to believe. Advances that seemed large shriveled in the need to cover everything from studio time to artwork. And there are complaints that despite the appearance of being pro-artist, companies rarely had their bands' best interests at heart.

The newest record labels plying yaogun have something of a commercial element to them: The appearance of a big financial backer. Pilot Music, 13 Month, Maybe Mars and Tree Music have all popped up since 2006 and boast large budgets and rosters. These newer, slicker labels are, like Rock Records/Magic Stone before them, showing that it's possible for rock music to be packaged in a way that encourages mainstream coverage and acceptance – one of the major battles yaogun has fought over the years. Just the impression of having a budget is a major hurdle to any kind of recognition – from consumers or reporters – and something that has in the past been an impossible task for cash-strapped labels. Modern Sky, in recent years, has also improved their image and reach through deals with corporate sponsors. Maybe Mars is a different beast from the others primarily because of its foreign component – Westerners compromise a large part of those in charge of the label.

While things look good on the label front, the question that needs to be answered, and quickly, is how long the investment can last, and how long sponsorship, event attendance or – gasp! – record sales are going to be able to keep them afloat. Because China, in one regard, is just like everywhere else: It ain't easy selling records.

Which doesn't imply that there is, or has been, a lack of records to sell. As the nineties gave way to the aughts, the musical landscape opened up tremendously.

Overload to Overloaded: Millennial Metal

The first metal band to make an impact after Tang Dynasty was Overload, which emerged out of the void left by Tang Dynasty's mid-nineties absence and took a very different metal to the masses. While the band was neither the earliest nor the only purveyors of extreme metal, they were the only band of the time that enjoyed a level of success beyond the local club scene.

"We were the country's first speed metal band," Overload's frontman Gao Qi told an interviewer, recalling early shows where audiences literally couldn't figure out what they were experiencing. The effect of the band's debut album, released in 1996, was that of a new kind of metal: One descended from a band like Slayer rather than, say, Rush or Bon Jovi (though there are certainly moments that bring the latter to mind, foreshadowing the band's future). There are, as with the music of his contemporary, Zhou Ren, elements of the dark and nearly-metal alternative rock of Alice in Chains, and of the Seattle Sound in general, but the main thread for Overload is weaved by Metallica.

Gao Qi's parents graduated from the Central Conservatory of Music; his father was a conductor, and his mother was a cultural liaison, going early to the United States. Gao didn't last long at Beijing Union University's Tourism School, joining up with White Angel, a cock-rock cover band training ground for many early rockers. In 1989, he formed the Breathing, which featured power ballads sung by the Stevie-Nicks-esque Wang Weihua, and for which he was the primary songwriter until his departure in 1991, when he started Overload. He had already helped to spread a metal beyond that of the Tang Dynasty and Black Panther schools through his short-lived radio show; Overload was a natural outgrowth.

The excitement with which the metal community celebrated Overload's debut was, with a quickness that out-sped Overload's metal, replaced by their disappointment over the band's follow-up. Where the debut opened with a depths-of-hell growl, the sophomore release begins with electro-lite beats and a pop star croon, signaling the distance the band traveled between the two releases. Gao's pop sensibility showed through even in the heaviest of his metal, but he took little more than that sensibility as the band moved forward. Overload's debut, he told an interviewer, represented the entirety of his metal understanding, and metal was not in the band's future – indeed, many of the songs released on the debut were already years old.

Gao's conscience is clear. He made great metal while he was a metal guy, and has since moved on. His fans don't see it that way, and that upsets Liu Wentai, an American-born bassist who plays with Overload as well as many others. Gao Qi's significance has been severely underrated in the wake of the band's popification, he said. "Everyone plays a role . . . There would be no longhairs on TV without Gao Qi." In addition to paving the way through performing music on television, Gao also performed on both small and big screens, his career as an actor – and soundtrack composer – not insignificant. But the important take-away with Gao Qi, from a metal perspective, is that he was an essential part of the puzzle. Without him, one wonders where metal might have gone. Like Tang Dynasty and Black Panther before him,

Gao pushes ever slightly the boundaries of pop in the general direction of metal. In their metallic incarnation, Overload had a large platform from which to preach a more extreme metal and things, from there, took off in a multitude of directions – musically and geographically.

More than just music fuelled the spread of metal, which is where *Painkiller* Magazine comes in. The team that put together the magazine's first issue, which hit the streets in September 2000, was not large – nor was the budget – a model that has been maintained into its eleventh year of publication as the magazine's distribution hovers around a rock-mag-average of twenty thousand nation-wide. The debut issue featured a collection of articles typical of the publication more than a decade on: Mötley Crüe, Pantera, Cannibal Corpse and other bands from around the world shared space with a death metal family tree and introductions to gothic and dark wave, as well as pull-out posters of Rage Against the Machine and Type O Negative. *Painkiller* is one of the major reasons that Chinese metal fans are so well informed.

The teams' day jobs (and their parents' houses) provided the monetary resources necessary to produce the magazine. "It was really hard. Nobody else was doing this, so there was no one to copy," said editor Han Ning, a slightly pudgy straight-laced dude who does not strike one as the obvious face of China's metal media. "The environment though, was also simple. We did it first. So we were fresh."

A major part of *Painkiller*'s operations is live music, the means by which the magazine came together initially. Instead of talking about the metal shows they'd like to see, they put one together. "Doing shows," said Han, "represented the fact that the environment exists." And that which exists can be reported on. Their debut issue was celebrated at a disco with a gig that drew so many people – somewhere between six and seven hundred – that they had to stop selling tickets. "It wasn't necessarily a metal crowd, because we didn't have a full-on metal scene yet,"

Han recalled. That was to change with the decision to continue publishing *Painkiller*, and view its mission as educational.

These days, the magazine puts together a growing number of concerts and tours not for only local bands, but for a large number of international high-level metal acts, from Swiss Goths to American thrashers, Swedish black metal and beyond. *Painkiller* has also been intimately involved in many music festivals around the country– managing stages, stocking lineups and also taking care of big-name visiting acts. It's an income stream – and not a large one – that is much needed. Since 2008, *Painkiller* has sponsored the Metal Battle, an international battle of the bands, in partnership with the Wacken Open Air Festival, the largest metal festival in the world.

Painkiller also spawned a record label, Mort Productions, which began, as so many others had, with a compilation. Mort's first release, *Resurrection of the Gods*, was essential, if less-than-ideally-produced (volume six came out in 2009). "At the time," said Mort founder Chen Xi, who goes by the online handle of Steelbath, "there weren't many metal bands. It was only because we found them that they came together." The year 2000, he said, was when death and extreme metal, which comprise the bulk of the label's catalogue, really started to emerge.

In stark contrast to the music of their progenitors, metal bands that came up in the late nineties and early aughts saw Death, Black, Speed and Thrash as the adjectives of choice for their metal. Chinese metal was especially linked to the international scene; as went trends in the West – industrial, goth, metal-core – so, too, did local variations thereupon crop up across the country. What's fascinating is that, on the one hand, you had all the makings of a Great Scene: bands involved in every element of creating a total package from logos to cover art to websites and merch; publications detailed in content and widely distributed and purchased (beside *Painkiller* there are a handful of smaller-scale mags); and a large and loyal fan base, often decked out in the aforementioned intricately designed attire, who are extremely well-informed about the international metal situation. On the other hand, there is much pessimism amongst the scene's observer-participants.

"There are two streams of metal fans," complains Lin Zheng, who co-manages the mostly metal 666 Rockshop, which stocks everything a banger might require. "Old school and new school. And they don't mix." This is not, by far, a problem particular to metal, but it's one that's bringing down the general level. And while healthy scenes exist in cities around the country, said Yu Yang, of *Painkiller* and *rockinchina.com*, the bands aren't living up to their potential, producing inferior versions of the overseas originals loved far and wide.

It's not so much that the work of Mort and *Painkiller* has been in vain. Particularly in the case of the magazine, foreign content has been the key to their success, while Mort has distribution rights for a handful of foreign bands, and is now also in the business of presenting visiting bands live. And introducing bands from the rest of the world to Chinese metal fans is in aid of creating the environment that will send Chinese metal back to the rest of the world. Talk of how local metal bands don't stack up yet to their overseas counterparts is related to guitarist Kou Zhengyu's concern about why metal is under the rock and roll radar: The audiences don't care enough about newer local bands – a complaint that has been leveled across the yaogun landscape. Just as Tang Dynasty still hovers atop the general metal heap, so, too, do the earliest extreme metal bands remain the most popular.

There is much talk of finding a *Chineseness* in yaogun, and there are several metal bands that have, more so than in other genres, made this foreign form local. Tang Dynasty did it with imagery and musical cues. Ditto for Spring and Autumn, a band that features Tang Dynasty's Kaiser Kuo. But the most interesting expression of Chinese-ness in metal bands comes not necessarily from a musical source. Which isn't to say that only bands with so-called Chinese characteristics are worthy of attention – or that all should strive to add some kind of ill-defined "localness." It is to say that bands that seem to be products of the places they come from tend to be the most intriguing.

In November 2008, Beijing's Ordnance released *Rock City*, their second album. Nine months later, news reports announced that that, citing the album's "attack on the current system" and the harm it did to the "national honor," the State Administration of Radio Film and Television (SARFT) had banned the album. The tune "Fuck You" may stand out from the track list as potentially scandalous – and it is, with its eponymous invective directed at the people that "say they Serve the People" and "say they're public servants." But the biggest problem with the record was the song "New Eight Honors and Eight Shames," which re-appropriates the words that will come to define the legacy of China's leader Hu Jintao. Hu believes that there are eight ideals to which every good citizen and Party member should aspire, and there are eight closely related but undesirable counterweights. Ordnance takes the idea and runs with it: "*Awaken the people / Don't deceive them . . . Take pride in freedom of speech / Be ashamed of the suppression of dissent / Take pride in the protection of human rights / Be ashamed of one-party dictatorship.*" The song, like most on the album, doesn't sound angry in a temper-tantrum type of a way. It sounds angry in a pissed-off-to-the-depths-of-my-soul kind of a way. As in, they're not just pissed off; they sat and thought long and hard about the why they're pissed off, and about the kinds of things that pass for honors and shames. And then went and thought long and hard about how to put that all into a song. It's a rare skill to have that song be just funky enough and hard-edged enough that, as a listener, you want to take them seriously. It makes you, too, start thinking about what kinds of things pass for honors and shames.

You hear these words sung in the growl of extreme metal and you start to wonder if maybe everyone else in the game that's singing about anything other than serious issues is wasting the medium, because it's a vocal method perfect for the expression of true anger. When Ying screams the titular phrase in "The People Must Resist," the *"fankang"* (resist), sounds close to "fuck," and it's a "fuck" that demands to be taken seriously. It's one of those lyrics that seem beyond language.

But what makes the band, the record and the ban most intriguing is that Ordnance rebel with Chinese characteristics. Not simply because of their insistence that they are doing their patriotic duty, but because they sing about it, particularly in "This is Ours," which lays out all the things that are "ours" – and, one should add, "aren't yours". What's interesting is that many (not all, but many) of the items on the list are those on which the government would eagerly join the chorus: Rights, Democracy, Freedom, The Future, Tibet, Taiwan, Changbai Mountain, the Diaoyu Islands, Our Bodies, Our Thoughts, Our Happiness, Our Soul. Perhaps it's the band offering a bit of payment on the debt they knew they'd owe once The Man saw the lyrics to the rest of the album, but it is clear that this, too, is what they believe. "It's not that (we're) opposed to everything," vocalist Ying Peng told an interviewer. "We have an aim . . . We've seen a lot of bad things, and we want to talk about them."

Bandmate Liu Lixin explained, "Whether we're criticizing or opposing things, it's because we want our government to be better and better," said Liu, who has a very real idea of what "better" might be. While taking a "tough line" on its own people, he says, China is "very soft" – too soft for Ordnance – in the face of international bullying. Call it clever or ridiculous, but Liu's use of that "tough line" against the authorities is certainly different. "The nation," he added, "is progressing." You wonder if their decision to submit the album for official approval was a move designed to test that progression, and whether or not it was a good idea to do so, since it kept them off stages for a brief period. But that progression continues, especially through Liu's deep involvement in moving things forward with his band as well as his venue, 13 Club, a much needed home for metal, and his record label Dime Records.

Another band whose Chinese characteristics are an essential part of their story – musically, philosophically, visually – is Voodoo Kungfu, the winner of 2008's Metal Battle. Though many believed that their extremely graphic fusion of black-industrial-nu metal with folk elements would conquer the competition and the Waken Festival, they came home empty-handed, but still full of the energy that makes them one of the most compelling performers in the country. The band, known for the literally bloody trail they leave in their wake, described itself to a local magazine as "new age war music." Li Nan, the band's chiseled oft-bare-chested, long-locked frontman is a former zookeeper who keeps a veritable reptile exhibit at home. The group has, on occasion, added to the traditional rock band setup a folk orchestra involving percussion, stringed instruments, throat singing and more. Musically, performances range from full-on unrelenting metal with shrieks, screams, cries and yells, to the contemplative peace of a lone horse-head fiddle evoking the wide-open spaces of, say, the Tibetan plain. Experientially, the shows are part religious ceremony and part anti-religious-ceremony: Non-musical elements, whether face-paint, freaky masks, banners, splattered blood or wandering priest-types being just as important as what is coming through the speakers.

But their local flavor has an insidiousness that is not just below the surface and, like Ordnance, there is a patriotism behind their anger. Their tune "Bruce Lee," at first listen, seemed like a joke of sorts: A high-intensity burst of pure energy in which the eponymous character's wordless kung-fu catcalls are channeled through Satan himself. When the room of judges in a Battle of the Bands competition heard that tune, we smiled at each other. But seeing, several years later, footage of a live show, the vibe is very different. Like a roid-raged preacher, Li tells the audience that China has been bullied by Europeans, bullied by Americans, bullied by (and here his voice changes into a scream, and is met by audience screams) Japanese. Chinese people, he continues, have lacked courage, idolizing a hermaphroditic thing – the Buddha statue in his hand. As he turns the statue around in preparation for smashing it (and another statue on hand), he announces that the next song is about a Chinese person of true courage. Li's Bruce Lee is not to be fucked with; neither is Li's China. It's a prospect equal parts exciting and scary – not unlike the band's live show.

Bands like Voodoo Kungfu appeal to the wider world in that one can hear (and sometimes see) clearly that elusive "localness" that so much of the outside world seems to expect from bands hailing from outside of rock's homeland. Which isn't to say that this is something that the bands set out to do – or ought to – just that it's the "Chineseness" that tends to be what outsiders are looking for. But Chinese metal, like all yaogun, won't be truly international until it stands up as metal, period. So the attentions of Wacken is certainly a good sign, and a potential salve to the complaints of folks who believe that more people ought to be paying attention to metal. *Painkiller* Magazine's Yu Yang has a positive outlook for the genre's future: "[Metal] is coming and it's growing by learning. And the audience is nuts."

Alternatives Emerge

"In the Beginning," the yaogun script reads, "there was Metal." But slowly, as so-called "alternative" was becoming, in the West, a new kind of rock music, the music that defined what was a large swath of land at yaogun's fringes still had yet to have a name. "We were called 'Beijing New Sound'," recalled Gao Jingxiong, of a few bands in the early nineties that didn't fit the metallic mold, including his own band, Underbaby, which would go on to lead China's punks. So it's not surprising that the second volume of Rock Records' compilation *China Fire*, released in 1996, featured a slightly different "now sound." Gone was the brightness of the first volume, released in 1992, where metallic power ballads were the main form represented, and where the Scorpions, Bon Jovi, Deep Purple and a bit of early heavy metal seemed to chart the direction of the participating bands. In the second crop of Beijing rockers – with the exception of Zhang Chu's folkie pop rock, which appears on all three volumes of the compilation – one hears the Cure, Primus, Nirvana and other influences making their way through the yaogun population, though there is still that early-yaogun not-quite-ready-for-the-stadium sound. But before Cobain took over completely, a few players were taking things in an alternative direction.

Dou Wei is one of the sources of the alt-ification of yaogun, beginning with his departure from Black Panther in 1992 and when, perhaps even more scandalously, he cut his hair. He formed Dreaming, a group inspired by his new love of the gothic Bauhaus. Though he may have been labeled a "Xerox machine," producing low-grade facsimiles of overseas glam and goth rock, his new direction signaled new yaogun territory. That it was pretty easy to find a new direction for yaogun in 1992 dulls slightly this claim, but Dou Wei certainly influenced a large number of those looking for a new sound outside of the hair-rock/metal paradigm. His *Dark Dream* album, one of the Big Three released in 1994, was a very different beast from the other two, as fellow Prominent Zhang Chu illustrates in the rock-doc *Night of an Era*: "Their music was really . . . " pausing a long time before finding the *mot juste*, "foreign." In contrast to the more extroverted performances of his peers – not to mention his former Black Panther self – his Robert Palmer-esque pseudo-dance and a bit of pacing during the 1994 Magic Stone concert in Hong Kong is the most movement we see from him. One wonders if Dou Wei, clad in a dark blazer, dark shirt and dark pants, is happy to be there. There are only brief glimpses of a smirk that seems swallowed up by an Artist who wants to be seen as Artistic, with little patience for anything as fleeting as onstage excitement. One man's "foreign," after all, is another man's "genius."

There's a fine line between ahead-of-the-curve and the ADD-esque constant search for something . . . *else*. Dou Wei has straddled that line for some time and for that, he is symbolic of yaogun's journey. Kaiser Kuo helped Dou and his fellow rockers transcribe "Last Christmas" by Wham! in the late eighties; reporter Steven Schwankert recalled the Cinderella poster prominently displayed in Dou Wei's apartment in the early nineties, and Dou's eureka moment upon receiving a Peter Murphy tape from a foreign friend. Meanwhile, Underbaby singer and guitarist Gao Jingxiong recalled how in the early nineties, they'd all take English names of their favorite artists. "Dou Wei's English name," he said, "was Simon LeBon." Somewhere between Duran Duran, Cinderella, Wham! and Bauhaus was Dou Wei – until, of course, those touchstones no longer applied. From MIDI to meditational, his musical tastes continued toward the fringes, covering improvised, ambient and experimental music. While often creating beautiful soundscapes, they are pieces that might not get filed under "music" by the many fans still hoping for at least a tune off of *Dark Dreams*, if not another taste of the original Black Panther hit "Don't Break My Heart."

On the one hand, Dou plays with this conflict. During his set at 2002's Snow Mountain Music Festival, audience members, frustrated with the "music" he chose to perform, hurled bottles stageward as Dou Wei, laughing, shouted "You've been tricked!" On the other hand, it's evident that he's also having trouble with the contradiction between his past and future. In a world where his former bandmates and many of his fellow early travelers are superstars, fans and media are confounded by his explorations, particularly since his musical legacy requires the kind of critical examination for which neither are known. Thanks to his interview style, many refer to Dou Wei by the poetic "*dui bu dui*" ("correct and incorrect") – the two longest answers one might hope to coax out of him. Assuming, that is, one can get him to sit down to talk on the record.

His fame in the wake of Black Panther came as he discovered a divergent musical path and he did not seem to take well to the attention that resulted from it. His relationship with Hong Kong pop and film starlet Faye Wong only increased the scrutiny, when paparazzi, not exactly a yaogun phenomenon, invaded the couples' lives; he still lives in a world where that relationship, which has been over for more than ten years, is considered one of his claims to fame. His latest run-in with the press ended when he set fire to a reporter's car, after gossipy reports about him and his second ex-wife made the rounds. (Thus can one – even one that might want to, say, interview him for a book only to be turned down in a way that makes one feel simultaneously honored to have gotten a response and personally insulted by that response – sympathize with his outlook.)

Though he'd "lost hope" in record labels – "they 'blindly worship foreign things'," he said, employing a four-character idiom that describes sucking up to foreigners, "and I figure they're not interested in my music" – it seems that someone's managed to convince him otherwise, and he continues to release music and push outward upon alt's boundaries.

When Dou Wei was still in his Bon Jovi phase, another important alt group was staring on a path just as far from where they would make their yaogun mark. The first description that tends to get applied to Cobra is "all-female," but the band's gender was not the only element that led the way to "alt." The band dwelt on the darker side of the yaogun spectrum, with new wave and goth coloring their sound, as was the case with many of the earliest bands that tended to be filed under "something different."

The band began on a subdued note; less a "let's do it!" cry, than a mumbled "you wanna?" Guitarist and vocalist Xiao Nan recalled the sure-what-the-heck beginning: "It was kind of cute, like: 'What should we do?' 'What can you play?' . . . It was just for fun, and we had no real thoughts of being on a stage."

"Sure, whatever," is how keyboardist Yu Jin remembers reacting to the initial idea.

"We were good at being professional musicians," said Xiao Nan, who is direct about her band's abilities in a way that would only be cocky if you ignore the fact that they had spent their entire young lives being told that they were the best there was. All of the members were highly trained, and at the top of the national heap on their non-rock primary instruments (accordion, piano, Chinese dulcimer, *erhu* – a two-stringed Chinese violin). They played music for a living in various "orchestras" that didn't nurture their talent so much as squeeze it for all it was worth. "I quickly got sick of [it]," recalled Xiao Nan, who never bothered to leave the Oriental Song and Dance Ensemble; she remains officially a member, despite her work for festivals, schools, labels and in bands of her own. Yu Jin, meanwhile, quit the Troupe in 1991 after eight long years. "I couldn't do it any more. It was scary . . . After Cobra started, the music was no good."

Beginning as a cover band, their reworked Cui Jian and folk tunes were a hit across the country. In one circa-1990 video, the band has at the tune that the Blues Brothers made famous, "Everybody Needs Somebody to Love." In the young ladies' hands, the good-time number has been put through the synthesizer and come out as an *oompah* rendition of the sort you might expect from a band of robots. Their guitar-less arrangement featured synthesized bleats more prominent than the lead vocals, which comprise sounds resembling those that might be the lyrics. They performed at the Modern Music Festival in 1990, but while the audience loved it, the band was embarrassed to be the only ones there without original material. Once they found their own sound, however, they were a completely different band. The fun they should've been having with "Everybody" comes through in footage of their first trip overseas to Germany as part of the China Avant Garde festival in 1993. The difference is immense; in and among the take-us-seriously music they appear comfortable in a way that seemed impossible three years previous.

As five of the very few female yaogunners, their identity was an issue. "All those years, we weren't really in the scene," said

Yu. "To most of the guys, we were girls first and musicians second." The media was already in a state of confusion over rock, and their gender took things to a new level: " 'What do your parents think?' 'Shouldn't you be at home raising a family?' 'Why Cobra? Such a scary word,' " recalled drummer Wang Xiaofeng, of the questions they were asked. "I think we freaked a lot of people out; they didn't know what to think." The same laissez-faire attitude at the band's formation reigned over the subject, until their trip to Germany, from which they returned with a heightened feministic awareness if not a mission. They countered an invite to tour the US that came on the condition that they change their name to the China Dolls and dress sexier not with insult, but with innocence. "We thought, 'How could we look sexy with these instruments?' And besides, we liked wearing jeans."

The band made it to the United States without a makeover in 1996, and were among the first yaogunners to see a record released officially in Europe, signing on with Network for the German release of their debut – despite Xiao Nan's confession that they had "no commercial thoughts at all." The band eventually came around and signed with Hong Kong label Red Star – who they'd initially turned down because they didn't see a point in a record deal. The band ended in 2000, upon release of their second album; there was a not-all-members reunion for 2004's Helanshan Festival, but all members remain musically active both inside and outside of China. Like Dou Wei, Cobra leaves a legacy of dark-tinged new wave that proved to be the bulk of the early "alt"; theirs was a rock that stayed away from the grunge that was to soon sweep through the nation.

If we believe metal guitarist Kou Zhengyu's statement that metal was yaogun's first mistake, then we should listen to what he said is mistake number two: "Everyone played grunge." The grunge model, he said, doesn't encourage subtleties, since, particularly early on, it depended primarily upon the contrast between a clean guitar sound and a distorted one; the whisper versus the scream; the creation of an effect instead of a composition. Yaogun's interest in Nirvana wasn't contemporaneous with the band's reign in the Western world, but the scene made up for lost time, and then some. In the wake of Cobain's suicide, his followers discovered different things in the grunge that had found its way through the scene.

Cobain's substantial legacy in China is intricately linked to Hao Fang's book on him – and the claim that Hao influenced record sales is not an exaggeration. Critic Yan Jun said that with the release of Hao Fang's *Radiant Nirvana* in 1997, "the whole underground spirit represented by Nirvana became reality . . . By this time, explaining to others 'we are an underground band' already seemed very respectable." Both the book and the man led many directly to the grunge and alternative that colored nineties' yaogun. But they also led to the punk that became an essential part of the pre-millennium period.

He Yong is also a 'gunner that is linked inextricably with both alt and punk – his music was tinged with the former; his life the latter. Born into a musical family, He knew from day one that music would define his life – especially, he said, when he got wind of "We Are the World." His father, a renowned *sanxian* (traditional three-stringed lute) player, inspired the boy with his own instrument, but also by taking him to that essential Wham! concert in 1986.

He's first band was Mayday, which one member recalled was put together before most of them could play. A few years later, Mayday was at Tiananmen Square; after the authorities accused them of involvement in "counterrevolutionary turmoil," He Yong headed for the countryside. In his 1992 article for *Spin* magazine, China scholar Andrew Jones paints a portrait of a troubled young rebel still dealing with the effects of the Beijing Spring. He believed that all Chinese had blood on their hands – himself included – and saw a bleak future ahead. It appears that He was never quite able to shake off the demons of which Jones wrote, though in performances like that of "Garbage Dump" in Hong Kong in 1994 – one of yaogun's all-time most breathtaking – he certainly tries. Ditto for the best tracks on his only album, simultaneously product and harbinger of that dystopian vision. The title track – which might be China's first punk tune – describes a society where people are "*. . . like bugs / Fighting and struggling with each other . . . we eat conscience / and shit ideology.*" It is a critique of the nation in which his generation lives: Old enough to remember China's original ideals and young enough to hope they might come to fruition, there is serious frustration over the "New China" where "People diet while others starve to death."

"He Yong was interesting because he was so in-your-face about things," said journalist Steven Schwankert. That in-your-face-ness served his music well, but not, perhaps, his career. That his dedication to the Old Beijing slowly being chipped away by so-called progress, "Drum and Bell Tower," became a radio standard and theme song was a small victory, because He's career through the nineties was a string of things going the other way.

At a 1996 concert, in what would these days be labeled Bjork-style, he added a shout-out to his song "Pretty Girl." "Who's pretty?" he asked, following it up with a zinger: "Is Li Suli pretty?" Witnesses say that the silence of the audience's collective jaw-drop was deafening. Li Suli was one of the Model Workers of the period, a bus driver whose care for her vehicle and its passengers was to be an inspiration for the nation. He had been warned that this show was not just an Official Event, but a Very Big Deal and an Important Opportunity for a 'gunner such as himself to show the nation yaogun's best side. Of course, that probably only made him want to flip the proverbial bird even more.

His reputation was already, by then, that of a loose cannon and crazy person, known for jumping on dinner tables and pianos – the latter done after calling out to Li Suli. After disappearing from the public view almost entirely since the late nineties, he only emerged briefly when news outlets reported that, in 2002, he attempted to set himself on fire, destroying his property and that of the neighbors. "I completely lost control," he said, and found himself in a mental institution for a brief stint. Only in the wake of his institutionalization did the possibility that He Yong might have psychological issues emerge. These days, he has mellowed out and slowly returned to the stage. Even as a shadow of his former self, he represents a journey that took a strength rarely found in all of yaogun.

Zhou Ren is an important bridge between the alt that stayed alt and that which went punk. His influence on the grunge sound of the late nineties is too-often overlooked, particularly in those pre-punk and -internet days, when grunge was the sound of the new generation of musicians. Zhou's star seemed only to flicker for a short moment, but his time on the landscape is far outweighed by his influence. A musician's musician, rockers of a certain age will complain that Zhou's true talent has been neither fully recognized or acknowledged. "He deserves at least ten pages in your book," one 'gunner told me, and similar sentiments span the spectrum – the age-old blessing-and-curse of being ahead of the curve.

Zhou's music confounded as much as attracted a range of late-nineties young'uns like early punk rocker Xiao Rong. Xiao needed clarification from Zhou as to whether Zhou's music was metal or punk, so that Xiao could determine whether it was actually as important to his musical life as he felt it was. The fact is that despite the seemingly irreconcilable distance between the longhairs and the mohawks, Zhou Ren's music settled right in between. The problem was that the groups themselves saw no middle ground, sending Zhou's music into the oblivion betwixt the two. Releasing one of Magic Stone's last albums before the label disappeared didn't help.

The music on Zhou's only album channeled the Seattle sound in a way different from others at the time. It was colored not only by his metal roots, but a love and appreciation of disco (the earliest Western music he heard was Donna Summer), funk (thanks to the education of American-born bassist Liu Wentai) and, most essentially, the kind of pop music that kept his choruses sing-along-able – a pop that was disappearing as alternative music became increasingly alt. "My music wasn't really for the masses," he said. The record's dark mood and his moany voice would seem to back that up, except that it comes across like an early Pearl Jam album: Yes, it's dark, but the voice that comes out of that darkness makes one uninterested in turning the lights on. Which is not to say that Zhou sounds like Eddie Vedder so much as it is to say that they're both the guy you'd want taking you through the abyss.

These days, Zhou seems genuinely comfortable – happy, even – with his place in history. "I'm proud that I'm considered important and a critical favorite . . . Maybe only a few people like [the album] but it's a definite point in history . . . All of us knew it was important." He is no longer surprised when young rockers tell him what his record meant to them. "Anyone around thirty years old playing music today," he said, "knows the album. When they were seventeen, for sure it opened their minds."

Deciding that rock was dead, Zhou, like many in the alternative scene in the late nineties, turned toward electronic music. In 2008, he decided to put the band back together. No doubt a new generation of seventeen-year-olds will discover Zhou in the wake of his return to the stage, where he stands out among his contemporaries for his live efforts. It's not that he screams louder than everyone else, it's that he better knows how to be heavy. His performance at 2010's Midi Festival showed a man in better rock shape than most of the other performers with whom he shared the stage. "In the end," he tells me, tapping his palm against his chest, "I'm rock."

The next artist that took up the grunge mantle was Xie Tianxiao, who did it more straight-up than Zhou. What the man who now goes by his initials (XTX) shared with proto-punk He was the idea that punk and alternative were not only about a particular kind of music, but rather, came through in a form beyond its sound. While Xie owes a musical debt to "Garbage Dump", there is a much larger I.O.U with Nirvana's name on it. Influenced by

He Yong, he literally embodied Kurt Cobain. Xie's wails seemed to emanate from the same vocal chords, his music less a rip-off than a co-production. He was Kurt reincarnated, with the same zombie-like gaze and skin-and-bones frame which gave no hint of his intense onstage potential. Like Cobain and Nirvana, Xie's band Cold-Blooded Animal was a force of nature whose best songs tap that eponymous beast's ferocity. Live, they literally transformed into something resembling their name, climaxing in a pile of people, instruments, sweat and often blood.

Soon after Cold-Blooded Animal's performances at the venerable South by Southwest Festival in 2001, Xie spent two years in the US before returning to Beijing to put the band back together, first as Xie Tianxiao and Cold-Blooded Animal, then eventually settling on just his own name, and, finally, initials. His rise to a stardom rarely seen in yaogun was, thereafter, quick, but had been a long time coming after many years of slowly climbing out of the late-nineties underground. These days, he packs the biggest venues and festivals in the country, despite his still unpredictably destructive live sets. The band's recent performances have involved a growing amount of a Chinese eight-stringed harp; the combination of the harshness of grunge guitars with the soft pluck of the *guzheng* has been something of which domestic audiences and media have been eager to grab hold. Musically speaking, there have been few better attempts at placing Chinese instruments into contemporary rock. The visuals couldn't be much better – save for Xie morphing into, say, a lithe sexpot in a tight-fitting traditional *qipao* (a tight-fitting, high-necked traditional silk dress) – but a tamer live set would be more fitting for the mainstream, which still isn't fully ready for the high-energy reggae-tinged grunge that Xie has performed lately.

In early 2011, Xie was busted with three grams of marijuana and released after a few days. Reports speak of others also swept up in the raid, but only mention Xie by name. The insinuation is that he has reached a level of fame at which he is high-profile enough to be made an example while his music remains outside the scope of the mainstream's comprehension – evidenced by an obvious discomfort and discord when he is placed amidst the vapid co-hosts that populate the nation's talk shows.

But he, and others, have begun to also use their access for good. In 2010, Greenpeace co-produced the video for Xie's "I Don't Love You." It begins with Xie calmly advising viewers of the effect that can be had from everyone doing their part, no matter how small – a stark contrast to the violence of the song. The accompanying visuals, including a horrific montage of seal-clubbing and general environmental destruction, come as Xie screams the song's title in his voice-from-the-depths. While Xie's music fits in nicely with Greenpeace's rogue image abroad, the organization had to dull things down in order to operate in China – Exhibit A in that case being their prior partnership with Catcher in the Rye for the pop tune "Green."

Meanwhile, a number of music festivals have taken on "green" themes and partnerships to varying degrees. Cui Jian opted for the more moderate World Wide Fund for Nature (WWF) when he became, in 2010, an Earth Hour Ambassador. The union of yaogun and the environmental movement has significance for both parties. Like yaogun, the environment has only recently left the list of untouchable subjects in China. That rockers are sought to spread the word signals not only the recognition that there are a significant number that might listen to what a rocker has to say, but that rockers are legitimate vessels for that message.

Another band that is dedicated to spreading a message is Thin Man. Their frontman, Dai Qin, remains a tireless fighter for yaogun's place in society, and has made great strides in the struggle. The band was the leading proponent of what became the most prominent millennial musical trend, when their eponymous rap-metal debut hit the streets in 1999. "We were good news for underground bands," said Dai. "We gave them hope." The wave of success the band rode, unknown to anyone aside from a handful of rock stars at that point, showed that "noisy" music can lead to rock stardom.

Frontman Dai Qin, who has come a long way from crooning pop in the clubs of the Mongolian grassland, is the kind of guy you can tell is a rock star. His walk, his clothes, his carefully-coiffed head of hair, his bracelets and his outfit let you know from a mile off that he belongs on a stage, screaming into a microphone. Talking with him, he's got that ability to make you feel like you're part of the Brotherhood which, only upon reflection, you know that you can't possibly join.

After quitting the Mongolian Beatles, Dai joined forces with American guitarist Chandler Klose, a guitarist in demand across the scene who had introduced Dai to grunge and alt-rock, and made a serious impression with their high-energy live show. By early 1994 they released a song on a compilation, but the recording process was bittersweet. Arguments over songwriting credits, said Dai, caused Klose to "lose faith in China," and broke up the band. Klose's departure hit Dai hard; after soul-searching – and musician-searching from his convenient perch as manager at short-lived live venue Angel's – he re-formed the band. At the time, said Dai, it was either take the Tang Dynasty-Black Panther route – that is, make "nice"-sounding rock – or give up on dreams of rock stardom. But they proved that theory wrong with the debut of their dark and mean rap-metal. "We were told we sold seventy thousand copies," said Dai. "But we definitely sold more." Other accounts have sales pegged at over a hundred thousand within six months of the record's release.

The band became rock stars. They were being flown to domestic gigs and getting real fees. They released an album in Japan and toured there three times, performing at the renowned Fuji Festival twice. "We had Benzes picking us up at the airport and we were staying at five-star hotels," Dai told one reporter. Thin Man became fat off yaogun. "We weren't talking about the music anymore. We were talking about buying a car or a house." Their follow-up didn't go over as well as they'd expected, while their third high-gloss record won national awards and many say they strayed from their underground roots. There are certainly elements of the band's music that have stayed relatively rock – the band's love of Rage Against the Machine still burns strong, as does an appreciation of much nu-metal – and Dai Qin remains devoted to bringing up bands.

His own band – and yaogun – was brought up when the chance to open for Linkin Park's 2007 Shanghai concert came their way. It turned out to be a disappointment, as the show only proved the distance yaogun still had to travel. Opening slots are a mixed blessing anywhere, but then, the idea of inviting a local band to open the show was a great gesture. It wasn't so much that Thin Man wasn't ready for the stadium as much as the stadium wasn't ready for Thin Man. Despite Linkin Park's rock roots, their fan base at Hongkou Stadium that November night was not drawn from the rock population. Thin Man, by all accounts, did as decent a job as could have been expected under the circumstances. But the crowd, who had come to hear Linkin Park and nobody else, booed Thin Man throughout their half-dozen-song set.

Dai continues to struggle to get yaogun and the mainstream to acknowledge each others' existence, his outlook defined by that young dude who, not so long ago, found salvation in rock and roll. "There are so many potential fans out there," he said. "Why shouldn't we let even more people in on what we're doing?" The band has scooped up pop awards and worked alongside the poppiest of pop producers. At each step of their development, Thin Man has been reminding any and every vapid host, hostess, awards-MC, interviewer and audience member – both above and below ground – of yaogun's contributions and potential, and that is why the once-fringe and now-almost-mainstream Thin Man remains an essential part of the yaogun story. Ten years and two records after their debut, Thin Man is still the embodiment of yaogun's hope; Dai Qin ever on the lookout for the next kid to save with rock and roll.

If Thin Man represents the underground's millennial hopes, its harsh reality was defined by Tree Village. Most residents of this community in the suburbs outside of Beijing, the center of yaogun's discontent, were out-of-towners. Many allied their neighborhood with Artist Villages that preceded them, both inside and outside of China, and it is easy to get caught up in a historical view that sees their work as Art, their music as Mission. It's easy to do so because those who resided in Tree Village chose for themselves a life that was nasty and brutish in order that they might dedicate it to yaogun, and did so in an era in which the best and brightest of their generation no longer turned to cultural pursuits, but, rather, to the then-mythologized pursuit of economic success. That the music they made didn't break through only further establishes the Mission's righteousness, and that it was about more than the music they played. They were an example that one could follow one's desires rather than what others decided was right, and the fact that they became impoverished to do so linked them to the tradition of artists, writers and poets from around the world.

The perennially dust-dusted "village" was comprised of a cluster of low-rise brick shacks; a few roads, lined with tiny hole-in-the-wall restaurants, outdoor pool tables, bric-a-brac shops and garbage, cut through the neighborhood that was less idyllic than its name or history suggests. Tree Village appeared as a musical destination in 1997, when the Midi Music School relocated to the area. By then the school had already become a major draw for young rockers across the country. Tree Village quickly became the first stop for out-of-town rockers scoping out a potential move to the capital. As yaogun spread around the country, Beijing had become, for most that yearned to rock, the only reasonable place to go. It had a population of bands, opportunities to perform, Midi's open-door rehearsal spaces, and, for a few, record opportunities. As more musicians moved to Beijing, the centrifugal force only increased, and Beijing's rock scene was soon overwhelmed by transplants.

Any sense of community that existed in Tree Village was belied by the music produced there, which, if by anything, was united in its harshness – a reasonable situation given the circumstances under which the musicians lived. Seemingly idyllic clips from the freeform documentary *Borders of Freedom* are deceiving. The swimmin' hole depicted therein was actually the village bathtub; the late-sleeping perennially-bedheaded shaggy dudes were, when not sleepily making their way through the village's ramshackle roads, confined to tiny rooms that served as both rehearsal and living space. The brief glimpses of live performance mayhem – the chaotic environment made more so by the handheld shooting – hint at a release that makes the poverty bearable. But these gigs, as the footage hints, were plagued by abysmal sound and technical problems, the result not just of under-equipped venues, but also musicians, audience members and club employees abusing the scant equipment available. Gigs, which were few and far between, were always far away and so, inevitably, a gaggle of 'gunners were stuck trying to scrape together enough cash for the trip back to their far-off homes in the wee hours of the post-gig morning. The film captures one such evening with an amazing combination of humor and sadness, following a dozen and a half bare-chested Titos, filthy from the evening's activities – not unlike their brethren ten years later at the Midi Festival – singing "The Internationale" from a heap of humanity on the back of a painfully-slow-moving truck.

At its peak, upwards of twenty bands inhabited the 'hood, including Mu Ma, Tongue, Ruins and Miserable Faith. Critic Sun Mengjin, visiting from Shanghai, was inspired by the communal aspects of the neighborhood, writing about the "solidarity" among residents and the tradition that saw whichever band that earned a bit of money treat others to dinner. When critic Yan Jun initially wrote about the area, he called it a utopia. Ilchi Qimude, who led nu-metal band T9 before forming folk act Hanggai, remembers the local restaurant that the rockers would take over. "We called it the yaogun diner."

Life in Tree Village was no-frills and difficult; musicians had very little hope for earning enough money to live lifestyles that were beyond Spartan. As one resident put it:

Tree Village bands were miserably poor, but still remained true to their ideals. In their view, if they went and did anything else, it would affect their work. So they would rather be poor . . . they just wanted to rely on music to support themselves. They weren't willing to do anything else.

In 2008, Yaksa lead singer Hu Song told a French reporter that though he believed Tree Village was a utopia where rockers and factory workers lived side by side, and the sound of practice sessions rang through the neighborhood almost constantly, it was essential that his band, and others, move on. "We were isolated. Life was too simple, too monotonous. It's better to meet different people and learn from their experiences."

Attracted by the musicians were documentarians, thesis writers, journalists and filmmakers. A decade after Tang Dynasty was cast in a film about the just-discovered rock scene, director Mabel Cheung – heavily-lauded in her native Hong Kong – set her sights on the scene, choosing to frame the film that became *Beijing Rocks* amongst Tree Village. Cheung, eager to include some *verite* in her cinema, had studied the scene via rock and roll road trips into Beijing, and was reportedly a big fan of *Borders of Freedom*. Until several days before production began, in October 2000, she had secured the involvement of several prominent Tree Villagers, for on- and off-screen roles in the production, but rockers angrily jumped ship upon seeing the revised script, which was a pretty-much by-the-numbers commercial love story. Though the rock scene is little more than backdrop to the film, there is value in the window into yaogun's past it provided – even if that window was heavily dressed. But the Village's experience with the production was emblematic of the spot in which yaogun found itself in the new millennium: That eternal struggle between staying true to itself and engaging with the rest of the world, and the conceit that the two are mutually exclusive.

Tree Village's legacy was more than theoretical. The music that was being made at Tree Village was primarily nu-metal, that combination of rap and metal defined by tin-sounding distorted guitars, and a delivery somewhere between hip hop's heavily-gesture-laden bursts and the primal screams of the loudest of the metal and punk bands. The bands that stand out from the Village pack tended to be outside of the rapcore tradition, though they aren't necessarily the groups that continue to perform: Ruins, Wood Pushing Melon, Glamorous Pharmacy.

Tongue, in particular, is a much-respected band that spear-headed the underground movement in the late nineties. Begun as a cover band in Urumqi, the capital of the northwestern fron-tier Xinjiang Province, the group moved to Beijing in 1997. They crafted an angular and industrial rock that was altogether new in yaogun. Part of what made their music so unique was their expo-sure to the various musical traditions of their home province. All of the members of the band were ethnically Han Chinese (who make up more than ninety percent of China's population), but the region in which they were raised – by parents sent west to pop-ulate the area in the wake of China's founding – was primarily comprised of a range of Central Asian ethnicities whose cultures are markedly different. The music was narrated in a growl more than sung by the especially-aloof Wu Tun. Wu would face directly across the stage, his energy focused not into shouting but using what might be best compared to the father who inspires fear in his children through lowering rather than raising his voice. After getting the extremely rare Cui Jian seal of approval, the band had a bumpy ride with record labels, two of which released products not fully approved by the artists.

Outside of Tree Village, meanwhile, another alt was brewing. Second Hand Rose, a band that combines prog-ish rock with tra-ditional Chinese instrumentation and comedy drew attention with a (male) singer, made and dressed up like a starlet, who whines clever and laugh-out-loud lyrics. While the band pro-duced some of the more interesting music of the decade, it seems strange that they should eternally overshadow the at-least-as-noteworthy (not to mention earlier-formed) Zi Yue, sometimes known as Confucius Says. Now known as Zi Yue Qiu Ye, the latter two words being the name of the bassist-singer-founder, the band blends the sounds of traditional Chinese music with a prog-inflected rock music and the kind of lyrics that, in addition to being delivered in a somewhat operatic tone, are appreciated far and wide for their intelligence and wit. Zi Yue is perhaps better known in mainstream circles than many other yaogun bands because of their music's appearances in film, TV and commercials, which, Qiu said, has helped with their image – sort of. "Now, people know that we are not bad guys, even though we do rock 'n' roll." What most people know about them – whether or not they know that it is Zi Yue – is the song that appears in a commercial for a popular melatonin health supplement that, following the incessant repetition of the fifteen-second spot featuring freaky animated senior citizens dancing in a variety of ridiculous costumes, sold gazillions of units. Qiu Ye told *China Daily* that the income from the ad "equaled the annual sales of an album," which means either the band got severely ripped off, or else they're selling far more records than anybody thought. Doing the commercial, he added, "was purely to make ends meet . . . There was no soul or spirit [in it]."

Zi Yue's music puts an emphasis upon Chinese elements in reaction to those that Qiu sees as having copied Western rock, and the band's work is critical of China's obsession with modernization at any cost. Qiu's opinions of other yaogun bands might well be the source of Zi Yue's strange position in the landscape: Respected by many, they seem to be removed from the scene at large. According to one report, his refusal to share a stage with punk bands that he deemed "thoughtless" hurt his reputation. The band's debut, produced by Cui Jian, almost didn't make it out: China scholar Jeroen de Kloet writes that drummer Zhang Yue's mother held a high-level position at a television station and was enraged upon discovering her son's marijuana habit.

She blamed the band, calling Qiu Ye a counterrevolutionary, and applied pressure upon the Ministry of Culture to find something wrong with the record to deny its release. While the sexual content of one song did wind up censored, as the band's manager told de Kloet, they simply out-waited The Man. When the record came out, in 1997, it was praised as a salve for yaogun's seemingly certain demise. "It is not only a pleasant surprise, but also a comfort," wrote one critic.

Because of the variety of people making and listening to music during the period, Ji Geng, a musician based in Shijiazhuang, a small city southwest of Beijing, believes the golden age of rock was from 1996 to 2000. Ji's own band, the oft-quirky and always-entertaining Omnipotent Youth Society, fits well with the alt bands of the era because of the stark difference between them and so many darker rock bands – in their hometown and across the country. Referencing bands like the alt-folk Neutral Milk Hotel as well as the grunge that Ji took to early in his listening career, the band creates fun-filled music that makes you not only want to sing along, but to dance along as well – a rare combination in yaogun.

The band that brings the alt posse to the present is post-punk outfit P.K. 14. Still going strong after nearly fifteen years, the quartet has risen to prominence both qualitatively and in terms of leading the scene forward. Originally from Nanjing, the band's frontman Yang Haisong may look like a slightly hip, introverted computer scientist, but he is a father figure to China's current crop of rockers, whether believes it himself or not. "I've been in Beijing since 1999," he told me when I asked him how it feels to be the big man on campus, "and I still feel like I'm outside of the scene."

Yang has also become a beacon and a booster for yaogun. His work producing the debut album from Sonic Youth-y Carsick Cars led to a key role in the creation of Maybe Mars, one of the busiest record labels of the last half-decade. His partner in the venture was American Michael Pettis, who left Wall

Street to teach finance at universities in Beijing. Having stepped away from the label, Yang continues his work in production and formed a Jesus and Mary Chain-inspired lo-fi noise-pop duo with his wife, Sun Xia. A testament to just how far above the scene his presence hovers is the amount of kids that approach him with the awe and embarrassment of being in the proximity of an idol, and how that rings familiar to Yang, who had the same reactions when spying the members of Tang Dynasty outside of a club a million years ago.

If Yang thinks he's outside of the scene, then Beijing's Lonely China Day is on another planet. The intense and introverted Deng Pei is the musical mind behind the group. "I want to achieve much with very little," LCD's press pack quotes Deng as saying. "Very minimal songwriting with the addition of many, many surrounding elements." The band's most recent album, *This Readily Assimilative People*, builds on their talent for less-is-more to create one of the best records to come out of China in years. Taking in post-rock influences, the band picked up a subtlety that ought to be – but likely won't be, knowing the general need for *more* – much-envied and -replicated across the scene. Even in the band's 2002 debut album, and certainly in their two follow-ups, one is often struck more by the space than by that which fills it. But the band does know how to fill space and, despite what many decry as an un-rock approach and setup (two guitars, two laptops, drums), they can crank it with the best of them. Comparisons to Radiohead and Sigur Ros are useful, not simply in aid of describing the cinematic and lately more electronic music, but also in Deng Pei's vocals, which, though chock full of poetic and philosophical references, act more as musical instrument than lyrical channel. What makes Lonely China Day even more interesting is that, like very few other bands, its music is colored by a Chinese-ness that is modest and concealed in the same way as its music's power: It exists with a subtlety that is obvious without being broadcast, hard to point to, but crystal clear through the headphones.

LCD's electronic and experimenal elements speak to yao-gun's movement in the new millennium. Like their late-nineties counterparts, 'gunners in the mid-aughts found rock at a creative standstill. While the late nineties saw a surge in electronic music, these days, when yaogun, more than ever, is about out-alt-ing the alt, experimental music's rise seems an almost natural progression.

Duo FM3 features long-time Beijing resident Christiaan Virant and keyboardist Zhang Jian, both of whom left the rock world behind, and have come to anchor the experimental scene. They quickly rose out of the confines of the Middle Kingdom, garnering international acclaim and performing in clubs, festivals and galleries around the world but might be best known for their extremely successful "Buddha Box." An anti-iPod of sorts, it is a small pastel-colored transistor radio-type device that plays various drone-y samples and sold tens of thousands of units.

Critic and poet Yan Jun leads the experimental charge, finding in the art form a relief from the rock music he'd seen as over and done with. He is clear that he doesn't expect, or want, to draw a large audience. "If there are lots of people [watching], they'll think we're not playing well. I don't want too big of an audience: I don't play that well." But because of the combination of Yan's reputation and a well-developed international network, a large number of musicians, audience members and media have followed him into the experimental world, against his wishes. The interesting thing about the experimental pseudo-boom is how it has attracted the attention of the mainstream Western media – and, to an extent, the Chinese media – who would barely acknowledge the existence of a *far* more developed experimental world on their home turf. Not to mention the fact that its leading light doesn't think it's worth all the fuss.

Much of the experimental scene seems to be defined by Yan Jun's observations of the country's chaotic music situation: "Chinese people don't know the best music system," he told the *New York Times* in 2007, when his influential weekly experimental series had already been going nearly two years. "There are no rules. No teacher. I can use this, I can use that – that's all interesting. In the West everything was created already. But here we don't know that."

A thought as scary as it is exciting.

Anarchy in the PRC

Kurt Cobain's music and story inspired grunge and alternative music, but a number of musicians came away from Nirvana discovering the punk that got their (anti)hero started.

Not all punks played punk music, though. Critic Yan Jun speaks of his hometown scene's "true punks": They may have listened to some punk, and even studied punk with their teachers – if they studied at all – but you wouldn't call the music they played punk. Like many residents of the rust-belt city of Lanzhou and other downtrodden towns across the country, they were desperate and unhappy, and their music expressed it as much as their lives did. The Lanzhou "punks", recalled Yan Jun, went to a Black Panther show and pelted the band with freshly-removed tampons. "Their music was a mess. They just started studying instruments and got right on stage . . . 'Yeah, I can't play, but fuck you, I'm doing it!' People would get hammered and bash into each other. Everyone else thought they were making yaogun lose face, and called them stupid." Yan said he met this type of person all over the country, stuck in the hopelessness of the middle and end of the nineties.

The punk scene grew in opposition to what yaogun had become: Formerly important, the money and fame had overshadowed the music; it had ceased to Mean Something. "Rock and Roll with Chinese Characteristics" by punk outfit 69 showed that it wasn't necessarily a brainless opposition: *"Use rock and roll to sell your conscience / Turn anger into cash . . . Use long hair to cover up the emptiness / Use music to deceive the truth."*

In addition to their objections of rock being smoothed beyond recognition, the punks were dismayed to find it reserved for a special class. When Gao Jingxiong, who would form punk progenitors Underbaby, first heard the Sex Pistols, it was a revelation. "Punk was for normal people," he realized. "Metal was for superstars."

P.K. 14's Yang Haisong had his punk epiphany listening to Radiohead. "The song that we focused on was 'Anyone Can Play Guitar.' That became our religion." And Yang – like many others in the mid-nineties – found many bands that preached the same ideals.

It's not that the punk bands that emerged were comprised of people who didn't know how to play, necessarily. "Lots of people then had studied music a bit," said Brain Failure frontman Xiao Rong, whether it was officially with a teacher or on one's own, playing along with the stereo. "The tool to connect [the feeling you have] to people is music. If you don't have the tool, or don't know how to use it, it's tough to do."

Wang Yue of Hang on the Box had different priorities: "From the beginning, we weren't so interested in the techniques of guitar playing," she said, likening it to visual art: Once she figured out what she wanted to do, her art history class was useless. "If I know I want to paint like Warhol I don't need to study Michelangelo. I heard the Breeders, Bikini Kill, that type of stuff, and that's what I wanted to play . . . I just needed a few things to help me get there." When I asked her about her lessons, and if they started with things like C-chord, it was unclear whether or not she was joking when she said, "I'm still not sure where C is."

Reflector's Tian Jianhua was attracted to punk in a similar way: "We didn't have good enough skills to play anything besides punk. So was an easy way to get into music . . . You don't need to play huge solos," he said. But the skate-punk that Reflector plays demands a fair amount of technique, and not just in order to keep up with the tempo.

But what one hears, in the pre-millennial punk, is the eschewing of the technicality of more complicated music in the service of an urgent message. "Why was punk interesting to me?" asks Brain Failure's Xiao Rong. "It's special because of its violence . . . It makes people pay attention."

Wang Yue was one of those people attracted to it, along with her friend and future Hang on the Box bandmate Yi Lina. Their lives were changed from the moment they saw their first show. The mohawks, the dyed hair, the sunglasses (inside!); they'd never seen anything like it. "You didn't know what made them special, but you knew that, in comparison, you were a jackass," said Wang, who couldn't sleep after that first show. "I called Yi Lina and said 'Our entire life before was completely stupid. We need to become like them: our taste in music, our attitude, our lives.' " It wasn't just that their lives changed, it was that they believed they *needed* to change their lives. That these two, who in many other times and/or places would have been the coolest girls in school – girls that had already Macgyvered a wardrobe, accessories and style of their own based on the rockers they idolized via *dakou* tapes – came to this realization demonstrates the intensity of the violence to which Xiao Rong referred, and how it's not so much about blood and guts, but about a visceral reaction to what's being thrown your way. Chalk it up to the indiscretions and idealism of youth if you want, but that doesn't make it any less of an essential choice that the new punks made.

The punk scene is generally considered to have begun with Underbaby. Brothers Gao Jingxiong and Gao Yang, weaned on the glimpses of MTV provided by the family satellite dish, took early to Nirvana, Depeche Mode and the Red Hot Chili Peppers. Their father, who owned a restaurant, disapproved of his sons' interest in guitars and drums but cleared out a part of a storage room regardless. That room became the brothers' apartment, studio and something of a headquarters for the growing group of young rockers-cum-punks that hung around with them, despite the tendency for the wall sockets to burst into flames when overworked. Their song "All the Same," which does more than just call to mind Nirvana's "Love Buzz," caught the attention of Magic Stone, who had the tune kick off the second volume of *China Fire* in 1996, a year after the band's live debut at a Kurt Cobain memorial show. Underbaby's big-label support was essential to the spread of grunge and punk beyond the small number of punk venues in which most bands remained, because it gave them access to bigger stages. But it took far too long for their record to come out; by the time it did, in 1998, not only had the scene changed (and Magic Stone disappeared), but so, too, had the band. Over the course of the time between Underbaby's record deal and the eventual release of the album, a punk scene emerged in Beijing that, for a brief moment, seemed to catch the world's attention. It was a time in which punk seemed poised to sweep through the nation, leading yaogun up through its late-nineties doldrums.

The posse of punks that first emerged from that scene may have sounded mad, but the Boredom Brigade was aptly named. Comprised of Brain Failure, Reflector, 69 and Anarchy Jerks, the double album that captured the four bands on tape is not just an essential window into the millennial punk scene, it is a damn good listen, overflowing with performances that would make both Kurt Cobain and Johnny Rotten proud.

It's no accident that the punk scene's headquarters wound up in the university district of Beijing. Arguably moreso than other types of music, punk was deeply connected to the foreign visitors that, by 1996, were increasing if still rare; visiting students comprised the bulk of those foreigners. They were lifelines to the outside world that was still mostly unknown to China and, more importantly, they were folks that could help guide the newly initiated through their own collections as well as the shelves of the *dakou* shops.

"We'd heard the Clash before, but there were some guys that were into underground American punk," said Brain Failure's Xiao Rong. "At the time, I didn't really get it, but now it makes me pretty annoyed because I see that it was like they wanted to bring the culture from their youth over here." He adds, however, that even though he wasn't a big fan of the hardcore punk music that was being passed around as potential models for bands – including the first incarnation of his own band – he doesn't look back with regret. Rather, he said it happened naturally. "I didn't like the music," he said. "But I thought it was cool." After all, they were the experts and he was just a teenager. Moreover, he was a teen who had just joined up, attracted to his first punk show by the belief that he might be able to watch people literally "go mental" – he meant it, he confessed, in the clinical sense. That he became friends and bandmates with the two most insane guys in the room that night shows how quickly and deeply he became attached.

The Brigade and the scene around them took off with a similar speed. When the Scream Club opened in 1998, the movement had a headquarters. Meanwhile, word of Beijing's scene was slowly getting out to punk communities around the world and in 1998, Tian An Men 89 Records released a compilation in France featuring the bands of the Brigade. It wasn't long before international media got interested in the story. Journalists flocked to the Scream Club, where they met kids with leather, chains, tattoos and mohawks; kids that quickly learned what the visitors were looking for. And thus, the balancing act between novelty and news: punk as both wacky fashion statement and the seeds of revolution against the Commies.

David O'Dell, Brain Failure's bassist and an early show organizer recalled "overzealous foreign journalists," and of shows stopped because of photographers crowding up front to the point that bands couldn't tell whether or not there were any actual audience members. Xiao Rong eventually came up with a strategy to avoid getting asked the same old tired and ill-informed questions during what became the requisite pre-gig meet-the-press. He told reporters that they'd have to get together and interview him in a group. "Everyone wanted to break the story, so none were willing to do it," he said. Problem solved.

While the international press corps came out in force, punks were dismayed that their local counterparts weren't interested despite efforts at inclusivity in promotional strategy and keeping ticket prices down. Of course, the international media was a blessing at least as much as it was a curse; nobody disliked seeing their name in an ever-increasing clippings pile, after all.

Riot girls Hang on the Box personify the blessing-curse of the surge in international coverage. What's ironic about the reaction to their sudden appearance in the international media is that it was precipitated by the appearance therein of fellow punks. Soon-to-be frontwoman Wang Yue got a call from Anarchy Jerks' Shen Yue inviting her to his upcoming gig.

"He said 'We're awesome. We've already been in all kinds of international media'," said Wang. "That's how he described his band." When Shen asked what Wang had been up to, she mentioned that she, too, had a band, and he suggested – out of politeness, said Wang, not out of a genuine interest in having them play – that Wang's band join in on the show. "I said yes. I didn't even think about it."

Of course, her band was only a band in theory – take that, Lester Bangs. Ten days later, they were onstage at Scream Club. Six months later, they were on the cover of *Newsweek*, earning enemies as they remained blissfully unaware that anything was amiss. After all, at the time, getting interviewed and photographed by international journalists was as much a part of being a punk as was the hours-long process of getting your hair ready for a night out.

The first time the ladies walked into the Scream Club after the issue's release they were treated with the same hostility that contributed to the band never quite being fully in the punk scene. "They started on us right away: 'Hey, look: Here come the cover girls,' " said Wang. The feeling was that HOTB hadn't earned it. Ironically, for a scene that eschews training, aesthetic standards, mass-market exposure and bias, they were derided as latecomers whose music wasn't up to snuff, chosen for the cover simply because of their gender. "I agreed with them," said Wang, fully able to admit that they weren't as good as the others. "But they weren't hearing it."

The article, said Wang, was another example of the Western media exploiting rebellious elements of Chinese culture to point out China's problems. (The headline atop the band's picture was "China: The Limits of Freedom"). Her language was tinged with that particular blend of punk and patriotism that one sees across yaogun: Our country has problems, sure, but it's *our* country and if it's going to change, it's going to be on *our* terms. Hang on the Box, after its *Newsweek* cover story, continued to plow through into the aughts with varying degrees of success and development. Signing with a Japanese label (Bad News) for a brief period, they toured the US and Japan before splitting, only to reform with different members. Their sound started out as a hybrid of heavily-accented silly English lyrics yelped on top of urgent if messy punk-tinged alt-rock, and while musically, things changed slightly over time, the lyrical and vocal concept of the band stayed pretty much the same – both in HOTB, which re-formed in 2010 with new members, and in Wang Yue's side projects, the bossa nova Brilliant Gia and the riot-grrrl Girl Kill Girl (drummer "Shengy" went on to play in experimental/noise group White and guitarist Yang Fan founded Ourselves Beside Me, which features moans, drones and a penchant for the weird).

The Boredom Brigade, meanwhile, was culled by half. Brain Failure and Reflector not only remained, but they have since become two of yaogun's best-known bands, developing their sound from their more hardcore days. Brain Failure has taken up the type of ska-inflected punk associated with Rancid, while Reflector went skate-punk *a la* Green Day; both draw audiences the size of which their younger selves could scarcely imagine.

Xiao Rong's first band took their cues from Sonic Youth and the Jesus and Mary Chain, a fact that he noted with a laugh over how everything old is new again: Those two bands may be two of the most popular influences in yaogun today, but the eagerness with which contemporary bands have taken to them seem to preclude the possibility that anyone before them had. Next came Xiao's requisite Nirvana days, followed by Brain Failure's hardcore days. He recalled being told – less suggestively than directorially – that the music he ought to be playing should feature less grunge and more punk, and the first incarnation of the band was more hardcore than he had envisioned. Re-forming in the early days of the millennium, the band signed with a Japanese label (Bad News, with whom they parted in 2009), headed to the US along with Hang on the Box in 2003, and suddenly, the world outside of China played an increasing role in the band's development. They hooked up with the Dropkick Murphys, a Boston-based Celtic-flavored punk band, finding in Dropkick founder Ken Casey a supporter, producer and booster. Casey recorded the band in 2004 and Brain Failure made its mark on the American circuit, hitting the Warped Tour and appearing on a variety of compilations and split-releases as well as on a video game. In addition to working with producer and Public Enemy bassist Brian Hardgroove, Chuck D contributed vocals to a track on their *Box on the Broken Ball* EP. But overseas experience and partnerships are not the sum total of the band's accomplishments. They remain an important band at home, and are eager to focus efforts there.

On the wall of one of Beijing's premier art galleries, there is a painting of Brain Failure at Tiananmen Square, signaling, depending on your outlook, either the depths to which the band has sunk or the heights to which it has soared. If you look at Xiao's image for long enough, you start to see that it's a combination of confusion and posturing, but the overall message is, "Ha!" – a simultaneous underground defiance and far-above-ground gloating. Has he sold out? Does he care? Xiao's relationship to punk, and to the mainstream, has changed over the years. "Last year in the mainstream media, I separated myself from the whole 'punk' thing," he told me in 2010. The statement is important for two reasons. Obviously, for one of the country's first punks, removing himself from the genre is big, but he did it because the word is misunderstood to represent things unrelated to him. But what might be more significant is the fact that there was a mainstream media that he could access. "I've deserted a lot of fans," Xiao said, "and they're disappointed in me. And that's exactly what's interesting to me. And that's rock and roll."

Another thing it is: pure punk.

Reflector, meanwhile, has also come about as far from the punk underground as is possible, the result of a seriousness of purpose that is belied by the fun that colors their music and live show. "I don't know what other bands do," said bassist Tian Jianhua. "But we have meetings. Not like 'let's have a meal together, and smoke and drink and maybe talk a bit,' but like *real* meetings. We'd meet for four or five hours, and talk through everything." That has resulted in a very professional image, both on paper and on stage.

It wasn't always thus. Their 2001 US tour opened their eyes, and not in an altogether good way. "We thought we were awesome before we went. We were really the only punk band left that was still making new music. We were kind of like the elders," said Tian. But after seeing shows in the US and playing with other bands, they had to rethink things. "They were playing the same instruments as us, but they were making them do different things." More meetings followed upon their return, and they got their chops up to snuff. But mastering their instruments didn't take the fun out of Reflector's music.

"I make sure the media understands that we *play* in a band," said Tian, emphasizing the Chinese word *wanr* ("wah-rrrr"), a verb that implies more fun than what one does with a guitar. The key for Reflector, Tian adds, is that people understand that they haven't been *played by* music. "We're still *playing*, after all these years." Reflector plays fun music, but it's music that is serious in its message.

The importance they place upon getting a message out there has led the band above ground, a place where, unlike many bands with a message, they are intent on staying. So when their recent album cover was censored, they didn't turn to underground distribution, they fixed it, believing that as many people as possible should hear what they have to say. "Our songs are about telling kids to choose your own path. To not listen to your teachers or your family, but make up your own mind," said Tian. "This is what kids should be hearing. We want as many young people as possible to be able to go into record stores and find our album and hear a different voice, so we do it above ground."

Doing it above ground, though, creates situations not especially yaogun. Fans fawn over the trio as if Reflector was a boy band. It makes Tian Jianhua visibly uncomfortable to even contemplate that it's happening. It's a discomfort, but you just know that the eternal punks inside Reflector relish the opportunity to poison the minds of so many. Indeed, the band has accepted the kind of offers that other bands might not, such as the chance to appear on major television shows, where they've taken advantage of the opportunity to spit in the proverbial eye of the mainstream.

While Reflector seeks not the superfandom of pop stars, another pre-millennial punk band seemed to chase after it. The Flowers didn't tend to hit the punk hotspots, but they were another sign that punk was changing. In 1998, the then-highschoolers caught the attention of "Jerry" Fu Chong, who was moonlighting as a promoter. After failing to get any labels interested in the band, Fu decided to release the record himself. Pollination metaphors abounded when New Bees Records released the Flowers' debut album, selling at least an unprecedented half-million copies.

The Flowers shot to fame so fast that many either forget or were never aware that they were spawned in the late-nineties underground. Because of that, in the initial phases of their fame, they brought not only yaogun, but also, more importantly, punk, into the mainstream, more through the references they implied than their music. Their sound was that internationally successful blend of the shine of pop music with the edge, extremely slight, of punk. That their pop-punk sounded like a less-polished Reflector (or, yes, later Green Day) isn't surprising, since they lacked the back story and chops gathered from years playing the music that made up the second half of the genre. Their "rebellious lyrics," as dubbed by the official English weekly news magazine, *Beijing Review*, were certainly safe for the nation:

> *We are not happy about anything we learned in class*
> *I just want to leave here as quickly as possible*
> *I hope the bell rings soon to tell us that class is over*
> *Class is over!*

Safe though they were, the Flowers benefited from the wave of international interest in the Beijing punk scene while simultaneously making the grade as clean-cut enough to jump into the mainstream, which was fine, since the band was in no way attached to the underground. But because their music had many elements of the kind of music that was being made underground, they still had an edge that hadn't been present in other music as commercially successful as theirs. Even Cui Jian, early on, approved. And, as sickening as it may sound to the punk faithful, there is certainly logic to the argument that it was, in fact, the Flowers that brought punk to the masses – sure, in one particular form, but if yaogun teaches us anything it is that the small victories are essential. And hey, didn't Green Day do the same thing in the US? Regardless, that edge didn't last long. Before they were much into their twenties, EMI came calling. The band that emerged from the major label makeover was much different from the one produced by New Bees, and it's at this point that any connection to yaogun ends (we might add that their legacy will likely be overshadowed by the "flaws" in the songwriting process that saw upwards of a dozen of their songs erroneously described as "original").

While not signing as many bands as Modern Sky or Scream, New Bees rode the success of the Flowers and established themselves as a player in the indie label scene. In 2000, New Bees signed Shanghai pop-rockers Crystal Butterfly, making them the second Shanghainese rock band to secure a label deal, but *not* the second band to release a record, as Crystal Butterfly's big shot turned out to be a dud. It was nearly five years after they were signed, and nearly three years after recording it, before their debut album was released. It was a huge blow to a band that had been a beacon for Shanghai rock, having dominated for much of the late nineties. Han Han, a giant-old-school-bespectacled indie rocker who plays in several bands and runs the small label Miniless Records remembers that when the band signed to New Bees, "everyone saw it as an example that you could be in a band and make a living." In 2005, Crystal Butterfly left New Bees, and has since stayed on home turf in their label dealings, releasing their second album in 2010 through Soma, the city's second "indie" label better known, perhaps, for their management of Shanghai's Mao Livehouse and for signing bands rather than releasing albums. (Shanghai's first "indie" label was Fanyin, which, in 2002, released the debut album by the Honeys that draws from influences like Depeche Mode, the Cure and Sheryl Crow).

It was around the turn of the millennium that Beijing's first punk wave ended with a slow burn. With notoriety came financial opportunities followed by in-fighting and the need for a reprieve. Beijing's nascent rave scene started to pull punks into its orbit, and an exodus saw many members of the community head to the literally greener pastures of the southwestern Yunnan Province, where time passes slowly and marijuana grows wild by the roadside.

Though it's hard to envision today, when "punk" bands top the *Billboard* charts, punk tended to get wrapped in a political package more than other types of music. Certainly, political attributes have been thrust upon yaogun across time and genre, but it's a subject that seems most directly associated with punk – and to an extent, alt – because the word tends to signify a musical direction as much as a lifestyle and way of thinking. The visual power of punk and the weight of all that the idea of China has come to represent, and suddenly, all punk is capital-p Punk: The Great Wall is sure to crumble under the weight of the Oi!

Such a discussion needs to be prefaced by some linguistic wrangling. China scholar Andrew Jones, wrote of those "eager to see China and Chinese rock only in politicized shades of red verses red, white, and blue." Eight years later, Tang Dynasty's Kaiser Kuo wrote that yaogunners have more in common with Guns N' Roses than with Bob Dylan. "The overwhelming majority of Chinese musicians who dream of rock stardom aren't interested in politics," he wrote. "Many are perceptive enough to know what Western journalists want to hear and cynical enough to repeat it to them."

Take Brain Failure's Xiao Rong. When punk blew up, by his own admission, he was young and unaware, searching for something cool rather than the cure for society's ills. The international media, he said, "put a political hat" on punk. "We never had any political meaning, but they said we were political, or they hoped we were." Which caused problems for people still feeling their way through the music and ideas behind it. "We were all young, and got all this attention and we start to wonder: *Are* we political? *Should* we be political? Is being political the cool thing to do?"

The real problem, he said, is in the conception of the term, and that's the key. "In China, if we were being called 'political' it means we're opposing the government . . . To me, there's only this meaning. So I never said 'Ok, we're political.' "

"We talk about our lives, and sometimes that means talking about political things," is the standard answer that Subs' Kang Mao will give to reporters. "But we're not political."

Li Yang of Demerit puts it slightly differently. "Politics aren't an easy thing to talk about," he said, in a 2010 interview (with an English-language publication). "Not because certain things are unspeakable, but because you have to understand their true meaning before you say anything." It's a sentiment that ought to apply equally to lyricists and interviewers.

Thus do bands that have had hats thrown their way – none of whom disputes the fact that they hope to influence people to action – get lumped into the "political" category against their wishes.

It's important to keep the discussion in mind as we head into the new millennium. A major difference between the current punk – and rock – landscape and the original scene is a microcosm of the difference between the generations known as post-eight-zero and pre-eight-zero, i.e., those born before and after 1980, a specious line, but one that generally separates those whose coming-of-age experience was defined by either confusion or abundance.

"We were educated in the communist system growing up," said Kang Mao, of Subs, who was born in 1977. "The economic explosion left us completely confused." To wit, she cites a song she remembers singing often in her childhood, "The Motherland is a Garden": *The flowers in the garden are bright and beautiful / The warm sun shines on us all.* Suddenly, said Kang, it became clear that the song wasn't true. The sun wasn't shining and the flowers had to find their own source of light.

"I was young, but I experienced 1989," said Reflector's Tian Jianhua, who was ten at the time. "But people born after I was, they don't understand anything remotely political."

Thus do we find primarily older 'gunners more engaged in the kind of grassroots-level behavior that defined the punk scene that started in the days before internet or cell phones, when it was essential to have hands-on involvement in every aspect of the music, from flyer design, copying and distribution to lining up gigs, studio time or creating music. These days, we'd call that DIY (do it yourself), and the fact that it would involve technology doesn't make it any less about doing it one's self. But there is a new phenomenon at work steering people away from the kind of spirit that defined the initial punk scene – and still defines a segment of it today.

American Nevin Domer, who moved to Beijing in 2005 mainly to get involved in the music scene, talks about the need for various levels of a healthy music scene. In order to have a healthy underground, you have to have a healthy above-ground. If bands can enter a system that creates mid-level rock stars, there is room for other bands to find their own way – which is what the punks did. If the above-ground system doesn't develop, you have a DIY-by-default system, where all bands are forced to do everything themselves, thus destroying the lure of the underground as a place one would choose to inhabit.

With the possibility of achieving mid-level rock star status a reality for more and more bands, Domer sees fewer and fewer that choose to go outside of that system. While Domer's heart – and, one might add, money and life, vis-a-vis his own band, Fanzui Xiangfa – is with the underground, his experience tells him it's getting harder and harder to bring people into the fold. "It's like pulling teeth," he said, of trying get bands to do some of the grassroots work he sees essential to the lower level of the scene. "All of them want to be pampered rock stars."

Or, perhaps more accurately, one might say they *expect* to be rock stars. The "Little Emperor" phenomenon, where single children are doted upon by at least two generations of the family – two generations that personally felt the kind of dearth unknown to urban residents in these boom times – tends to create a generation of divas, who expect the treatment with which they were raised to continue into their adult lives.

But there are bands, particularly punk bands, that are countering that trend. "These days, rock isn't related to politics," said former pop singer and rock producer Wang Di, who is of the "Rock is Dead" school. "There's no tradition of criticism . . . We're suspicious of [it] . . . Look at punk: It's totally fashionable now. I like it, though. But does it have real meaning in this society?" Many have noted the decline in the Importance of rock music, both in terms of yaogun's content and also in terms of the desire of artists to Make a Difference. But, alas, there are exceptions to all rules, and Pangu is nothing if not an exception.

While punk, in theory, identifies with the underdog in general, it's hard to envision a punk band *actually* gaining a following among the underrepresented. But Pangu's cause attracted a downtrodden worker in the band's hometown, who donated what little money he had to the band to enable them to buy instruments. "I have no hope," he told them. "You guys go out and do it." Pangu confronted that hopelessness head-on, with a music that challenged – lyrically and musically.

Pangu's brand of punk is infused with their hometown's history. Nanchang is the site of the first shots fired in the Chinese Civil War, and the birthplace of the Chinese military, the People's Liberation Army. Pangu's Ao Bo sees the band's mission in terms his revolutionary forbearers might find familiar: "This is what the Communist Party requested that people do!" he said. "Didn't Mao Zedong say that wherever there is oppression we must resist it?" Of course, in contrast to others, Pangu now must do the resisting from outside their homeland.

Agreeing to 2004's Say Yes to Taiwan festival in Taipei was either their boldest move or biggest mistake. Suffice it to say that relations between Taiwan and the Mainland are strained, and that the latter does not take kindly to events like this particular festival, celebrating, as it was, the soon-to-be re-elected leadership devoted to Taiwanese independence. In short, the festival was more than just a gig, and the band was not going to come out of an association with it unscathed. They had already been stirring the pot with their unsubtle calls for change and action. But calling for Taiwanese independence at the 2004 festival, specifically by saying (again, in a Bjork-y move) "Protect Taiwan!" took things too far. In transit in Thailand en route back to China, they realized they'd be arrested if they returned home. Sweden accepted their request of asylum, and the group is now primarily based in Taiwan.

Particularly in the years before their exile, Pangu's following was intense. David Frazier, a journalist who has followed the band closely, speaks of meeting "a steady collection of rockers . . . with a consistent story, namely that . . . they suddenly found a band that was telling them the truth through rock and roll." He recalls hearing the same type of thing over and over, " 'Before them, I listened to Cui Jian and Zhang Chu and He Yong, and I thought that was great. But then I heard Pangu and realized that everything they were saying was all wrong.' "

"Lots of people," said Ao Bo, "finally found their hope with us."

Ao, too, was once inspired by Cui, but the moment he heard Pantera's *Cowboys from Hell* – an album he acquired by asking the shopkeeper to give him the "loudest, heaviest thing he had" – things changed. In 1995, he decided it was time to form a band, and recruited two of his fellow machinists-to-be. The next logical step was to figure out how to acquire and play their instruments. With a bit of borrowed money, the RMB50 (about $6 at the time) donated by a fellow worker – "That was a *lot* for him at the time," said Ao. "That's how poor everyone was." – and the drummer's dowry, they had almost enough to cover the gear they needed; learning to play the acquired instruments wasn't exactly a priority. "From the beginning, the goal was to say something . . . We wanted to make sure people understood what we were saying . . . We weren't doing this to be artists," said Ao. "I knew it was going to be like Nirvana, Pantera and Cui Jian combined. I knew that we weren't good enough to do it, but that's what we wanted to do."

Their first show, on the streets of Nanchang, wound up separating the real punks from the rest. The idea was simple: A bunch of bands show up outside a record store and play. Speakers and a drum kit were brought in on a three-wheeled bike they borrowed, and the band set up. But no other local bands – and there were other bands – would dare play. "You don't think of what might happen until *after* you do it," said Ao, still, almost fifteen years later, confused as to why other bands didn't show. "That's punk." Reflecting on their earliest shows, Ao sums up the punk philosophy better than anyone: "We could never play better than back then, because now, we have experience, so it's not real punk. Punk is about the first time always being the best."

Ao was a reader of Yan Jun's columns and thought the latter would like Pangu's music; he was right. Yan connected them to Wang Lei, who held court in Guangzhou as king of the southern scene, having released a number of inventive if overlooked records. Wang's interest in pushing the boundaries of experimental and industrial rock inspired the band moved to Guangzhou; they released two albums in three years through Wang while performing regularly at Unplugged, Wang's club.

Pangu's 2001 self-titled Scream Records release was the band's most-widely distributed album. You'd probably expect to hear something a lot more punk-sounding than this, but in Pangu's case, punk does a better job describing the band's outlook rather than the type of music they play.

The record is difficult listening. Production is horrible. The performances are a mess. But beyond the harsh sounds is a seriousness that is so intense, it's as if there was no time for production, or to learn the instruments. The band was expressing the life they led. The horror-movie screams and shrieks scattered throughout "Hopeless" recalled the kind of desperation you can imagine inspired their Mission. "You Won't Let Me Rock" may be a great conceptual theme song for yaogun in general, but for Pangu, the sentiment was soon to take on a meaning that not even the punks themselves could have envisioned. Ao, a policeman told a reporter looking around Nanchang for the band's legacy four years after their exile, "was a serious matter." Listening to this record, you understand why they'd want to keep an eye on him.

That they got the album released officially at all is either the result of official malfeasance or just plain old dumb luck: Even

Scream Records, after all, had to submit all of their content to Ministry of Culture censors before receiving a barcode. "We went to our closest friend in publishing, and he had some sixty-year-old censor it," said Scream founder Lü Bo. "For some reason, [the censor] didn't mind."

The band's discography since their debut is a difficult thing to keep track of, including, as it does, a regular stream of singles, EPs and albums available for free online put out with such speed as to enable Pangu to be one of the only bands that regularly record songs about contemporary events. "Ao says what we wouldn't dare say," wrote Yan Jun in 2001. He continues to do so from exile.

They have written songs about Zhang Lin, the Chinese writer arrested for posting an essay online with Pangu lyrics; about Taiwanese and Tibetan independence; about a band called Beijing-Fucking Olympics; and more. The band wrote several songs in tribute to Yang Jia, the cop-killer that became a national phenomenon in 2008: Charged with riding an unlicensed bicycle, Yang Jia claims he was beaten. He sued the police, unsuccessfully, and then, taking matters into his own hands, walked into a police station in the Shanghai suburbs, threw Molotov cocktails, and started stabbing police officers, killing half a dozen before he was stopped. For the killing spree, Yang was sentenced to death. The not-insubstantial amount of support he received in the wake of the sentence was the result of his embodiment of widely felt frustrations. "You want to give me an explanation, I'll give you an explanation" was both a quote attributed to Yang Jia as well as the title of a song which puts the band in the killer's mind:

I'm not crazy
I'm innocent
They broke the law
It's the police who are guilty
Kill, you want to give me an explanation
Kill, I'll give you an explanation.

"We want to be the child who says out loud that the emperor has no clothes," Ao told the *Taipei Times*. "But aside from telling the truth, we also want to overthrow the emperor."

Since 2004, Pangu has had to find a spot from outside the Mainland to plot their overthrow, while punk bands of all stripes blossomed across the yaogun map. Many of these punks are uninterested in Pangu's mission, but there are also some making efforts to let their fellow citizens in on the flaws in the imperial wardrobe.

Formed in Wuhan, which, by the late nineties was laying the groundwork for a healthy punk scene of its own, Subs moved to Beijing in the first years of the aughts. In 2005, they were invited to perform at the Oya Festival in Oslo, which is when, in the interest of full disclosure, our paths crossed. As one of four Chinese music industry representatives also invited to the Oya Festival, I was told that the band needed help getting some shows together to make a tour out of the festival invite. Several emails, phone calls and weeks later, I was on the Scandinavian road with the band as tour manager, road manager, roadie, driver, translator and then some. Before their first European trip, the band had already made a name for themselves in China. Theirs was not the straight-up punk of the Boredom Brigade, though their approach to it is certainly of a type idealized by those early punks.

Their high-energy live show and the fact that their singer is a woman with a power and presence matched only by the intensive and explosive music that backs her up has brought them their renown. Critic Yan Jun sees those two factors as contributing to the total package. "Lots of audiences have been attracted by Kang Mao's screams. But what really makes them fall in love is the group's completely genuine attitude. The band has put their lives into their music – when they perform they're like people madly in love." Just as arresting as the on-stage antics of a Subs show is the image of the entranced crowds I have seen from Beijing to Bergen.

Subs, like many other post-millennial bands, have chosen English as the language of the bulk of their lyrics and have, in recent years, added more Chinese. "I sing in English not because it's the language of America," Kang said, "but because English is the language of the world." Having had the pleasure and curse of not only reading through but attempting to edit said lyrics, I can say that this likely wasn't the best choice she's ever made. Her linguistic decision seems to fly in the face of the band's motivation and mission to highlight "things that are more important than money," but she is clear: "The Chinese audience may not understand the English lyrics, but then, they wouldn't get it if it was in Chinese either." That there are times when English speakers are equally in the dark is beside the point. Pronunciation and syntax are the first victims of Kang's wail, but as long as one doesn't read along with a lyric sheet or watch subtitled performances, one might well be swept up in what can only be interpreted as Important Things. She has gone from self-proclaimed "Scream Queen" to, according to the band's 2010 album, *The Queen of Fucking Everything* and neither title is an exaggeration. Their punk music combines their love of hardcore a la Fugazi with the garage rock of the Sonics; they have added post-rock and post-punk and new wave to the mix. In addition, there is far more straight-up singing than ever before. Our Scream Queen isn't exactly choosing a new vocal direction, but she is, finally, ok with melody. Which doesn't mean she can't reach down to the very depths to unleash howls of hell – in a good way – but that now, there's something that your average rocker might sing along to – again, in a good way.

One of the band's most impressive songs features the ultimate in rock and roll revenge, when Kang Mao takes her father's put-down and puts it to use. "My father told me that if I play rock music I'll have four 'Nos,' " she tells audiences before the band breaks into "Down," the title track of their 2006 record. Throwing out numbers is one of the oldest semantic tricks in the Chinese book. Mao sought to destroy the "Four

Pests"; Deng Xiaoping brought the "Four Transformations"; Jiang Zemin had the "Three Represents"; Hu Jintao listed the "Eight Honors and Eight Disgraces." Add Papa Kang's Four Nos to the list: "No money, no family, no job, no future." Kang brings her father's list into the rock scheme, using rock's own numbers game, employed since the beginning: the count-off. If we were the type to look for larger messages in the song, we might look to the choice to include audience participation in the tune's opening count – "*One, two, three, four*" – as a bringing-together of all rock fans in opposition to Father Kang's, and society at large's, disapproval of the rock lifestyle chosen by those who scream along with Kang Mao the first four numbers. Later, Kang breaks down the four. "*One: no money, keep the naked body / Two: no family, like the first day / Three: no job, throw away old cage / Four: no future, come down to rock 'n' roll.*" If "up" is where society wants its citizens to go, the band has said many times, "we choose down." "*I am happy and downward,*" Kang sings, summing it all up nicely.

In contrast to that of Kang Mao, we have Joyside's count-off on 2004's *Drunk is Beautiful*, an almost-too-perfect demonstration of the difference between the two bands' brands of punk. "I Want Beer" begins with a bouncy bass line, atop which, several bars later, comes the count, which starts out with an energy and volume you'd expect for a punk band about to sing about how, when there's crud all around, beer is the answer. As quickly as it takes to get from the "one" to the first millisecond of the word "three," singer Bian Yuan's digestive system takes revenge and his opening call sinks like a blimp with a fast leak: "**ONE! TWO!** sr − (*gulp-belch*)" is what comes out, and you feel the discomfort of what sounds like it might be day-old beer, but we'd know better than to expect there was any alcohol *that* old in the vicinity of this band. Joyside does for booze what Anarchy Jerks did (and Misandao does) for Oi!, namely, abuse the hell out of it. Their reputation for drunkenness – a tradition begat with the soothing effects of sauce that calmed first-show jitters – is directly related to their reputation for hit-and-miss live shows.

"Eighty percent of their shows are bad," said one fan, a student at the Drama Academy who helps promote rock shows. "But the twenty percent is *really* good." That rock fans would have to see nine shows before they might catch the band on their game would seem the ultimate in disrespect, but Joyside's fan base is, confusingly, far from insulted and there is something in their throwback to early punk 'n' roll a la Stooges, New York Dolls and Sex Pistols that has won over the masses. Frontman Bian Yuan resembles his idol Jim Morrison in many ways – greasy mane, ever open-collared shirts, tight leather pants – but is a shell of the Lizard King in his lyricism and singing, the former overloaded with garbled drunken Chinglish, and the latter the result of a range that encompasses not much more than the distance between speaking and moaning. It would be a stretch to call Joyside's philosophy nihilism, because it would be a stretch to imply that they have anything resembling a philosophy – and because nihilism doesn't necessarily involve enough beer. Before disbanding in 2009, they did tighten up a bit with a more-polished surf- and post-punk-influenced rock. But it's hard, with a band like Joyside, to know whether you want them to get better at their instruments or to stay sloppy, because there's something about sloppiness that feels authentic.

Joyside's Maybe Mars labelmates Demerit are a different breed of punk and, again, their count-off is a perfect encapsulation of that difference. The title track from Demerit's 2008 *Bastards of the Nation* introduces singer Li Yang atop a distorted riff with a "**ONE TWO THREE FUCK YEEEEEEEEEEEEOOOOOOOOOOOOW-WWWWWWWWWWWWW!!!!**" that sounds as if he's saying it as he rips the head off of the "you" about which he proceeds to sing. Demerit, in case you weren't sure, means business. But they perform a hardcore accessible to those who might be turned off by the term, because for all the onslaught that their music rains down, there are respites of pleasantness. "Street punk" is an oft-used descriptor for the band, but there's more melody than you might expect; there is certainly more than a little Mighty

Mighty Bosstones in Li Yang's vocal delivery, which is Cookie Monster, yes, but a Cookie Monster that's been schooled in pop. Particularly on the occasions he gets to breaking it down and talk-screaming through what sounds like a megaphone with low battery power, he even brings to mind Chuck D. The "whoa"s and "la"s that might be surprising to someone looking for a hardcore record show a deep appreciation for hooks and melody, and the guitar work, especially the rip-roarin' solos, is obviously a product of the band's love of the metal of Motorhead, Judas Priest and Iron Maiden.

But amidst the rip-roarin' is a band that knows to what end it rocks. Demerit has a message. "I don't want war; I'm against the manufacture of weapons; I'm against bloodshed regardless of skin color; I hate grandstanding public officials," said Li. "I could feel how unfair these things were, so I put them down in my music – that's where those lyrics come from."

Demerit's producer was Public Enemy's bassist and musical director Brian Hardgroove, who is quick to shower praise upon the band whenever he gets the chance. "I've adopted them as my little brothers," he told one reporter. "I went [to China] because of why I started playing music to begin with . . . Because I'm more of a social-political individual, and music is the best tool. For Americans, we need to look outside of America. We're very isolated here. I'm a citizen of the world, and we have to start behaving as such. What's happening in the Chinese music scene is a great example of what should've happened in America." In addition, he said, his relationship with Demerit wasn't unidirectional: "It's great to be able to show them a thing or two to help them on their way. But I think the generation of musicians coming up in China might have a few things they can show us, too." And Demerit is doing just that, having secured a slot on 2011's Vans Warped Tour.

The Era of the Festival Dawns

After several false starts and nearly-festivals, it was only in 1999 when things really kicked off with the Heineken Beat Festival in Beijing's Ritan Park. The festival was almost derailed after the 1999 bombing of the Chinese embassy in Belgrade because event organizers decided that the unrest resulting from anti-American protests was enough to necessitate a delay – the US embassy was a block from the park. Blues legend Robert Cray couldn't make the new July date, but a range of others made the trip two months later including the Dirty Dozen Brass Band and Gilberto Gil. Local talent at the festival included former Cui Jian keyboardist and pop-star-in-his-own-right Zang Tianshuo, Beijing-based rhythm and blues revue Rhythm Dogs and the People's Liberation Army's Marching Band. Heineken Beat returned for two more installments, each a bit more pop-oriented than the last. The festival was essential in bringing China events up to international standard, in terms of the quality of the experience both in front of and behind the stage.

The summer following Heineken Beat's 2001 edition was to have seen big things happen in Beidaihe, a coastal city three hundred kilometres (nearly two hundred miles) directly east of Beijing. Every summer since the founding of the Republic, top central leaders headed to the city to escape the heat of the capital. As a result, the town is well known for its connection to high-level political intrigue, inspiring an oft-quoted "one diplomat" to dub Beidaihe "China's smoke-filled room." That a cancellation of the planned festival seems to have come as a surprise to organizers is more of a shock than the cancellation itself, and would lead one to think that it wasn't bravery that led them to Beidaihe – these were, after all, the same people who, in the midst of all the Woodstock talk, neglected to draw an overt link with the fact that the 1968 festival was celebrating its thirty-second anniversary on the very weekend their event was scheduled. How organizers thought they could bring a rock festival to the town hosting vacationing Party leaders is mind-boggling. But the reason for the cancellation – at least, the reason given to the *Wall Street Journal* by festival organizers, was a shock of another kind: The site, the paper reported, was "drowned by tides." There are several problems with that statement – should we allow that it might actually be true, which, let's be honest, we shouldn't – not least of which is the fact that it's been a long time since we had to guess at the movement of tides. But the biggest problem of all is that, in a nation where silly, inadequate, frustrating and downright impossible excuses were, and are still, nothing new, Beidaihe organizers didn't even have the decency to use the generally-accepted catch-all buzzword for cancellations or closures, which even in the millennium's second decade shuts down venues and events: safety. Granted, safety seems a plausible reason to board the doors, but only if you know the specifics of the safety problem – which one never does. Without specifics, there are no potential solutions, and therein lies the evil beauty.

By the time the festival could be rescheduled – after the tides, presumably, and national leaders were out of the way – the *Journal* article said, "most bands had other commitments." Knowing how eager artists are to jump at opportunities such as this one and knowing, too, the dearth of any opportunities, festivalian or otherwise, for a yaogun band in mid-2001, the words "feeble attempt at spin" only begin to describe the forces at work here. Somehow, even a line like "there's no power available" would have made more sense. In the face of the news, one wonders about festival organizers' vision of "A Chinese festival, but one that would also have a big effect in international music circles."

While no Chinese festival yet has made a big impression outside of the country, the sudden proliferation of festivals has certainly made people pay attention. That the rise is a sign that things are looking good for yaogun is an important half-truth at the very least. Music festivals are, indeed, an increasing occurrence around the country, especially as local governments have come to see value in backing such events. Despite the fact that the word "rock" still has to stay out of any event's title, the employment of the word "festival" ought to be interpreted as a legit nod in yaogun's direction.

Festivals make both a good and bad model upon which to base a judgment on the rock scene. Many events are barely worthy of the f-word. Most remain one-offs, despite the "annual" prefix often slapped somewhere in the event's name, and those that return remain plagued with problems. In 2003, I attended the First Annual Lattetown Music Festival, named for the condominium complex in southern Beijing where it occurred. It saw a half-dozen metal, rock, funk and punk acts aid in the promotion of luxury housing. Alas, we still await the festival's second installment. In 2005, organizers of Beihai, Guangxi's International Beach Tourism Culture Festival added a yaogun component to their celebrations – which already included the Miss Bikini World competition. The cryptically dubbed "Carnivalesque Party of 1 vs. 120,000" featured Cui Jian, Black Panther, Tongue, CMCB and others.

One 'gunner who performed at Beihai may not have seen it as a giant step for the Cause, but he certainly wasn't complaining. Xiao Dao is the keyboardist for the industrial-rock band Tongue, not exactly the kind of band one would expect to be basking in the southern Chinese sun alongside bikini-clad models from around the world, having spent their share of cold and hungry nights in Beijing's artistic ghetto, Tree Village. But hey, it's the New China. "They're using beautiful women to support and promote yaogun," Xiao Dao said. "You gotta use as many ways as possible." Of course, he was quick to add, "they" aren't really interested in promoting rock. "The local government is looking to attract investment, they want to do an 'event' . . . But the government has no idea what rock is. Slowly they're getting an idea."

Thus, do we have festivals cropping up in more and more cities. Indeed, my chat with Xiao Dao took place right after the bikini-competition-cum-rock-fest, in Inner Mongolia, backstage at the Gegentala Grasslands Music Festival. There, on the grass-lands, spirits were high; bands – several of whom, including Cui Jian, were fresh from Beihai – had been shipped from far and wide to a festival that was promising big things for years to come. In actuality, it was an attempt by the local municipal-ity and a Chengdu strawberry magnate to garner attention for a tourist spot and bring in a few bucks while they were at it. There was no second installment. Xiao Dao also pointed out that the Carnivalesque organizers didn't really have a full grasp of what they were presenting. "They called the bands *zuhe*," he said, re-ferring to the word for "ensemble" rather than the word used to refer to rock bands. But then, water under the bridge, really: "There were tons of girls with bikinis! Girls from all over the world! They did kind of a fashion show, then bands went on."

While the Midi Music Festival has come a *very* long way from humble roots, it's likely that the festival won't be resorting to fashion shows to attract fans – crowds haven't been a problem for years. The Festival's first installment was an in-school affair in 2000, offering students at the then-seven-year-old Midi School of Music a big-stage opportunity to strut their stuff in front of their peers. Since the first years of the aughts, it has emerged as the most successful festival story of the new millennium, and the model to which others strive. In Midi's early days, just having a festival was a big deal, and that meant fierce loyalty. When 2004's May festival was canceled – with days' warning – the Midi School had no choice but to host something resembling a festival, when fans who had left their hometowns before the announced cancel-lation started arriving on the school's campus. A similar situa-tion created October 2008's mini-festival. The Olympic year was not a good one for the festival most often invoked to represent the rock and roll state of affairs in the Middle Kingdom: Post-poned in May, rumors had the event slated for locations around the city before it was canceled, rescheduled, and canceled again. With days' notice, the festivities – and droves of fans, despite the cruddy weather – returned to the school from whence it all began.

Midi's 2002 event was significant not only for its move out-doors, but for the widening of the audience. For the first time, the Titos, the Iron Henchman of yaogun, weren't the only ones around: Midi had gone Maxi. And festival fever was in the air when, months later, the Lijiang Snow Mountain Music Festival captured yaogun's attention, as well as that of a large number of international media outlets.

In the northwest corner of the southwestern province of Yun-nan, nearby the once-mythical and recently-official Shangri-La – three thousand-plus meters above sea level and fifteen kilome-ters (about nine miles) outside of the ancient town of Lijiang – lay China's rock and festival prospects. With artistic director Cui Jian at its head, few media outlets neglected to christen the event a Sino-Woodstock with visions of a New China blossoming at high altitudes. Of course, the real link to the mud-soaked sixties' festival was in its strategic scheduling for rainy season, but what was expected of Snow Mountain was that it would bring a new level of rock and roll experience to the masses. Alas, the masses seemed not up for the trek. Ticket prices, in the days leading up to the festival were cut in half. Three thousand were reported in attendance on the festival's first day; day two attendance is said to have doubled – a far cry from the tens of thousands predicted. Organizers knew they were in for a tough time: " . . . there will be shortcomings" one told the *South China Morning Post*, emphasiz-ing the trailblazing nature of the event. In a trend that was soon to become widespread, the Lijiang city government had spon-sored the event in order to attract tourism to the city.

Niu Jiawei, who was at the festival as manager for Second Hand Rose, one of the eighteen bands on the bill, remembers the festival as messy. "Artists started asking me for help . . . so I wound up working for everyone. I think I ate like two meals in three days."

Organizers tried to remain optimistic even as the rain poured and the mud flowed. "I've been tired, but I've never been this tired; I've seen chaos, but I've never seen chaos like this," one festival manager told a reporter. When asked about the festival's future, he replied, "Next time, we'll have to make money, and for sure hold it in a big city. But," he added, "we won't do rock music. Maybe it'll be jazz."

Next time came, if later than anticipated, but remained relatively rock. In 2007, Cui Jian once again headlined – along with a handful of pop singers – and upwards of forty rock and folk bands filled out the lineup. The following year, Emma Ticketmaster, the short-lived conglomerate that was the international ticketing company's foray into China, took on the festival and out, for the most part, went the yaogun. Avril Lavigne headlined, as did DJ Deep Dish, while trad-Chinese-meets-prog-rock Second Hand Rose and Shan Ren, a hybrid Yunnan-folk-meets-rock band brought the rock. In 2010, the fest went primarily folk, and local. Three years after the initial Snow Mountain Music Festival, fans once again converged upon a far-flung locale when Huang Liaoyuan – he of the 80,000 *yuan* profit-margin from Xinxiang – coaxed a few first-generation 'gunners out of retirement for a three-day event dubbed "The Glorious Path of Chinese Rock and Roll." He Yong, Luo Qi, Cobra and others that either hadn't performed in years or else hadn't appeared on the same bill since the earliest days headed west to the desert outside of Yinchuan, Ningxia. The festival piggybacked on the Fifth International Motorcycle Tourism Festival, uniting bikers and rockers; those that didn't ride out could, once again, take a rock-and-roll train. It was, says Huang, the first concert since his Xinxiang event that made money.

Midi, meanwhile, has expanded. That Midi was even able to move off its small edge-of-the-city campus, which it did in 2004, was a huge step; that the festival then agreed to Haidian Park's request that it move again – and that Haidian Park made the request in the first place – was an even bigger step. There's no doubt that Midi's mainstreaming has added to the recent rising tide in festivals, but it is not the only reason. With every few steps forward, backward-stepping is not far behind. Rugs have been pulled, recently, from under Midi and Modern Sky, while the 2008 Beijing Pop festival – whose previous events hosted Nine Inch Nails and Public Enemy among others – was strategically cancelled from within: "It's not because we've been told not to [do the festival]," festival director Jason Magnus told *Billboard*, "but because we don't want to take the risk." And he's got a point, what with the climate that year – Bjork in April, a massive earthquake in Sichuan Province in May and the Olympics in August. Of course, the fact that these incidents occurred shouldn't, in an ideal world, have any bearing on a festival's ability to occur, exist or welcome overseas performers. But the fact that things can go pear-shaped without warning means the music festivals – at least, the type to which Midi, Modern Sky, Beijing Pop and yaogunners in general aspire – is not something that officialdom is ready to embrace fully.

But whether festival foundations were ever solidly in place is a legitimate question that rarely gets asked, and will likely never be totally answered. Permits are one thing, but pieces of paper, even with the more-valuable-than-gold Official Seal stamped upon them, can only go so far. Take 2008's Midi Festival: Reports indicated that it was cancelled because the local police wouldn't provide security for the show, security that is a requirement for any event outdoors. That the police were happy to supply security to the myriad sites and events related to the Olympics three months later tells us where priorities are – or aren't. And this is all despite the prior successful Midi years, when the powers that be seemed convinced that there was nothing wrong with a little outdoor fun. The Beijing Pop Festival and, in 2009, the Modern Sky Festival dealt with a different, and arguably more restrictive, city district. On the one hand, Public Enemy and Cui Jian performed together in 2007 for Beijing Pop; on the other, two years later, the Buzzcocks and thirteen other international acts were told to stay away just days before the Modern Sky festival was to begin.

"It's very important we work closely with government to let them understand that rock and roll is just a cultural event,"

Beijing Pop's Magnus told a reporter in 2006, but clarified his sense of the obstacles. "It's not so much that it's rock but that it's a standing event. If we were doing a seated indoor event it would be very easy. We'd just need a performance visa. But there are no seats and we have a lot of artists and spectators. So it was difficult getting permits."

And, thus, does the conversation of festivals turn to one of psychology and coping mechanisms. "My attitude is 'whatever'," said Zhang Fan, head of the Midi School and Festival. "It's the only way you can get things done." Thirty overseas bands and two hundred local bands were booked and set for the 2008 festival before it was cancelled last-minute. "We did so much work, and suddenly, it was over. I came out of the last meeting, and sat down on the curb and thought, 'Now what?' " For Zhang Fan, there are two potential paths: there is the Sex Pistols and there is the Beatles. And though he was, in his day, a kid that leaned toward what he called the "fuck" of the former, his festival has not thrived on Anarchy in the PRC. Indeed, for several years, the festival's promotional materials have quoted John Lennon's Imaginary hope that some day, all will be joined. What went through Zhang's mind, sitting on that curb in 2008, was "There was only 'Let it Be.' " There was no other way, he said, adding that his job was to make better the sad song now confronting him. In China, he added, "you can only develop through patience." On the one hand, you want to shake Zhang by the scruff of his shirt and get him angry about how The Man is trying to stop his festival – and *History* with it! – but then you realize what he, and yaogun, is up against. Not a government bent on the destruction of rock and roll, but a Machine of enormous proportions that goes far beyond permit-issuing government departments.

In June of 2001, at a week-long outdoor concert at a shopping-center, I was granted a glimpse into that Machine. I had been to several of the previous days' festivities, and noted that, while most of the crowd was bewildered, there was also a smattering of loyal yaogun followers in attendance. And the bands played on, through the rain, and through the consternation and confusion of the bulk of the audience. But on the week's seventh day, after a slew of rock bands had already taken to the stage, "they" pulled the plug. There was no word on who "they" were, but what was most shocking was that, while the few foreigners among the crowd starting throwing mini-tantrums demanding answers – *Who was responsible for this?! Why was it happening?! Why should this night be different from the previous nights?!* – the locals were zen about the whole thing. "This is China," came the answer to our queries, explaining exactly nothing. But to the speaker, the line between question and answer was crystal clear, despite the sigh and a shrug that inevitably followed the line. Pretty soon there were only a very few of us left who still cared, burning with our questions unanswered: *Why the hell* were the rock fans *just sighing, shrugging and heading home*?! How could they *just leave*?! What's more unstable: A crowd of rock fans watching a concert, or a crowd of rock fans *prevented* from watching a concert?

Here's the thing: They had a point. "It doesn't matter *why* it's cancelled," I was told. "It's cancelled." Trying to figure out the reasons behind it was fruitless; put that energy into your music, and you might just come up with something that works for you. Or, go the zen route.

"You have to go slowly," said Zhang Fan. "And you have to go around, not straight through. Straight through is a lost cause ... It's all about finding a way to not be *over*," he added, emphasizing the most important words by using English, "and to *keep going*." "Over" is something that Zhang Fan sees as a sword ever-hovering just above yaogun's proverbial neckline; "they" can make you "over" if things get out of hand. "It's really difficult. If you think our leaders are saying ridiculous things, you can't just get up at a festival and yell about how they're jackasses," he adds. "Everyone knows they're jackasses. You can be mad, but, what can you do?"

You could sing out your complaints. Which was fine, basically, until you'd like to release an album, when you'd have to send your lyrics in for inspection, and more often than not, cultural authorities tend not to see the poetry, and then bye-bye big stages. A band like Ordnance, for example, had played all kinds of sensitive material at Midi and other festivals around the country and it was never a problem. But the moment they put the words down on paper and passed the paper on – and they couldn't have been ignorant of the consequences when they did it – things changed.

But there is more language at work than the carefully-chosen words sent upward to officialdom, or inward to soothe the post-cancellation blues. "Festivals say things like 'we use the language of Woodstock'," complains critic Xiao Yu. "There is tons of copying going on. They say things like 'we'll have tons of people at the festival, so we'll need an electro stage, a small stage and all that.' Well, who told you that this is the way you have to do things?" He points to a 2009 festival just outside of Qingdao as emblematic of the problems at work. "They lost money . . . The organizers were great. On the one hand, they were after a kind of utopia vibe; on the other, they said 'We're doing a music festival, so we gotta have an electronic music stage, we gotta have sponsors and we gotta have government support.' Trying to put these things together, it's absurd."

Likewise, for the bands: "Which bands are going to say they won't play at these festivals? Who's going to say 'I don't want to work with the government or commercial interests?' " asks filmmaker Sheng Zhimin. "You realize that people still want to be rock stars."

Considering the pace with which each festival's scope expands, there seem to be endless opportunities for achieving, at least for a moment, rock star status. It seems that an event ain't a festival unless it has stages of at least three types. In 2005, the four-day-long Midi Festival added a second, "experimental" stage to its festivities (headed up by critic and experimental musician Yan Jun). The next year, it added two more: a second "rock" stage and a dance music stage. In 2007 came a fifth, hip-hop, stage. Beijing's Strawberry Festival 2010 had six stages. This type of thinking big comes at a price; rarely is there a discussion of whether or not there is enough content to justify adding genre-specific stages. Additionally, performers at these festivals, wherever they are held, tend to stay the same. "Aside from Cui Jian," said radio DJ Zhang Youdai, "there are very few bands that can play for an extended period of time . . . and [there is] a shortage of qualified technicians and gear."

In 2011, gear is not a problem, but arguably a lack of a large number of technicians continues to pose an issue. There are a few more festival-worthy acts, but not as many as one might think. There is a big difference between *experienced* festival bands and *good* festival bands. Because prime time was ready before the bands were. Stages (ok, *a* stage) on a scale not unfamiliar to any festival-goer in the West have been regularly hosting bands since Midi went big, in the first few years of the twenty-first century, when attendance went from a few hundred into the thousands and past the ten-k barrier. But the kings of those stages change infrequently, even among different festivals. What is interesting is that many caught up in the rock scene have long spoken of how China doesn't have its own U2; a band that can attract at least as many people as Cui has, or more, and make the crossover into the mainstream. "If bands like that existed," said Zhang Fan, who has been inviting many of the bands at his festival back year after year since the early days, "they could play Midi every year."

One wonders what, if any, major festival on the global map invites the same artists year in and year out, particularly those that appear in the "headlining" slots. (Though the concept of "headlining" is not necessarily the same in China as abroad). Or why it is that there seems to be some sort of seniority situation at work. The old-school headliners wind up being a necessary part of the festival's identity, even as these artists start to wonder whether or not the gig is worth doing. "We could do it," the singer of a band long scheduled for Midi's 2010 festival told me prior to the festival, "but what's the point?" Presumably, if there were more bands *fit* to headline, this might change the overall situation for festivals around the country. Audiences would be attracted by the acts rather than the prospect of a nice day out, and the cycle could benefit from a boost of energy.

"It's like how it is with everything else," said filmmaker Sheng Zhimin, a man who has witnessed and participated in yaogun's journey. "Yaogun has no history, and suddenly, we have everything. It wasn't an evolution . . . There's been lots of exterior changes – festivals, live venues . . . But all of these are fake . . . Rock has become a kind of cool."

If yaogun itself is a foreign concept that has scarcely had three decades to develop, the idea of a music festival is one not familiar – despite its ubiquity – to the bulk of the population. The Midi Festival tends to be a model for events nationwide and the measuring stick for the general health of the nation's festival – and, by extension, its rock – scene. And there are a lot of ways it resembles its overseas counterparts. It is full days of rock bands rather than a gathering of a handful of big-name acts; it attracts fans, bands and artisans from around the country; it is held outdoors, in a park; and has attracted a growing number of international acts of varying degrees of fame.

"In China, cultural events of any kind are rare," observes Liu Chang, a Midi School graduate who has worked on the Midi Festival since 2007. "People go to restaurants – they don't even really go to bars . . . The concept of any event like that is blurred. Most people who go to the festivals probably have no knowledge of the music or any band. To them it's a simple gathering."

Lü Bo, the man behind Scream Records and booster of metal and punk in particular, offered words of wisdom to Hong Kong newspaper the *Standard* after 2006's Midi Festival, saying that we might want to hold off on the celebrations just yet. "I wouldn't regard sixty thousand people attending Midi as a symbol of rock's success. When we get sixty thousand seeing a single Chinese band, then we can say rock has made it."

He Yong of Magic Stone's Three Prominents, after performing at 2010's Midi Festival, said yaogun can't rely on festivals to grow. He believes that they are only a part of a puzzle that includes media, industry and infrastructure: "If you don't work really hard at it, fewer and fewer people are going to come. Why do people go to festivals in the first place? The important reason to go would be to see someone in particular." That, on the whole, people aren't going for anyone in particular is a worrisome sign.

Filmmaker Sheng Zhimin agrees. "The fact that a lot of people are going to the Midi or Strawberry festivals, it doesn't represent strength or the popularity of rock," he said. "Actually, it might represent the opposite."

Many argue that a major factor holding things back is that the live scene isn't preparing local bands for the kind of large-scale event in which so many want to – and with relative ease *can* – participate. The more festivals that occur, the more opportunities there are for the increasing number of bands; the more bands there are, the more bands each festival hosts; the more festival stages on which each band performs, the more experience they gather, and – whether or not there is any improvement – the more experience they gather, the more apt they are to be invited to the next event. Thus, the festival scene becomes a sort of freaky factory, secure in their never-ending supply of raw materials, ever cranking out product, but somehow skipping the quality control stage.

Currently there are a growing number of festivals being put together for the first time, and inexperience is only part of the problem. As festival veteran Patrick Deng put it, these first-timers see the events as promotional, "so why would they need to do them more than once?" What this creates is a great situation for mediocre bands and residents of cities around the country – the former are eager, abundant and available to perform, while the latter are easy to please and generally indifferent to what's on stage. That China would need a healthy or flourishing festival *scene*, as opposed to a couple of beacons to light the way until there was enough content, interest, qualified staff, sponsorship, etc. goes unquestioned.

Radio DJ Zhang Youdai points out an important piece of the puzzle. "The more international acts that pass through, the more local bands will realize how far they need to go," he said. Of course, these days, international acts are an almost-daily occurrence in the major rock cities on the map, but most are not models for the festival stage. "Chinese bands have never seen a show. When I went out of the country and I saw shows, I realized how important this is."

It's not all bad news. Guo Chuanlin of Black Panther produced the Ice and Snow Festival, a series of weekend concerts at Beijing's Olympic Park in the first two months of 2010. The Midi Music Festival celebrated its twelfth year in 2011 and Modern Sky's eponymous festival has been annual since 2007, its Strawberry event since 2009 – and both brands have taken their shows to other cities. Zebra Festival began in Chengdu and has expansion plans because of a large amount of international attention and headlining pop acts. Meanwhile, festival programs, though occasionally decimated with last-minute changes, have been opening up to artists including Public Enemy, Nine Inch Nails, Avril Lavigne, Mr Big, Yeah Yeah Yeahs and more. Previously and with few exceptions, international artists came through embassy partnerships that saw mainly acts of little fame take to festival stages; bigger acts are starting to pass through with more regularity.

Which is not to say that the presence of international artists in and of itself is proof that the festival scene is ready for prime time. Certainly, though, artists of a certain level tend to stay away from engagements until conditions are worthy of their status – not to mention technically prepared to handle them. And the ability and desire of a festival to pony up for big names – both domestic and international – represents something significant about the festival in the context of the international scene. And, particularly in Midi's case, this means that things have come a long way. In 2009, Cui Jian made the trek to Zhenjiang for the relocated Midi Festival while 2010 saw performances from Tang Dynasty and He Yong, two artists whose combined audiences dwarfed even the most popular of the current crop of 'gunners. With the festival now the "next big thing," the country is lousy with folks looking to cash in. Festivals are adding Taiwanese and Hong Kong stars to beef up lineups and draw pop fans, signaling a new commitment, ability, and desire to bring in names with mass appeal. The more players in the festival game, the worse the overall batting average, and the more likely audiences and artists will be turned off the idea of shelling out money for – or showing up to play at – the next Big Event.

Writing Toward Normal

As the musical offerings of the nineties bloomed, so, too, did the infrastructure surrounding it. Publications appeared offering a new generation a chance to fill the shoes left by the first generation of critics. When "underground," "punk" and "alternative" were all exciting new philosophies with fascinating possibilities for bands, the critics of the nation were linked by Yan Jun's publication of *Sub Jam: Spring of New Music '98*, a collection of music writing from around the country – from authors including Shanghai's Sun Mengjin and Beijing's Hao Fang. It collected writings on local bands and scenes, introducing bands that would go on to be important to the story of yaogun into the new millennium and beyond, and bringing critics into the fold as well. While there was a growing number of venues in which to write critically about rock, one must keep in mind Hao Fang's observation that *Radiant Nirvana* wouldn't have had the same effect if rock was a normal thing. If rock was a normal thing, there would have been more than a handful of *yaogun* books in Chinese.

In 2007, critic and blogger Wang Xiaofeng wrote that a dozen years of searching netted him ten books on the subject; "and only one" – Hao Fang's *Wild Blooming of Wounded Flowers* – "that took my breath away."

Nobody is more aware of this than Hao Fang, and not for egotistical reasons. When a friend came up from Hong Kong and asked Hao to take him to a shop to find books on rock, they only found books that Hao had written or helped get published. "He thought I was amazing because I was involved in all of this. I think it's funny," said Hao, but it's obvious he doesn't find it ha-ha funny. Like Cui Jian, Hao is eternally uncomfortable with his rockstar status – and they both are rockstars, even if only one of them performs.

"Music writers my age, including myself, shouldn't be writing," Hao said, adding that it's necessary – not to mention past due – to "bring up the next batch of writers to do it better than us." It was this philosophy that guided his tenure running the Chinese *Rolling Stone* for the first year and a half of its existence, and the results have disappointed him. "The books written recently aren't inspiring kids to play rock . . . I want kids to read . . . and be inspired to play."

"Lua" Zhou Xingyue could be considered one of Hao's disciples, working under him at *Rolling Stone* as what she calls a "rock journalist." She's changed her opinion of rock critics over the years, having gone from idolizing their words to sending them assignments. "We have very famous critics, but they don't understand music making," she said. "There are very few Chinese critics I can read."

In 2003, Shanghai critic Sun Mengjin wrote a State of the Yaogun. Inspired by witnessing the racist slurs and projectiles hurled toward 2003's Midi Festival stage when Japanese band Brahman was to begin their set, Sun called for immediate introspection. Yaogun, he believed, needed to figure out where it was going. In the article, "Yaogun's Mess," he pointed out the space between the mainstream and the underground and the need to bridge it. One way to do so, he argued, was to make more room for pop-flavored rock. "Ordinary people," he wrote, "start listening from pop rock." Point being that we want more people listening, and one way to do that was to make nicer melodies – a task that he said most rockers weren't up to. It's a simplistic answer to a large problem, and it's only one of many items that need work, but it's as good a place as any to start. Because yaogun's mess might be tied to the idea of underground: That it's not supposed to be accessible. Poppy bands are frowned upon as not rock enough.

Tai Ran fronts one of Chengdu's longest-running bands, Ashura. He has been dogged for over a decade about how his band is too pop for rock. "But that's wrong. Rock is doing what you want, so we're definitely rock. People say rock is an attitude. I know people . . . that aren't related at all to music, and they're really rock."

There are many young bands playing great pop rock in the clubs of the nation while older artists seem to be moving in that direction: XTX, Second Hand Rose, Ruins and more have been mainstreaming their sounds – while garnering larger audiences along the way. These bigger audiences can only help yaogun on the whole.

The real question that needed attacking, particularly for Sun, was whether or not yaogun *wanted* to increase its ranks. For Sun, it was a given that yaogun should welcome the outside world. It's not clear that others see it that way.

Like Sun, Hao Fang is all about expanding the flock, and expresses concern over the rock magazines that have, since the late nineties, emerge and spread through the landscape. "If I didn't like rock, I'd look at [rock] magazines and think all people related to rock were crazy." The question is what ought to be the mission of a rock mag. For Hao, it's obvious: They exist to bring people in from the outside, and if they don't appeal to the outside, yaogun will remain isolated. Evidently, magazine makers disagree.

Tongsu Gequ (*X Music Magazine* in English; the Chinese trans-lates as "*Pop Songs*") and *Wo Ai Yaogunyue* (*So Rock!* or literally "*I Love Rock and Roll*") both chose the relative safety of Shijia-zhuang, a small city of just under ten million located an hour's high-speed train-ride southwest of Beijing – close enough to the heart of yaogun and far enough from the not-too-long arm of the law. Both magazines include CDs with their publication. *X Music* took on editor Chen Peili around 2000, when the then-thirty-seven-year-old took the magazine in the rock direction. "There's not a lot of competition" between the two magazines, said Chen, while recognizing there is a limited number of poten-tial readers. "It isn't any magazine in particular that's really our competitor, it's the internet in general."

Zhao Liang, an editor at *So Rock!* agreed. "There's so much information out there," he said. "People don't need us as much." Thus, *So Rock!*'s outlook changed. Realizing they "couldn't be *Rolling Stone*," they cut their musical content down to below half of the magazine. These days, they thrive on attitude: "We call ourselves an 'unprofessional entertainment magazine'," he told me. "Our style is to introduce music and make rock an attitude and energy." For better, or worse.

They may have begun with the desire to promote Chinese bands, but that no longer seems at the top of their list. "Nobody will come to like rock through reading *So Rock!*," said Hao Fang, and it seems to me that the magazine would take that as a com-pliment.

"Our attitude changed," said *So Rock!*'s Zhao. "We used to pay attention to music. Now we want to look at society . . . Our view of society influences our view of music . . . Everyone's out-look has matured and expanded."

"Matured" might not be the first word that comes to mind in discussions of *So Rock!*. In a 2009 issue, a new editor wrote of her devotion to "following *So Rock*'s great road to bathroom reading." A sampling of covers from over the years reveals the following: "Jesus Loves You," said one 2005 headline atop a large photo of a Christ action figure, below which continued the thought: "But I think you're a cunt." "Hey Jude/Don't . . . Give a Fuck," said another from 2008, atop a picture of an infant flipping the camera the bird.

But the magazine is known for its biting, opinionating reviews and social critique, and its *Mad* Magazine-style gutter humor belies its bite. June 2009's issue, twenty years from 1989, you'll note, featured the familiar image of Edvard Munch's "The Scream" with an x-marked patch over the screamer's mouth on the front cover. On the back was the phrase "Never mind the machine here's the *So Rock!*" in cut-and-paste ransom-note homage to the Sex Pistols atop a photo of a shirt that said, in Chinese, "So you've got a tank?" Inside that issue, articles on Pete Seeger; the American Civil Rights movement; and, most daringly, a reprinting of famed Chinese writer Lu Xun's (1881-1936) essay "In Memory of Miss Liu Hezhen," about the government-sanctioned killing of several dozen protesters in 1926.

The reality of the situation is somewhere short of Revolution. The magazine is Fighting the Power, and not doing so without, on some level, making the authorities aware. But because of the magazine's limited influence, they are given some leeway to operate. Much like the case with so much policing the world over, until the authorities are given a reason to crack down, which would most often come in the form of a direct complaint, things remain status quo. "Nobody is looking to bust [these magazines]," one observer commented.

What's interesting is where Zhao Liang of *So Rock!* and Hao Fang meet. Both are convinced of the need to bring yaogun's artists down to earth. When rock started, said Hao, its practitioners were already placed on a pedestal because of the weight of the cultural mission. "Maybe it started at too high a place," he said. "In the past, Mao was a god . . . people said 'how could you make him out to be a normal person?' Rock is the same. We need to see it for what it is. We need to pull it down, put it in a more mainstream position, judge it and understand it."

"We used to make bands into heroes," said *So Rock!*'s Zhao, who added that all too often, writers "*chui niubi,*" which isn't literally to say that they were "blowing cow's vagina," but that they were eager to make folks sound more amazing than they were. Which is a natural thing for a rock music magazine to do in order to justify – to say nothing of make attractive – one's existence. But lately, things have been different. "More and more of our content is negative. We used to think about how much great stuff there was. Now we focus on what's wrong." Like Hao, Zhao and his colleagues went through some soul searching over the course of their rock and roll ride. "We used to look at rock from a utopian perspective, that it was the most effective way to change the world," he said, but that's where the similarities with his elders' ends. "But now, looking at domestic rock, I wouldn't say that we've lost hope, because I don't think we put a lot of hope in it."

Hao Fang, though, put a lot of hope in rock, and like others who have similar investments in and dreams for the music, he's not alone in his disappointment in the current generation. What links most critics who have been watching yaogun for more than five years is their conclusion about the current state of affairs. It's not that they're unhappy with how things are, it's that they're disappointed. It is the feeling of seeing something you've devoted your life to regress in the hands of those charged with continuing the legacy. Of recent years, one Chinese critic said:

> I go to a show, and these guys stand on stage for five minutes and they think they're foreigners. I come to see a show, not to study a foreign language. I don't want to see a band that's trying to get overseas. Are they [Chinese] bands? They could be from anywhere.

Through Round Eyes

According to the ancient logic, anyone from outside of China was, by definition, inferior, backward, barbaric, completely uncultured (it was called the Middle Kingdom – i.e. the Center of It All – for a reason). As a product of foreign soil, then, rock music's reputation preceded it. Recall Radio DJ Zhang Youdai's meeting with a central official who heard that rock music had brought down the Soviet empire; combine that with Ronald Reagan's virulent anti-Communist message, and you can see why, at the highest reaches of authority, there might be a palpable worry that this import would threaten the stability of Chinese society. Rock's rebellious reputation in China was at least in part due to its Western roots.

But in the eighties, as we have seen, there was a new interest in the outside world that had been anathema to Chinese culture for so long. Along with Japanese pop music, European philosophy and the English language, rock music began to attract a segment of the population. And, despite the risks and logistical difficulties of international relationships, foreigners were never far from the action. From the age of rock parties, foreigners were a significant presence, something that continues to this day in rock venues across the country. Particularly in the early days of the party scene, foreigners could get away with things that locals couldn't.

One major reason that the foreign community in Beijing was, and remains, important to the rock scene is cold, hard cash. "At the time, most of the people that would pay to get in [parties] were foreigners," recalled party promoter and filmmaker Sheng Zhimin, who used to charge the equivalent of around $5 for entry into his events in the early nineties. "It wasn't so cheap for Chinese people. And you know, friends of the band, or our friends, they wouldn't pay. And we needed money to pay for the gear, pay the bands." Sheng remembers the key to an event's success was figuring out how to get into the foreign students' dorms or apartment complexes, off-limits to Chinese, to put up flyers. "We'd figure out a way to get in, which was usually finding a foreigner willing to bring us in, and we'd put photocopied flyers on as many doors as we could until security grabbed us and kicked us out."

So-called "expat rags" – the in-country version of entertainment guides known around the world – emerged naturally as foreign populations increased. Their events listings, reviews, features and classifieds proved not only lifelines to the growing number of non-local locals but also boon to the party planners like Sheng, who no longer needed to go right to the doorsteps of their most spendy audience members. The English-language entertainment guide phenomenon across the country has snowballed, with blogs gone big and paper-and-ink mags celebrating decade-plus anniversaries.

In addition to the diplomats and journalists that first arrived after China's opening – and tended to be met with official suspicion that made forming relationships difficult – the first main points of entry for foreigners in China were universities. One might imagine a Western student arriving in the Middle Kingdom in the early eighties, armed with little more than a few cassettes and a Walkman, quickly becoming king of the world. Marco Polo could only take notes and hope to bring what he learned in China back home; our student had the chance to repay the favor by enlightening young Chinese with his collection. Ditto in the nineties when, armed with a little bit of knowledge, one could help guide a new generation through the piles of *dakou* tapes and CDs. "I'm certainly personally responsible for some peoples' bad tastes in music," admits German Udo Hoffmann, who moved to China from Germany in 1989. "Since the beginning, it was unavoidable that the tastes of foreigners coming into China got through."

Coloring any cross-cultural meeting was, recalled Graham Earnshaw, "a sense of how uncomfortable the authorities were with any kind of cross-pollination." And that discomfort was also felt among average folks, not generally eager to test the limits. Earnshaw and his bandmates in the Peking All-Stars helped to test those limits, performing in a variety of locales. These rare shows were essential to the development of a scene: Listening to tapes is one thing, but the live experience is something altogether different, especially in the first years of the eighties.

Certainly the authorities' fears jibed with reality, in a way: Earnshaw is quick to admit that there was evangelism at work with the All-Stars. "We were aware of the fact that we were the only people doing this. We believed that this music was powerful, and feel-good music, and we wanted to spread the word." They planned events that they believed would attract the most Chinese audience as possible, because up until the mid-eighties, the rock scene was almost entirely centered around the foreign community.

The Beijing Underground was another significant member of the then-percolating scene, comprised of an international group of expats performing covers and originals, who even put out a cassette. An Associated Press look back at international music news of 1986 mentioned that "rock music cracked China's cultural wall," citing the Beijing Underground's – rechristened the Mainland Band – tour of south China, which, the report said, was sponsored by the government. Reaching out far beyond the foreign community, their efforts directly led to a growing interest in and awareness of rock music. ADO would grow out of that band, and go on to back Cui Jian before its members created names for themselves – guitarist Eddie Luc Lalasoa Randriamampionina plays alongside Cui to this day. The members of ADO were the first foreigners that large numbers of up-and-coming rockers would hear and also, more importantly, meet in the early days of the party scene.

Taking advantage of the post-Tiananmen period, in which the cultural landscape opened up, the United States Information Agency (USIA) sponsored the visit of guitarist Vic Trigger in November of 1990. A lecturer at the Guitar Institute of Technology in

Hollywood, Trigger was sent to Guangzhou, Shanghai and Beijing to teach rock theory and guitar. A local host had requested, according to Reuters, "an older musical expert, preferably over fifty, who would be able to persuade the Chinese musicians to play their music a little softer," but rock won the day. A classical player at the Beijing Guitar Association told a reporter that he'd been "converted." In addition to lessons, there were tapes: Three major record companies granted Trigger unlimited access to their libraries in advance of the trip, and he left tapes in Shanghai and Guangzhou schools with the stipulation that students be allowed to listen and copy them as they saw fit. Trigger found students that were as excited about the music as they were challenged by it.

"There will be world-famous Chinese rock and roll groups," Trigger said, "but they aren't there yet."

In the mid- and late-nineties punk scene, foreign involvement certainly affected the music's direction. "I do think me and David [O'Dell] and other foreigners felt a sense of responsibility," said Anna-Sophie Loewenberg who, along with O'Dell and a handful of others, was involved in the punk scene at its genesis. "I'm sure that I'm the first foreign woman that anyone [in the punk scene] ever knew." She and O'Dell in particular had come out of punk scenes in the US, and were met with enthusiasm as their local friends found out more about the music. O'Dell writes of how he was often the only foreigner around, a situation he was alternately proud of and frustrated by – feelings not uncommon among foreigners in China throughout the ages.

Punk rocker Gao Jingxiong recalled something of a common occurrence: "One time a bunch of us were hanging out on the street. A foreigner rode by on his bike, and then we saw him turn around and come back. We talked a bit. He was American, and he gave us *Appetite for Destruction*, and then left." Not long after getting that Guns n' Roses record, Gao Wei and Gao Yang formed Underbaby.

While there was no doubt that foreigners were a boon to scene, there was also, said Hang on the Box's Wang Yue, a frustration born of patriotism. "It *is* upsetting," she said, of the foreigners' role in the scene. "We've got 1.3 billion people, how was there *nobody* doing this stuff? It makes you think: Is there something wrong with Chinese people?" The feeling, she said, looking back at her early years in the scene, is that somehow Chinese people needed the help; that without the foreign intervention, a scene wouldn't have emerged.

But there was discomfort on the other side as well, and it comes from the foreigners' simultaneous role as observer/outsider and participant. Because Loewenberg is right: It *was* her scene, too. But then again, foreigners can pack up and go home, so there will always be a divide. On the one hand, you can sympathize with those that were trying to make a difference, but you can also sympathize with a guy like Xiao Rong of Brain Failure, who felt that he was having things thrust upon him.

Members of any scene want nothing more than to see it grow and evolve, regardless of where one happens to be, or be from. But there is a feeling that it's a colonial impulse. That it comes from the same place as that smile I've felt myself and seen on the faces of other Westerners, upon catching a glimpse of yaogun. The smile that says, "Aww, isn't that just great! Chinese people interested in *our* music." The smile that says, "Sure, your album's not great, but you guys – and by 'you guys' I mean your People – are new at this and so it's pretty alright for a start." It's a feeling that comes from thinking not in terms of "Good" but, rather, in terms of "Good for China," in which a line like "What amazing energy they have onstage" glosses over the shortcomings of a band still finding its sound.

But foreigners don't only play a role in judgment. "China hasn't come up with a real rock culture. It's a phenomenon," said Cui Jian, adding that there are only a "few" small clubs in a "few" big cities. "Does China really have the basic rock culture foundations? I don't think so. If there weren't any foreigners in these cities, there couldn't be these clubs." It's hard to know if he's grateful or embarrassed by this situation.

Certainly Cui's own music was influenced by foreigners and though he was the first 'gunner to play with foreign musicians and learn from their legacy, he was far from the last. Endless numbers of yaogun bands either contained or were influenced by foreign musicians, while the distance between all-foreign and all-local circles closed over the years.

Yaogun Meets World

If conditions for yaogun were created by the combination of local and foreign forces, then meeting of East and West – though not the be-all and end-all – must be an important part of yaogun's struggle for meaning. If we live in a world that is connected, yaogun should see the world and the world should see yaogun.

The first time that the world saw yaogun, in 1982, it's questionable whether or not it was witnessing actual yaogun. French producer Marc Boulet had built up a small collection of recordings from the fringes of the rock and roll world when he came to China to cover Jean Michel Jarre's 1981 tour. Friends in Hong Kong told him about a band called the Dragons, who boasted a back story featuring work camps and daring escapes. Boulet rushed to nearby Guangzhou (aka Canton) to record them. Though yaogun came from and was centered in Beijing, Guangzhou's proximity to Hong Kong granted its residents access impossible elsewhere via the radio and television waves. It was plausible that Guangzhou birthed the Dragons.

When *Billboard* announced the release of a "clandestine album" from "what may be the Republic of China's [sic] first punk rock group," there was, to be sure, disbelief. But the disbelief was rooted in the odds against which the band emerged, not over whether or not they had actually emerged. That there is debate over their existence is not strange in the world of yaogun, where so much information goes unchecked, unquestioned and unknown. Xiao Dao, who runs two Guangzhou venues and spent much of the past two decades in the local scene, knew of the Dragons, but not of the debate over their roots. He assumed they were the real deal.

Within the small, international and tight-knit punk community there was little debate upon the release of the Dragon's album *Parfums de la Revolution*. At the time, nobody seemed to believe the record was made in China; word had gone around that it was a prank. Except, that is, Boulet, who assured me, via e-mail, that "The information contained [in *Billboard*] is detailed and accurate." Boulet's relationship to China is beyond reproach. He spent many years there, authoring several books on the subject. Yet more evidence suggests that the Dragons were either France-based Chinese expats or just plain-old Frenchmen than Guangzhou-based punks.

If forming before you master your instruments makes a band the embodiment of rock, where does one file the "classically trained" Dragons and the racket they made with vocal chords, guitar, drum and *erhu* (two-stringed Chinese violin)? Cui Jian, the yaogunner most ahead of the curve, had just discovered Kenny Rogers; these guys were jamming to Johnny Rotten. The first signal that something might be, well, rotten, is that neither the term "punk" – which did describe how early 'gunners were living – nor the genre were widely, or even narrowly, known in rock circles until the nineties.

There is magic in music that is both amazing and awful; confronted with the Dragons on record, you don't know whether you ought to wash out your ears or root for the veracity of their story. Their versions of the Rolling Stones' "Get Off of My Cloud" and the Sex Pistols' "Anarchy in the UK" are Exhibits A through Z in the trial against singing – using the term loosely – in a non-native language. Their take on "Anarchy" was "the most anarchic version yet," wrote critic Robert Christgau – which might be fitting, but might just be plain bad. Boulet said that while he never met the man behind the Pistols, he was told that Malcolm McLaren "wept with emotion" upon hearing the Dragons "destroy" the tune.

It's hard to figure out why Boulet would continue to insist that the Dragons were a full-fledged Chinese punk band despite the evidence to the contrary. He'd won the battle, showing the media, both underground and mainstream, for the over-eager malleable institution it was. He'd punked 'em. Who was he trying to punk now?

Coverage of the band showed that the world was eager for stories from the Other Side that showed rock as an outlet for protest. Though the album was not a commercial success, it was successful in a different way. It helped pave the way for yaogun's encounter with the West. Exaggeration, factual errors and shoddy reporting are still abound in the coverage of yaogun, but that's not the lesson here. The point is that the world was ready for yaogun. Now it was up to yaogun to get ready for the world.

There have been many attempts at bringing, through musical rather than media channels, yaogun out of the Middle Kingdom. Cui Jian was the earliest yaogun export, performing at the Seoul Olympics in 1988, in the UK and France in early 1989 and around the world in the nineties and onto today. The Chinese Avant-Garde project took a half-dozen bands to Germany in 1993. Cobra hit legendary rock clubs CBGBs and Wetlands as well as the Michigan Womyn's Festival and elsewhere in 1996. Five years later, Cold-Blooded Animal hit Austin, Texas's South by Southwest festival, and Reflector toured the US west coast. As was the case with overseas bands performing regularly inside of China, Chinese bands regularly getting to the outside world only began in the early aughts; it's still news when a band goes out on a Japanese, European or North American tour.

Magic Stone's Landy Zhang, foreseeing the problem that still plagues yaogun bands trying to make an overseas impression, suggested to Cui that he try and find his own description for the music he was playing. "Once you call it 'Knife Songs'," he told Cui, referring to the song and Cui's belief that Chinese rock was "Like a Knife," "you and the West are no longer hooked. And when you perform in the US, they won't introduce you as the rock and roll band from China . . . It would be something that belongs to the Chinese." In an interesting twist, Cui Jian's music has wound up being just that: Something that belongs – and is of interest – almost exclusively to the Chinese. "In the big American venues," Cui told me in 2005, "it felt like we hadn't even left China . . . There are more foreigners at our shows in smaller Chinese cities than there are overseas."

Nonetheless, Cui, who has gotten flack for having foreigners on his management team, said that overseas tours have always been part of the plan. "We've always been thinking about overseas and think it's very important."

Cui is not the only one looking abroad, and more and more 'gunners are setting their sites beyond their homeland. The key though, is what kind of impression they are making. "It's great to have a chance to play overseas," said Su Yang of Catcher in the Rye. "But there's no real significance . . . If you're singing in English, it's bad English, the audiences don't understand. If you're singing in Chinese, they can't understand." Of course, as we've seen and will see again, *what* is being sung isn't always as important as the fact *something* is being sung, since there are all kinds of ideas projected upon and gleaned from the performers.

In ancient times, when reporters were first let in to Deng Xiaoping's China, there were many enticing stories to be had on the subject of Western culture for those in search of "news of the weird": spiritual pollution eradication campaigns that threatened pop music; the Chinese fascination with disco; AV exhibitions selling recordings priced in the weeks-of-salary; senior citizens ballroom dancing in public. When dudes grew their hair long and ostracized themselves from society in the name of rock music, there was more to write: Rock in China! It was, at the time, both a legitimate societal investigation and a back-page novelty story. When yaogun and the Beijing Spring coalesced, another rash of reportage followed.

But with rare exceptions, yaogun coverage into the late nineties and arguably through to the present, never strayed from the model forged in the spring of 1989. Facing the oncoming tanks, Chinese rockers rise up to face the turrets with guitars. This is where rock and roll's political wing guided the editorial direction of the casual China watcher. While reporters saw music for change, 'gunners were often playing for chicks.

In the documentary *Beijing Punk*, we see hardcore punk band Demerit's Li Yang, drunkenly staring at the off-screen filmmaker from whence this statement comes: "You guys are fucking crazy, you're doing punk music in communist China and you could get shot by the government."

We could stop there and deconstruct that sentiment, but let us, instead, allow Li Yang to respond: "We have beer."

The international attention upon – or, possibly more accurately, the attraction to – yaogun, is simply an extension of the general interest in the particular way in which Western phenomena enter the Chinese context. Though there are now more people covering it and many more outlets from which to do so, what is important to remember is that it's nothing new. The amount of actual yaogun that has been performed overseas is new, but what's interesting is to what extent yaogun's reception abroad is colored by the legacy of its international coverage. Having witnessed more than a few meet-the-press engagements inside and outside of China – not to mention having been the one being met on many occasions – I can attest to the depths to which this legacy irks 'gunners. What one finds, with only rare exceptions, is reporters eager to talk to 'gunners but interested only in the non-musical aspects of their interviewees. This is unsurprising given that the bands are known less for their music than for their citizenship, and they are of more interest to the general reporter than the music reporter. How this plays out in overseas concerts is simultaneously interesting, sad and inspiring.

In 2004, I went along for the ride on the China Music Lab tour of France, which showcased industrial rock group Tongue, electro-dub artist Wang Lei and Kazakh-folk group Iz at clubs and festivals around the country. At the tour's first stop, Rennes, an audience member responded to Tongue's music by screaming "Jackie Chan!" There are jackasses everywhere, and surely not even this one thought that there was a direct correlation between the band and the movie star, but the point remains that an overseas audience approaches a Chinese rock band differently because they will always be Chinese first and rock band second.

"Chinese musicians in the overseas media will never be musicians," said Brain Failure's Xiao Rong, switching to English for emphasis. "They're *objects of the underground.*"

In anticipation of their first US tour, Hang on the Box's Shen Jing expressed that very sentiment to the *San Francisco Chronicle*: "I just hope that we can leave people with the feeling that we are a great band not because we are Chinese or because we are women but just because you can enjoy our music."

In Scandinavia in 2005 and 2006, on the road with garage-punk band Subs, just as in France in 2004, I witnessed good yaogun's potential for taking sheer curiosity and transforming it into a fandom that takes the "China" out of the rock. In short, yaogun is like anything else done well: First, it attracts you, and then it wins you over.

Generally, the first stage of this process involved disbelief that there was rock music in China, which created a curiosity to see just what it was that a Chinese rock band might *look* like. Because folk bands just *seem* more Chinese, if not in look – Beijing-based Mongolian folk act Hanggai, who has toured extensively in Europe and the Americas, often performs in traditional Mongolian costumes – than in sound, with traditional instruments being more obvious signposts. But with few exceptions, yaogun bands don't *look* like one might imagine a Chinese band would look.

"Hanggai is good for people that want to see China. When people see Subs, they might think they were tricked; they're not a China band," said Xiao Rong, whose band Brain Failure has made repeated North American tours over the past near-decade. "Tricked" doesn't best describe the reaction of audiences to Brain Failure, he said, and it certainly didn't describe the reaction to Subs' overseas shows in my own experiences.

There was something amazing about observing the slow physical transformation that accompanies the audience's mental transformation over the course of a Subs set's first few songs. By the time Kang Mao has screamed her way through the first song, the crowd generally wears the kind of smile you might see on a mother's face when her child gets through a piano recital performance without any glaring errors. The smile that says, "Wow! How cool is *this*!" When they realize that Subs is serious – that is, when they focus on the distorted heavy punkish rock music that the band is playing and get past the pidgin English with which Kang might speak to the crowd and the grin on at least the bassist's face, who is quite clearly pleased to be on the stage more so than a band this serious ought to be – their smiles change to grimaces, but grimaces that imply that they are *listening*; that they are *hearing*; that they are *digging*. These are, after all, audiences of people generally disposed toward rock music, so it's not as if the band needs to win over the enemy. But the transformation is clear.

"We felt that the audience, when they were jumping around . . . they didn't see us as Chinese, or Japanese or whatever," Subs' Kang Mao said after a European tour. "They saw us as a punk band. And even more, they liked us. That made us happy."

There is a flipside to all that, though, and it is something that every yaogun act with even the slightest aspirations of visiting the rest of the rock and roll world must face. In the lead-up to Subs' first European tour, we discussed the promotional language. They knew that their first time out they were going to be

"CHINA subs." Eventually, they could be "CHINA SUBS." Then, after that, they could be just plain "Subs."

"Why must we say we are MADE IN CHINA?" read the band's 2006 tour poster. The band knew the answer, but they didn't like it.

6

WHAT A LONG, STRANGE MARCH IT'S BEEN

Yaogun changed you and me.
China changed rock and roll

SMZB "GO! CHINA! GO!"

Rock Star Over China

Over yaogun, there hangs a question, unanswered and often-times unasked: What lies at the end of the tunnel? In the standard rock and roll narrative, the dude (as we know, more often than not it is a dude) picks up the guitar with visions of fame, fortune and conquests of a regular sexual nature. But in a country where playing rock doesn't get you arrested anymore, what kind of fame and fortune could possibly come from the yaogun effort? Sometimes, there are also visions of doing something, of making a difference, but lately this hasn't been high on the rock and roll to-do list anywhere, let alone in China. And as for a difference, well, it's been a long time since there was "Nothing," and in these days of not just Everything, but Everything Always, it's not so much that nobody's speaking – there are, in fact, too many voices. The problem is that nobody seems to be interested in hearing. Whether or not either fame or change occurs with any regularity is beside the point. What's important is whether or not these are the goals. Because if they're not, why rock – and, further, why care?

In the yaogun context, simply surviving is the goal: I rock, therefore I rock. Every 'gunner worth their salt knows deep in his bones that the rock star life is no different from the pop star life, the cult of celebrity being a special thing in China. Inherent in the idea of the Star is something that, for the most part, precludes the rock and roll fantasy: official recognition, which marks the end of all things rock. Particularly in China, where "official" has a particular (some would say, and not necessarily be right or wrong, *political*) meaning, this is far from the goal of most 'gunners. But it happens.

"There is such pressure to sell out," said former journalist Graham Earnshaw. "The Party's success in buying people out has had significant impact on the growth of rock." Disco was co-opted; in 1991, Party classics (not that party; the big-"P," Communist Party) used the best of Boney M to spread the word using disco beats in *Red Sun*. But yaogun, certainly at the club and festival level, never quite got co-opted in that way, existing in something of a no-man's land, where it wasn't either allowed or banned outright. Those rockers that did break through to the mainstream, save one, did so by pretty much handing in their membership cards.

If one could be lifted from the pseudo-underground status of yaogun up to a height worthy of Famous, little would distinguish one from the latest traditional pop star. It's not surprising that it's the first generation bands that have broken through. They started in an era where there were few competing voices and a newly discovered hunger for what they were producing, launching them into the limelight from day one. They were, generally, not only trained as musicians but spent their lives around musicians, being, as they were, descended from performers who lived amongst their colleagues. These artists may have been absent from the spotlight for any number of years, but their place was held until they were ready to return. Their fans, along for the nation's transformational ride, were the early beneficiaries of a system that created new freedom and wealth, and, like ageing early rock stars everywhere, it is their fans that have the spending power to keep them atop the country's charts and stages. Many of them continue to produce – if they continue to produce – the kind of music that lends itself to mainstream success. As opposed, that is, to the yaogun world, in which melody, associated as it is with pop, is something that often tends to be avoided at all costs.

As is the idea of "Famous." In the mainstream Chinese context, fame is completely anathema to yaogun. A person well known in yaogun circles is not Famous; it's the break into the mainstream that bestows that kind of title, and at that point the yaogun ends. Given what lies ahead for those who break through, it's little wonder few have chosen to go on to the next level. Media coverage and experiences would be familiar to the *Seventeen* or *Cosmo* crowd rather than that of the original *Rolling Stone*; China's own version of the not-so-rock-anymore mag took headquarters' lead and ran with it, leading to a product geared more toward creating stars than reporting on rockers. Television is a form for which the word carnivalesque only begins to describe its madness. What this mainstream media presence represents, though, is the proverbial deal with the devil – minus all of the fun and rockin' stuff: pats-on-the-backs and jobs-well-done from the political leadership. So it's unsurprising that, on the one hand, rockers avoid it, but that, on the other hand, there are plenty who aim for it.

"I consciously try and limit my television appearances," singer Zheng Jun told a Beijing-based English magazine in 2003. "Otherwise people will think I've departed from true rock and roll." It's also clear that those who broke through from yaogun, like Zheng, who garnered popular success alongside Black Panther, would want, when speaking to yaogun ears, to sound removed from it.

And let us not forget that the mainstream has at least as much disdain for yaogun as yaogun has for it. In an interview with Andrew Jones in 1990, the *tongsu* songwriter Li Lufu checks through the list of reasons that rock is foreign, both in terms of citizenship and culture. He speaks of rock as a "way to let off steam about oppression and depression. It's like a public toilet where people can express things they otherwise couldn't express." It's something that's allowed in the West, but not in China, he said: "Rock is anti-tradition, anti-morality, anti-logic. You can hear that in the lyrics . . . Its development is not in tune with our national spirit." Thus, he concludes, is Cui Jian "only representing" an ideology. "Real rock couldn't develop in China."

Though Li was speaking in what is essentially the ancient past, there remains a large segment of the population that agrees with him. And that's what yaogun is up against. "It's not a few leaders, but billions of Chinese people," Cui Jian said in the rock-doc *Night of an Era.* "The way they think just conflicts with rock music . . . Chinese people don't appreciate the beauty of rock. Being critical is never a kind of beauty in Chinese aesthetics." Which hasn't stopped Cui, and has, in fact, made his rock more real than anyone else's.

Which all demonstrates why most believe that only once has true yaogun stardom really struck. Certainly there are rockers other than Cui who have achieved fame, but often their music is caught up in what might be more than a semantic debate among yaogunners, who are a population that, on the whole, holds, deep in the bones, a love-hate relationship with fame and an inability to reconcile it with real rock. After all, like everywhere else, fame and street-cred tend to be mutually exclusive. Many believe that bands like Black Panther and Tang Dynasty lost the right to the yaogun label a long time ago.

It's not that yaogun revolves around a single person. It's that there isn't anyone else who embodies yaogun quite like Cui Jian. Nobody has been going for as long, or has achieved the success and credibility among a range of audiences as Cui. While others make the claim of never having changed their attitude or music, it is simply not as believable when compared to Cui, who doesn't have to make that claim himself. Citizens of all stripes line up to talk about how he's stayed on the path. It is demonstrative of the state of affairs that Cui is often credited for his perseverance, because his path is unique in the enormous amount it requires.

"Why I admire him so much," said Wang Di – who, back in his pop-singing days, was in Cui's original band – to China Central Television (CCTV) in 2010, "is because there are so many things that people think are impossible to do; he doesn't just persist at them – he gets them done."

While the stardom acquired by rockers around the world often produces and enables a certain kind of freedom – reckless abandon may be more accurate – Cui's stardom seems to bring with it more pressure, both from within and without, than anything. In the late nineties one source recalled discovering Cui's disappointment in his status as a Rock Star. "He said 'I want to be a songwriter.' I said 'But you're a rock star.' He seemed to take it hard." Which is an interesting contrast to recent 'gunners, who look to Kurt Cobain without seeming to catch his own disdain for the fame thrust upon him. With Western media looking for its own version of a Chinese rock star, and a domestic media looking to make superstars out of anyone on a stage, too many young rockers believe their own press clippings and run with it. So while Cui is reluctant to acknowledge his fame, we see young bands expecting the rock star treatment, despite the impossibility of this kind of stardom occurring in China.

Cui seems to keep his perpetually-ball-capped head down. The shaky reputation that bubbles below yaogun's surface means that any misstep by the genre's most famous practitioner could result in its downfall. He may show up at club gigs, and was still playing them every so often in the first years of the twenty-first century, but his reputation exists well above the so-called underground of yaogun, and just below the level of mainstream superstar. It is a shaky line upon which he treads, and it's a walk that requires the stability of a yaogun scene that doesn't yet exist. Because while yaogun is starting to find a foothold in the mainstream, it's not quite there yet, and besides, it's not outrageous to believe that somewhere there are shadowy figures just waiting for some yaogunner to do something stupid enough to inspire a snuffing out of the entire landscape. Right now, Cui is the only one with his neck out far enough to be chopped. The amazing thing is that, despite being swiped at in the past, he continues to put it out there.

Cui spent most of the nineties unable to perform where he wanted in-country, despite no official ban (meanwhile, he played shows around the world and released three albums at home). He re-emerged in the early aughts with a "Live Vocals" anti-lip-synching campaign. Many simply viewed the campaign as a safe, not to mention completely un-rock-and-roll, way to curry official favor, but it couldn't have been about just that. Sure, grizzled Party veterans expressed shock that the People were being cheated by singers who, gasp, *didn't sing*, and took action. But why should yaogun care? For one thing, in the historic see-saw of *Tongsu v. Yaogun*, it was definitely a point for rock, and all of yaogun benefitted from being on the side of good. Another thing: It wasn't just about fake singing. It was about fakery of all kinds. In an ideal world, a pop music fan would be confronted with a new reality: "Wait a second . . . If the singing's fake, what else is fake?"

Unlike most of his fellow rockers, Cui is still devoted to the idea that "the rock stage is my battlefield." The fact that the official English-language newspaper *China Daily* printed that very sentiment shows just how far both Cui and yaogun – and, sure, while we're at it, China – have come. Yaogun's potential for fighting is important particularly in light of the fact that yaogun is, officially, slowly becoming just another kind of music. But Cui, like very few others, continues to employ the discourse of rock's potential to fight.

And that's important, because one wonders how much fight he might have in him, when "Nothing to My Name" is not only yet another song covered, first, for the 1993 television series *A Beijinger in New York*, by pop crooner Liu Huan (who would, at the Beijing Olympics' opening ceremonies, sing alongside Sarah Brightman), and then, by billions in karaoke halls from Peking to Peoria. Further, the song that changed the world is now a nearly-ten-dollar cocktail (vodka, melon liqueur, Malibu rum, pineapple juice) you can sip in Shanghai's swanky JZ jazz club. Which, to understate the case, is a long way from whence Cui – and yaogun – came.

It's hard to know if it demonstrated the distance traveled or the circle that leads things back to tongsu when, in 2009, "Nothing to My Name" was introduced to a new generation of musical consumers via China's version of *Pop Idol*, *Super Girl* (in 2009 the show's Chinese name was changed to *Happy Girls*). In much the same way that *Idol* did in the territories it conquered, *Super Girl* changed both Chinese television and pop music by putting the next generation of pop stars through a simultaneous grooming and audience-approval process. The difference between *Super Girl* and the competitions of tongsu's earliest days, when shows of this type dominated television, was the appearance that the pop-making machine was now less a top-down imposition upon the public and more of a democratic bottom-up process with phone and text-in voting. In August 2009, one of the eponymous ladies, Huang Ying, who wound up taking third place in the season's contest, took a stab at Cui's anthem.

There was something discomfiting about seeing the shiny-jacketed and mini-skirted Huang, hair done up tight and glittering, perched upon a small square platform, surrounded at a safe distance by a bevy of glow-in-the-dark heart-placard-hoisting pop fans, bathed in the light of a thousand flashing bulbs and backed by several walls' worth of what seem to be laser light shows borrowed from vintage planetaria. Everything about why yaogun doesn't belong on television was present in the two-and-a-half minutes it took for her to belt out the tune. The over-the-top acid-trip lengths to which set dressers, lighting and camera crews, producers and directors go to out-wow each previous episode; the over-produced nature of show and stars alike; the fancy camerawork hiding perhaps more than revealing. Atop the mini-stage, Huang seemed to be having a grand old time, crooning, fist-pumping and dancing like the pop star she's aiming to be; the song was less about a burden she carried preventing her from enlightenment than a stone upon which to stomp in the trip to the top – the precise kind of behavior which so confused Cui and his fellow travelers back when the song was written.

"Twenty years ago," wrote one commenter, "Cui Jian 'sang a red song yellow'," yellow being the color of the illicit, red the color of the nation and the Party; the implication being that Cui turned an official event illicit, by singing "Nothing." "Twenty years later, a Happy Girl sang a yellow song red."

Ding Taisheng, of record label Modern Sky, who was one of the judges of the competition, looks at the episode in two ways:

> On one hand, having rock songs sung on the highest-rated television show in the country has a small benefit: At the very least, it lets people know that this kind of music is this good, and this moving. But of course, no matter how well she sings it, she doesn't have the background or life experience to be able to express all of the things that the song represents. But for an entertainment program, you can't have your hopes too high.

But let us find the element in the scenario that turns it all around, and does so in the tradition of the man who penned the song in the first place; the man who is still fighting. It doesn't matter if it was the studio band, the cameraperson filming them, or the producer that knew the meaning of the English on the house-band guitarist's t-shirt. Heck, even though it'd be a slap in the face to the song's composer, it doesn't even matter if the show's house band was actually playing their instruments. What does matter is that, brief though it was, the t-shirt was shown. And what matters is what it said: "OBEY PROPAGANDA."

It's arguable that the Happy Girls stage is the biggest upon which Cui's music has, of late, been featured – for better or worse. But the biggest stage upon which Cui has stood, in the international scheme, certainly seemed to be the one he shared, albeit briefly, with the Rolling Stones.

To many, the Rolling Stones's Shanghai concert in 2006 signified something major – for the Stones, for Cui Jian, for China, for yaogun. The Stones got to strike one of the few geographical territories left that they haven't personally dominated – and one they'd had their eyes on for nearly thirty years – off the list. Surely Mick Jagger appreciated that moment when he expressed his relief that, thanks to the censoring of five Stones tunes, Chinese culture officials would "[protect] the morals of expat bankers and their girlfriends," the group he understood (correctly) would comprise the bulk of the audience. Cui was invited, last minute though it was, to sing alongside his heroes. China, and yaogun, was to see its own hero alongside the world's biggest band, bringing the rest of the nation along for the ride.

But the overall effect of the Stones' performance was less than flattering. The mostly-foreign crowd didn't exactly affirm China's place in the world of rock so much as prove that Shanghai's financial industry can afford the exorbitant amount of money it costs to let its hair down every once in a while. Rather than coming off like a confident rock star worthy of the world's stage, Cui was less outshined than out-rocked. Anyone would be intimidated finding themselves in the presence of the Rolling Stones – and the nervousness was amplified by the fact that the invitation came just two days before. When Cui joined the Stones for "Wild Horses" in Shanghai, though, the significance for yaogun wasn't exactly clear.

Emerging onto the Stones' stage strumming an acoustic guitar, Cui was met with little fanfare, as it seemed to very slowly dawn on the audience what was happening – one almost hears the collective whispers of those aforementioned girlfriends explaining to their banker boys why the dude with the ball cap is worth their attention. Strumming minimally during the opening verse, Cui's duet with Mick on the song's first chorus definitely *feels* historic. But things got away from Cui during the singing of the second verse, and they didn't improve. Even knowing how Cui swung and missed, the thought that he might've hit the third verse's "*I have my freedom*" still sends tingles along the spine. Alas, he may have messed up the lyrics, but he did announce before leaving that in this, yaogun's twentieth year, he's made a "reservation" with the band to meet back in Beijing, soon.

To label the meeting of Cui and the Stones a major landmark for Chinese rock is to misunderstand both China and yaogun. The Stones, no doubt, felt the weight of the moment, which, for them, represented their 30-odd-year journey to the Middle Kingdom. Cui felt the weight of the moment. The expat bankers felt the weight of the moment. International journalists felt the weight of the moment. But China had no idea there was a moment, much like rock critic Lester Bangs had predicted back when the Stones were first talking about China.

Of course, when Bangs asked, "What if nobody liked them?" unlike the Shanghai concert's promoters, he could scarcely have conceived of a Stones China show attended primarily by Westerners. A Chinese fan's discomfort at seeing a Westerner at the concert wrapped in a Chinese flag was, to many, something of a symbol of the whole endeavor. "It's actually tragic if you think about it: A foreign performance borrowing Chinese land, but Chinese people cannot come because of price or other issues," the 23-year-old told the *New York Times*. We are not in the territory, anymore, of yaogun. While there was something about that moment when rock royalty East and West united, there was more that was missing.

Though Cui is likely to have a long and full career in the years to come, it will be difficult to top the way that things came full circle on New Year's Eve 2010 and New Year's Day 2011 when Cui found himself turning the tables on his old orchestra.

"Comrade Cui Jian has worked very hard, and he is a good comrade," said a spokesman for the Beijing Song and Dance Ensemble (now known as the Beijing Symphony Orchestra), by whom Cui Jian was employed to play trumpet. "But since he got interested in pop music, he more and more concentrated his attention on pop music, rather than the work of the orchestra." Thus did the spokesman suggest, in 1987, that Cui think about employment elsewhere.

Twenty-three years later, Cui got to be the spokesman as he stood on a stage flanked not only by his band, but also by his former employer. Reviews of his combination of classical and yaogun were gushing, but that's neither here nor there, since rock has met classical before – though we might point out the unexpected booty-shakings of the string section that might be somewhat unprecedented. But one thing you can't argue with is that in the form of this union, after a twenty-five-year fight, if yaogun didn't win the war, it certainly made serious progress. Sticking to the war tip, Cui invoked his song "The Village Attacks the City," named for a phrase that guided Mao's revolution as it won over the countryside before liberating the urban centers and, then, the nation. Comparing rock to the village and classical music to the city, he said, "You can't underestimate the countryside, and you can't underestimate rock. Our rock population is larger than classical's. Otherwise, how could I be standing in front of an orchestra today?"

Take that, The Man.

One last thought on Cui, his place in the yaogun pantheon and his, and yaogun's, potential for the world. Twenty-five years after the release of an artist's first recording, that artist achieves eligibility for entry in the Rock and Roll Hall of Fame. If, as Cui's own website suggests, his career begins with *Rock and Roll on the New Long March* (rather than with the pop albums that preceded it), he becomes eligible in 2013 – alongside Nirvana and Fugazi, two bands not inconsequential to the yaogun landscape. No, shooting for the Rock Hall of Fame is *not* aiming too high. The Hall honors the "contributions of those who have had a significant impact on the evolution, development and perpetuation of rock and roll." Let us put aside the issues of timing, since it'll be another half decade before anyone else is eligible. There is, simply put, no other yaogun artist past or present worthy of the honor. And the only way that yaogun can be placed on equal footing with the rest of the rock world is for Cui to be placed on equal footing, because if he can't represent rock in the People's Republic, nobody can – or, more importantly, nobody *should*.

All of this talk of Cui might well be moot anyway, as the current crop of Chinese rockers and fans – and youth in general – seem to have little interest in him and in the historical perspective wherein one ought to know from whence one comes.

"We don't care much about the older generation," said Zhang Shouwang – guitarist and singer in Carsick Cars, one of the bands garnering a large amount of the late-aughts' media attention – to the *Asia Times*. "I don't really listen to their music, including Cui Jian. As new bands come, the old ones demise."

It's a flip and controversial statement, and, yes, a rock and roll one to be sure, but it is also a statement that displays a lack of understanding about what got him where he is today. And there's nothing *less* rock and roll than choosing to live in a vacuum.

Going Official

In addition to being some of the most ideal opportunities for a true engagement with the rest of the world, Beijing's Olympics and Shanghai's Expo were two of the biggest hurdles faced by yaogun in the new millennium and demonstrate the constantly shifting climate in which yaogun operates. "Because of the Olympics" was the answer to many a question asked in the weeks and months surrounding the Games when faced with delays, closures or general messiness; ditto for Shanghai and its Expo. When veterans of Olympic Games past reminisced about their host cities' transformation, it involved memories of a city-wide festival, where people from around the world gathered in après-event revelry of all kinds. Not so for Beijing or Shanghai, where an intense devotion to Total Event Control affected the cities' cultural life directly, despite the fact that part of the thrill of both events is how the world comes to meet in ways and places outside of official events and sites. While the Expo site buzzed with a billion visiting troupes, bands, artists and more, Shanghai itself was a virtual desert, deprived of even much of its own entertainment and culture – to say nothing of the opportunities for outside-of-Expo appearances that became even harder than usual to arrange.

Not even yaogun was spared this Total Event Control. Shanghai rock band Top Floor Circus felt the weight of the Expo upon their backs when they took Beijing's Olympic theme song, "Beijing Welcomes You," and created two versions of their own for Shanghai – "Shanghai Welcomes You" and "Shanghai (Doesn't) Welcome You". In classic Top Floor form, the songs succeeded in using humor as rock and roll weapon like no other band around. They succeeded, perhaps too well. The songs questioned whether it was the people or the currency that was being welcomed to their city and at what cost.

Alas, Shanghai authorities weren't laughing, and called the band in for a chat, pledging to watch closely the band's future performances. The song, as well as any reference to or videos of it, seemed to have been wiped clean away from the internet. "We will never perform the song again," the band's drummer was quoted saying. Rock venue Mao Livehouse, too, was sucked into the storm. The Top Floor Affair resulted in a visit from the powers that be, who found problems with the club's legal status. The takeaway: When China is showing its best side to the world, yaogun should stay away, far away. But on the positive-ish side: Yaogun can still be controversial.

In Olympic terms, one doesn't exactly yearn to look back upon the madness that was Beijing's Opening and Closing Ceremonies, but one goes there in search of what little yaogun might take from them. As the curtain came down on director Zhang Yimou's acid-trip through Chinese history – like a fifties musical in the grandest of the Technicolor style, but, with, say, an exponentially larger budget, and with, well, *more*, with just a dollop of even more on top, and Sarah Brightman – there was a taste. The preview for London's 2012 Games that ended the spectacle featured Jimmy Page atop a double-decker bus, shredding a version of "Whole Lotta Love." Critics said that the London preview paled in comparison to Beijing's spectacle, but from a yaogun perspective, nothing could be further from the truth. He probably didn't know it, but Mr Page's antics showed the nation – which likewise may not have known it, occupied as it was covering itself with the meticulously-scrubbed version it showed to the world – that way, way down inside, they need every inch of ... Well, you get the idea.

Two years later, another Games, and Vancouver had rock all over their ceremonies, with performances from Bryan Adams, Joni Mitchell, Nickelback, Avril Lavigne, Neil Young and more. And just before that, not just rock and roll in the White House, but a president deferring to a rocker: "I'm the President," Barack Obama said during the introduction to Kennedy Center Honoree Bruce Springsteen, "but he's the Boss." Put Bruce alongside previous Honorees like Bob Dylan, Brian Wilson and even non-Americans Pete Townshend, Paul McCartney and Roger Daltrey, and then look at the list of performers that have graced the White House stage, and one's yaogun-focused mind begins to reel.

We're a long way off from seeing Cui Jian perform for the leaders of his nation. But yaogun has received some mainstream support and there is a reason to think it might find more. In an interview with the mayor of Beijing, Bai Yansong, popular host of current events show *News 1+1* on the state-run CCTV network, spoke of how it was important that the city give rock some breathing room; that it should be "tolerated." He said that the rockers, the poets, the artists and all other "Beijing vagabonds" and "warriors" of the literary and art circle, "are the city's core driving force for cultural productivity." Of course, the reaction to his statements – which also included the suggestion that Beijing may want to offer graffiti zones – was that of shock. Explaining further, he added that rock music "wasn't what everyone thought." Rock "includes folk," he said, likely seeing that the eyes of people around him as he spoke threatened to pop out of their sockets. While it's nice to know that Bai has yaogun's back, we still have a long way to go when the suggestion that the city of Beijing might get involved with rock music is almost as shocking as the fact that the host of a CCTV news show might believe such a thing.

It's been argued, by, among others, Lu Zhongqiang, of Beijing record label 13th Month, that yaogun ought to look to the Chinese cartoon industry as a potential model to which it might aspire. Premier Wen Jiabao was less than enthused while sitting through episodes of Japanese cartoon Ultraman, his grandson's favorite. Discovering that China was a net importer of animation, he spoke up. At an animation studio in March 2009, Wen complained, to the gathered crowd, about his time with his grandson. "We should be cultivating a domestic animation industry," he said. Turning to the animators, he said: "Your work is meaningful. You should play a leading role in bringing Chinese culture to the world . . . Let Chinese children watch more of their own history and their own country's animation." Funding became available, content laws kept the bulk of the airwaves for local products, and suddenly, Chinese animation got a kick in the pants (and you know that Wen's grandson got more than that from his classmates). Could yaogun not go the same way? Perhaps a teenaged Wen III will stumble upon a rock show and start spending his time with Gramps listening to music. Upon discovering that the kids would rather rock than yaogun, who's to say what Premier Wen, or other leaders will do? If yaogun could be seen as a similarly shining example of culture the nation can be proud of, there is no telling what future might lie ahead.

The question is whether or not yaogun is taken seriously. If cartoons can be serious business, why not yaogun? Ask former Foreign Affairs Ministry spokesman Qin Gang. In answering – sort of – a question about the Chinese government's reaction to the release of Guns n' Roses' album *Chinese Democracy*, he provided a window into one of the current official views on rock, which is a long way from the days when officials feared it would bring down the nation. "So far as I know, not many people are fond of this kind of music because it's too loud and noisy. Besides," Qin continued, addressing less the question than the questioner, "you are a mature adult, aren't you?" The answer is interesting on several levels: You don't know whether Qin is the coolest bureaucrat ever or the embodiment of The Man at its most evil. You also begin to wonder if Qin is that good on his feet, or if he knew that the question would be coming. If he knew the question was coming, then doesn't that mean the Ministry might actually care about rock? And is that a good thing?

But what seems more realistic is that rock music is a punch line, at best; something with which only the immature concern themselves. It's hard to tell what yaogunners would like more: to actually be banned, giving them street cred, or to maintain the status quo, whereby their existence is recognized just below the level at which they might be pointed out, like some sick game of Whack-A-Mole, with a glass sheet hovering barely above the board, preventing the rock and roll moles from both mocking The Man by popping their heads up or feeling the wrath of the governmental hammer. Yang Haisong of P.K. 14 is conflicted about the situation, "Because the government doesn't care about us, we aren't forbidden from playing. Maybe we're not dangerous. It's sad."

It has been said many times over that the current generation doesn't need rock. But no generation before needed rock either – until, that is, they got it, and it became their very life force. To this day, there is no shortage of people that believe they need rock, and it is those people that will create the yaogun that will move things forward.

Despite the proliferation of documentaries, articles and books, to say nothing of the increasing numbers of Chinese bands performing outside of the Middle Kingdom, we are not witnessing the pinnacle of yaogun's glory.

Critic Yan Jun agrees. The task of the years since the complete destruction of the Cultural Revolution, he said, was to rebuild the country's inner and outer worlds, and experiment with all of the new phenomena available. That thirty-odd years has been enough "to shock the world," but not enough for the "real creation" that takes things to the next level.

Successful yaogun, like any art form, does far more than "shock." Awe, to borrow a phrase, comes closer to that which should be strived for. Yaogun's international success thus far, which has seen bands perform abroad but not make serious industry-level dents, has fallen into the former category, and certainly yaogun on the whole benefits from the export of any of its members. But this is only a small step. Yaogun has to get its own house in order before it can legitimately join the rest of the world. Yaogun has to be more than simply something novel; it has to become something Good.

Though the country has come a long way, yaogun remains besieged on all sides: by a society intent on homogeneity; by a nation obsessed with the acquisition of wealth; by a culture so devoted to its millennia-long history that there is little interest in or appreciation and support for new forms of expression; by the enticing prospect to cash in, abandon the yaogun path and join the mainstream; and, perhaps most significantly, by the indifference of the bulk of the population. Which, to many, is exactly the way it should be; that only when faced with those kinds of obstacles can yaogun truly rock.

Yaogun ain't done yet. The best is yet to come.

One Last Scene from the Scene: May 2009

When you're staring down from a festival-sized stage at an audience composed of equal parts security guards, confused and obviously-uninterested tourists, and goats, it's hard to know whether to laugh, cry, get angry or simply head into the nearby mountains at a full sprint, not stopping until you've reached the top of the furthest peak you can find, ripping your clothing off as you run, screaming like a banshee the entire time. Because, has it really come to this? Nearly a decade of your young life up in the music scene, and the number of eyes watching your band, a band of which you are eminently proud, not only barely reach a hundred, but don't even all belong to beings of the same genus as you. You could have booked a Tuesday night gig and gotten more (human) attendance, without leaving the comforts of your hometown.

The setting, you have to admit, though, is gorgeous. Grey, a bit cold, but gorgeous – especially when the fog lifts and you can see the enormous river valley and surrounding mountain landscape. Scary, though, when you think about the bus ride in the thick fog that brought you here, along with scores of other Beijing-based yaogunners, and suddenly, when you can see the condition of the roads and the depths of the valleys into which the roadside cliffs fall, your jokes inspired by erratic driving that began with "The Beijing rock scene was decimated today . . . " take on a new level of horror.

You know that the chill-out time the past three days – in the post-apocalyptic gated community transplanted into this so-called National Park hours outside of Chongqing, the megalopolis home to more people than any other municipality on the face of the earth – was a good, if cold and patience-testing time. But you were also hoping that when you took to the stage of what you were told was going to be a great three-day Festival on the May Day weekend of 2009, your performance was going to be seen by more than livestock.

There were people, you know, that attended the festival's previous days, thousands of people, but, alas, you've been scheduled for Sunday at noon and, Monday being the first day back to work after the three-day weekend, even the stage crew thought they'd be packing up – and, indeed, were in the throes of doing just that as you arrived at the stage. And when, from the stage, you watch a herd of goats elude their shepherd and bust through the fences of the audience area, headed, like lemmings to their ear-splitting demises, toward the stage, the fact that there is no fear of goat-related injuries demonstrates, without a single doubt, that you are playing for nobody.

You play, nonetheless, and you can literally count how many people are watching you. And instead of hightailing it into the mountains, you take it all in, knowing that, in every possible sense of the word, nothing rocks quite like yaogun.

Sources and Further Reading

There is more yaogun out there to hear than space here to list. For further listening, updates, news, appendices, footnotes, stories and more – call them the book's liner notes, if you will – visit *www.jonathanWcampbell.com.*

Lyrics (used with permission):
"Zhongguo tese de Rock n' Roll" ("Rock n' Roll with Chinese Characteristics") by 69 (© Scream Records)
"Yi wu suoyou" ("Nothing to My Name") and *"yi kuai hongbu"* ("A Piece of Red Cloth") by Cui Jian
"Fang xue le" ("School's Out") by *Hua'er Yuedui* The Flowers (© NewBees Music Production Co. Ltd.)
"Lajichang" ("Garbage Dump") by He Yong
"Rang shijie chongman ai" ("Let the World Be Full of Love") by *Baiming Gexing* The Hundred Stars, lyrics by Guo Feng
"Gonglu zhi ge" ("Highway Song") by *Tongku de Xinyang* Miserable Faith
"Xin ba rong ba chi" ("New Eight Honors and Eight Shames") by *Junxiesuo* Ordnance
"Gei ni yi ge shuofa" ("I'll Give You an Explanation") by *Pangu*
"Sleeping in My Car" by Roxette (written by Per Gessle, © Jimmy Fun Music)
"Zhilia" ("Trick") by *Ershou Meigui* Second Hand Rose
"GO! CHINA! GO!" by SMZB
"Down" by Subs
"Likai" ("Leave") by *Yehaizi* Wild Children

Books

Our Band Could Be Your Life: Scenes from the American Indie Underground 1981-1991 Michael Azerrad

Psychotic Reactions and Carburetor Dung: The Work of a Legendary Critic: Rock 'n' Roll as Literature and Literature as Rock 'n' Roll Lester Bangs; Greil Marcus (editor)

China's New Voices: Popular Music, Ethnicity, Gender, and Politics,1978-1997 Nimrod Baranovitch

In the Red: On Contemporary Chinese Culture Geramie Barme

Mao: The Unknown Story Jung Chang and Jon Halliday

Postmodernism & China Edited Arif Dirlik and Xudong Zhang

On the road with the Rolling Stones: 20 years of lipstick, handcuffs, and chemicals Chet Flippo

China's New Cultural Scene Marie Claire Huot

Like a Knife: Ideology and Genre in Contemporary Chinese Popular Music Andrew Jones

Asia and Global Popular Culture Richard King and Timothy J. Craig

China With a Cut: Globalisation, Urban Youth and Popular Music Jeroen de Kloet

Multiple modernities: cinemas and popular media in transcultural East Asia Jenny Kwok Wah Lau

China Underground Zachary Mexico

Comrade Rockstar: The Life and Mystery of Dean Reed, the All American Boy Who Brought Rock 'n' Roll to the Soviet Union Reggie Nadelson

I'm Coming to Take You to Lunch: A Fantastic Tale of Boys, Booze, and How Wham! Were Sold to China Simon Napier-Bell

Sound Kapital: Beijing's Music Underground Matthew Niederhauser

Rhythm, Riots and Revolution David A. Noebel

Inseparable: The memoirs of an American and the story of Chinese punk rock David O'Dell

The Insider's Guide to Beijing 2005-2010 Adam Pillsbury (editor)

Live at the Forbidden City: Musical Encounters in China and Taiwan Dennis Rea

Rock Around the Bloc: A History of Rock Music in Eastern Europe and the Soviet Union Timothy W. Ryback

Mick Jagger: Rebel Knight Christopher Sandford

The Search for Modern China Jonathan Spence

The Long March of Rock 'n' Roll (Der Lange Masch des Rock'n'Roll)" Andreas Steen

Back in the USSR: The True Story of Rock in Russia Artemy Troitsky

Piao yidai (*Vagrancy Generation*) Xu Xinjun

Yaogun xunmeng (*Seeking the Rock and Roll Dream*) Xue Ji

China Pop: How Soap Operas, Tabloids, and Bestsellers Are Transforming a Culture Jianying Zha

Articles/Theses

"Beijing Days, Beijing Nights" and "Official Bad Boys or True Rebels" Geremie Barme, 1991

"Birth of a Beijing Music Scene" Matthew Corbin Clark, 2003

"Tongue: Making Sense of Underground Rock, Beijing 1997-2004" Jeroen Groenewegen, 2005

"Beijing Bastards" Andrew F. Jones, *SPIN* Oct 1992

"Red Sonic Trajectories: Popular Music and Youth in Urban China" Jeroen de Kloet, 2001

"Beijing Rocks: Rockin' in the Not-So-Free World" Steven Schwankert, *The Wire* Sept 1995

"Der Lange Marsch des Rock 'n' Roll" Andreas Steen, 1996

"*Zhongguo yaogun lan tanzi*" ("Yaogun's Mess") Sun Mengjin, 2003

"Wok and Roll" Rob Tannenbaum *Details* Magazine, Nov 1998

Internet

English

Beijing Beat @ cluas.net

beijingdaze.com

beijingscene.com

thebeijinger.com
beijinggigguide.com
cfensi.wordpress.com
thechinabeat.org
chinamusicradar.com
cityweekend.com
danwei.org
theglobaloutpost.com
kungfuology.com
layabozi.com
New Sounds of China at londonhuayu.co.uk
rockinchina.com
shanghaiist.com
smartshanghai.com
timeoutbeijing.com
tsquare.tv

Chinese
douban.com
mogo.tv
music.sina.com.cn
neocha.com
painkillermag.com
wa3.cn
wangxiaofeng.net
wooozy.cn
xiami.com
yanjun.org
yaogun.com (Japanese)

Films/TV
Jean-Michel Jarre: China Concerts, 1981
Wham! in China: Foreign Skies, 1986
The Year Punk Broke, 1991
Beijing zazhong (Beijing Bastards), 1993

Toufa luan le (Dirt), 1994
Gate of Heavenly Peace, 1995
Ziyou bianlu (Borders of Freedom), 2000
Beijing le yu lu (Beijing Rocks), 2001
PBS Frontline "China in the Red", 2003
Midi Music Festival (2004-2010)
Hou geming shidai (Post-Revolutionary Era), 2005
Gonggong wangguo de lvxing (A Tour of the Public Kingdom), 2005
Lehui Beijing (Surviving Beijing), 2005
Yaogun duoduo (China Rock), 2006
Rockstar, 2006
Modern Sky Festival 2007
Feixing rizhi (Air Diary), 2007
Beijing Bubbles, 2008
Global Metal, 2008
Rock Heart Beijing, 2008
Zaijian wutuobang (Night of an Era), 2009
Yaogun zhongguo le sheli (Dou Wei, Zhang Chu, He Yong, Tang Dynasty Live in Hong Kong 1994.12.17), 2009
Beijing Punk, 2010
PUNKIT!: Beijing to London, 2010
Voodoo Kungfu with the Traditional Folk Orchestra, 2010